Quakers in the Colonial Northeast

Quakers
in the Colonial Northeast

Arthur J. Worrall

Published by the
University Press of New England
Hanover, New Hampshire and
London, England
1980

Copyright © 1980 by Trustees of Dartmouth College
All rights reserved
Library of Congress Catalog Card Number 79-63086
International Standard Book Number 0-87451-174-7
Printed in the United States of America.

Library of Congress Cataloging in Publication Data
Worrall, Arthur J   1933–
Quakers in the colonial Northeast.
Bibliography: p.
Includes index.
1. Friends, Society of—New England—History.
2. Friends, Society of—New York (State)—History.
I. Title.
BX7639.W67   289.6'74   79-63086
ISBN 0-87451-174-7

University Press of New England
Brandeis University
Clark University
Dartmouth College
University of New Hampshire
University of Rhode Island
Tufts University
University of Vermont

For Janet

Preface

IN 1911 RUFUS M. JONES, Amelia M. Gummere, and Isaac Sharpless wrote *Quakers in the American Colonies*, a volume in the Rowntree series in Quaker history. Since then many books on Quaker history and related subjects have appeared, rendering the Jones volume somewhat dated. Consequently, over a decade ago Kenneth Carroll of Southern Methodist University, soon joined by Edwin Bronner of Haverford College and eventually by me, proposed to bring out new volumes to replace Jones's work. Our intent was to incorporate recent scholarship and to use all relevant Quaker records.

I have sought to explore the Quaker experience in the Northeast from the time Quaker missionaries first appeared in 1656 until 1790. The dates are approximate but necessary. Some background information precedes the discussion of the Quaker invasion, but only to explain the experience and outlook of early Friends. By concluding in 1790 I was able to demonstrate the effect of Quaker reform. It was clear by 1790 that reform, not war or some other cause, lay behind the large number of Quaker disownments (expulsions of members), and its consequent decline compared to other denominations.

For financial support I am indebted to several institutions and organizations. Indiana University awarded me a fellowship and travel funds. Thanks to the support of Harry Rosenberg, then chairman of the Department of History, Colorado State University granted a sabbatical leave. The Joseph Rowntree Charitable Trust supported research in England. Grants from the Rowntree Trust, the Chace Fund, the Shoemaker Foundation, and the Friends Historical Association all supported publication.

In the course of research and writing I have been fortunate to have had the generous support and friendship of a number of people. Both Edwin Bronner and Kenneth Carroll have been generous with advice, encouragement, and material assistance. Thyra Jane Foster, formerly archivist of the New England Yearly Meeting archives, introduced me to the New England Quaker records and to Quaker worship and provided hospitality on several occasions. Mary Cook, onetime archivist of the New York Quaker records, her sister Katherine, and Day Bradley all helped to make research in New York rewarding. Edward Milligan and his staff at the Friends House Library in London, especially Malcomb Thomas, generously provided documents and advice and made our family welcome in numerous ways. The staffs of the Rhode Island Historical Society, the John Carter Brown and Rockefeller Libraries at Brown University, the Newport Historical Society, the Old Dartmouth Historical Society in New Bedford, Massachusetts, the Nantucket Historical Society, the Massillon, Ohio Public Library, the Public Record Office, and the British Museum were patient, courteous, and generous in meeting my demands. At Colorado State University Loretta Saracino helped me obtain books and film from other libraries; Jack Hadley drew the graphs and Lisa Eckert the map. Reiko Urano typed several manuscript drafts. Ronald Cooksey checked my data on Rhode Island Monthly Meeting; Fred Anderson read the manuscript and made valuable suggestions. Hugh Barbour, J. William Frost, and John Moore read the manuscript for the Friends Historical Association. John Moore graciously permitted me to use articles previously published in _Quaker History_. Eugene Berwanger and Mark Gilderhus, my colleagues at Colorado State University, made incisive comments on the manuscript. David Horne, then director and editor of the University Press of New England, corrected more stylistic mistakes than I like to admit. Irene Neu of Indiana University has been a valued friend, critic, and supporter. Trevor Colbourn now President of the University of Central Florida, despite administrative burdens, has given constant encouragement over the years. Finally, my family has endured enough elation and frustration over this book to last them their lives. Our children, Tim, Beth, and Tom have been temporarily uprooted for my research and writing. To my wife Janet, also an historian—who at times delayed her own research and served as critic, contributor of ideas for graphs and maps, and typist —the book is dedicated. It would never have appeared without her sympathetic criticism.

Fort Collins, Colorado   A.J.W.
July 1979

Contents

PART I
From Heretics to Dissenters

The Popish Inquisition newly erected in New En-
gland; whereby their Church is manifest to be a
Daughter of . . . Babylon, which doth drink the
Blood of the Saints.
              —*Francis Howgill, 1659*

[The Quakers] sowed their corrupt and damnable
Doctrines, both by word and writings, almost in
every Town in each Jurisdiction, some whereof were,
That all men ought to attend to the Light within.
              —*Nathaniel Morton, 1669*

Friends, God has raised you up to chastise us for the
vile Contempt and Affront which People generally
cast on the Light of God within them; and for our
usual and criminal Rebelling against the Light.
              —*Cotton Mather, 1725*

Chapter 1
The Quaker Invasion

"LET ALL NATIONS hear the sound by word or writing. Spare no tongue, nor pen; but be obedient to the Lord God; go through the work; be valient for the truth upon earth; and tread and trample upon all that is contrary."[1]

George Fox's frequently quoted words written in Cornwall's Launceston Prison in 1656 were typical of the outlook of early Quakers. Hardly the benign, benevolent, charitable people they are today, Friends in this first, prophetic period of early Quakerism did not care to suffer the mass of mankind to go unconverted. They attempted to subdue the evil in the world by convincing the unregenerate of truth as they saw it. They went beyond England in the 1650's to the European continent and unleashed a torrent of preaching, in English, upon uncomprehending princes and multitudes. In the enthusiasm of the time, two Friends reached the Ottoman Empire, where they obtained an audience with the sultan. Two others, John Luffe and John Perrot, were less successful in Rome, where they were denied an audience with the Pope, and authorities left them to the none too tender ministrations of the Inquisition and the madhouse. John Luffe was hanged. Perrot, after three years in Rome's insane asylum, was released.[2]

With the notable exception of Rhode Island, the northern colonies in New England and New Netherland did not receive Quaker missionaries with enthusiasm when Friends first came to them in 1656. By 1662 four had been hanged and an unknown number whipped, fined, imprisoned, and banished for encroaching on Massachusetts' godly experiment. Plymouth and New Haven carried out a similar if less severe policy. While no other Friends were executed thereafter, Massachusetts and Plymouth yielded but grudging toleration during the balance of the seventeenth century. New Haven was so forbidding that Friends did not convert many residents there, nor did they enjoy any appreciable success after the creation of an enlarged Connecticut in 1662. New Netherland, after an initially severe persecution, permitted Quaker settlers to worship with less harassment than most New England colonies. Tolerant Rhode Island proved to be the strongest of the early Quaker areas and the exception to the hostile reception given Friends in other northern North American colonies.

Generally, historians who have studied Quakers in seventeenth-century New England and New York have, like Quaker pamphleteers of that era, given their attention to Massachusetts, site of the greatest conflict and relatively few conversions. They have thereby denigrated events elsewhere. I have proceeded colony by colony so as to treat the impact of Friends more evenly. Even so, emphasis is given to Massachusetts, which remains the chief site of both conflict and debate.

English Background

The Society of Friends originated in England, an offshoot of the Puritan Revolution. There are abundant parallels with earlier radical religious groups, and some historians have found Quaker origins in them, but it is certain that without the chaotic conditions of mid-seventeenth-century England, Friends would not have appeared or spread in the manner they did. Just as the England of the Puritan Revolution provided the occasion, early Quaker leaders, themselves conditioned by events of Civil War and Commonwealth, provided the impetus. Like the majority of those converted—or "convinced," to use the Quaker term—they shared in the fundamental uncertainties of the period, at least until they came together as the Society of Friends.[3]

Among the leaders, the most prominent, to later generations at least, was George Fox. Fox had begun to feel the stirrings of a religious experience as early as 1643, and he went about the countryside in the south of England during the rest of the decade seeking persons of similar belief. Usually, historians have taken Fox's efforts in the North, in the counties of Westmorland, Durham, Lancashire, and Yorkshire, as the beginning of organized Quakerism—specifically in 1652, when he brought together in that region groups of separatists called Seekers.[4]

Fox was a charismatic figure, typical of many early Quaker leaders. A man of medium stature but with a commanding air, his presence, to take his own words at face value, confounded opponents and converted many others. Fox and several other early Quaker ministers were responsible for the growth of Quakerism by virtually a geometrical progression from an initial group of a few hundred in the early 1650's.

They found especially receptive areas in the valleys and moors of the North of England, in London, and in the West.

Large sections of England's northern counties had been long neglected by the church. Even the Reformation left much of this area unaffected, and Puritanism had had little influence there. The North was consequently without strong religious attachments before Fox began his ministrations. Like several other sections where Quakerism took root, this area was economically backward and its people poor; for over a century they had suffered from enclosures and from depredations of landlords. That England's remote North was open to Quaker preaching and receptive to the radical religious and political strains that were a part of the Quaker message was due in large part to this combination of poverty and religious neglect.

Other sections of England where Quakerism developed were more prosperous and had had exposure to religious ferment since the fifteenth century. One can only speculate on the cause of conversions, but at least a major ingredient was the sense of alienation caused by the economic, political, religious, and social unrest of the first half of the seventeenth century. The same difficulties had also led to emigration of middle groups of English society: merchants, craftsmen, and yeomen. Indeed, as Richard Vann has suggested, the Society of Friends may have consisted at the outset of all classes but with a tendency toward the upper middle, while the second generation may have numbered a higher proportion of lower classes. Several students of alienation have indicated that groups which have had a significant place in society, a place that seems to be eroding, are as likely to be alienated from society because of radical change as are poorer classes, and perhaps more likely. To a great extent the rapid change and dislocation of the seventeenth century must have readied people who had known both religious concern and economic uncertainty for conversion to the radical religious message of Friends.[5]

Quakerism gave a sense of meaning to groups of poor people who were unexposed to the thrust of religious change and to those who had known prosperity (or its possibility) and had already passed through many of the stages of religious excitement. It brought certainty where so much uncertainty existed. The radical Puritan message of Fox and other first-generation Quaker ministers stressed the workings of God on man's spirit. To these early Friends all people had a seed or an Inward Light of Christ within them. At a person's election, this seed or Light could be magnified and could grow. If one sought to cultivate the Light, one would be saved; if not, one would continue unregenerate. In taking this position, Friends made clear that all persons at their own election could be saved. They did not accept the prevalent Calvinist view that men were predestined to be saved or damned. Equally pernicious to Puritan clergy was the Quaker belief that one did not need the preachings of a learned, salaried ministry to cultivate the Light and be saved. [6]

Orthodox Puritans were bound to be suspicious of the Quakers' unpaid, sometimes unlettered, and essentially self-appointed ministry as well as their suggestion that the seed of God in man was sufficient for salvation. To orthodox Puritans, Quakers had restrained God by this mode of thinking, by insisting that He had bound Himself to yield salvation to all who would accept Him. He was hardly the arbitrary and almighty Deity whom Geneva Calvinists and their English descendants made Him out to be. Choice for salvation or damnation, according to Friends, was not God's, it was man's, and, worst of all for the Puritans, it left decision on salvation to the individual who might easily confuse his impressions of salvation and individual perfection with the workings of the devil.

Such confusion was a very real threat to early Quakers, for there were Ranters who, like the Friends, followed the leadings (that it, the guidance) of the spirit. Unlike the Friends, however, they argued that salvation led to personal perfection and an exalted state that put them beyond man's law, and they went out of their way to flaunt their freedom from ordinary moral constraints. Such religious perfectionists were a threat to the state, and if their excesses led to anarchy, civil authorities would have to restrain them. Since, like Friends, they also claimed to be following the leadings of the spirit working within them, opponents frequently confused them with Quakers. [7]

In this expansive period, other beliefs and practices got Friends in trouble. Though Quakers accepted Scripture as having a measure of authority, they asserted that the Bible was not the only or the final standard for belief. They argued that there could be other revelations, for God continued to reveal himself to man and recent revelations might even be superior to the written word of the Bible. Quakers also seemed to deny the historical, Biblical Christ in their assertion that a seed of Christ was in all men. How, their critics asked, could Christ have died, ascended into Heaven, and still be present in man?

The certitude of Quaker ministers about the seed of Christ within appealed to the poor and religiously deprived people of the North and to alienated Englishmen elsewhere. To many in the North Country belief in the Inward Light and rejection of clerical ministrations were attractive because both clergy and church had ignored them. Their religious beliefs, such as they were, had of necessity been inward. The Quaker message found receptive audiences, which had developed doctrines strikingly similar to Friends before George Fox and other Quakers came among them. These North Country Seekers received Friends as prophets and accepted their scheme for salvation during the troubled times of the Commonwealth and Protectorate. To other alienated Englishmen, Friends' beliefs brought the certainty of a new faith and an explanation for the ills of their day.

In accepting Quaker spiritist beliefs in the setting of the Puritan Revolution, the Northcountrymen passed on practices and attitudes that set their stamp on Quakerism. Refusal to use "you" in the singular was one of these customs. Friends came to require the traditional and egalitarian mode of speech of the back country North "thee" and "thou," and as a consequence came to provide their persecutors with readily identifiable means of detection and grounds for persecution. Quakers also refused to swear oaths, reading the Biblical injunction not to swear to mean not to swear an oath. Friends also permitted their women—even encouraged them—to act as ministers, an unseemly act to the majority of Englishmen at the time and perhaps to many of the English women too.

New England Background

New England was an inviting target for Quakers. Puritans had founded Massachusetts and her neighboring Puritan colonies of Plymouth, Connecticut, and New Haven to establish Bible Commonwealths in America. They were at once havens for harried Puritans in England uncomfortable under William Laud's persecution, and (at least so later Massachusetts clergy thought) models for the English Puritans to copy once they had come to power. The most radical of the Puritans went there, it seemed, before civil war broke out in England. Perhaps because of a fear of the consequences of this radicalism both from England and within these colonies themselves, authorities in the new settlements, led initially by Governor John Winthrop of Massachusetts, clamped down on the most outspoken settlers. It should come as no surprise that far from establishing a sense of toleration, restraint instituted before 1640 obtained the very opposite. The one visible exception, of course, was Rhode Island, settled by malcontents driven from Massachusetts.[8]

Trouble arose early after the founding of the Bay Colony. Roger Williams had challenged the legality of the charter and both the wisdom and the Biblical justification for establishing a New Zion. For essentially religious reasons, he found forced worship repugnant, and because of his opposition had to flee to what was later Providence, Rhode Island, to escape forcible repatriation to England.[9]

Williams' opposition was not, however, the greatest challenge faced by Massachusetts leaders. In the 1630's a much larger number of dissidents, many of them of a mercantile orientation, organized themselves around a Boston housewife, Anne Hutchinson, against the original clerical and lay leadership. For a time it seemed that the Hutchinson party would control Massachusetts; but John Winthrop and the orthodox clergy won the struggle for power, and Anne, with most of her mercantile followers, departed to found Portsmouth, Rhode Island. Massachusetts remained safe and orthodox, and Rhode Island began its quarrelsome early history.[10]

The challenge was serious, and New England leaders outside Rhode Island, particularly in Massachusetts, were wary of any similar threats to their experiment. There was a marked similarity in the beliefs of Anne Hutchinson and Quakers. Like Friends, the Antinomian party led by Anne had followed an essentially spiritist argument. She attacked what she thought was clerical insistence on the covenant of works. Her position was similar to later English radicals' arguments as it emphasized the individual seeking salvation rather than clerical supervision. Opponents also thought it placed the self-recognized regenerate above the law; hence it was a danger to civil order. It was primarily for these reasons that Massachusetts expelled Anne Hutchinson and her followers. A further point should be noted: many of these people were merchants highly alienated from their society, like later converts in the towns of London and Bristol in England.[11]

Enclaves of dissent were to be found in several sections of New England. To Massachusetts authorities the most threatening area was on Aquidneck in Rhode Island, settled by Hutchinsonians. Their gathering in that permissive colony meant that when Quaker missionaries appeared almost two decades later, they found many people ready for Quakerism. But there were other dissenting locales too. The isolated towns of Sandwich and Falmouth in southern Plymouth colony, like much of the English North, had groups to whom spiritual mysticism was attractive. Unchurched, without clergy to oversee them, they were open to the Quaker message. So, too, was a very small minority of Salem, in the section known as "The Woods." They seem to have rejected both that community's church and the town's increasingly mercantile nature. Towns north of Salem would also supply converts when Friends appeared. These towns were not of the Massachusetts mainstream and had been settled by one-time supporters of Anne Hutchinson—reasons enough for being open to dissenting views.[12]

The outpouring of disgruntled English settlers did not stop at the boundaries of the New England colonies. Unwelcome in all of New England save Rhode Island, many of them moved on to Long Island, then under the control of more tolerant authorities in New Amsterdam. Safely across the border from New Haven and Connecticut, they settled the towns of Flushing, Hempstead, and Jamaica—English towns in a Dutch colony. To the consternation of Dutch authorities they rarely employed clergy. If in Dutch eyes their religious dispositions were not quite so bad as Rhode Island's—that "sewer," as two Dutch clergy referred to it—like many Rhode Islanders they adopted doctrines like those of the Antinomians. In many instances these were doctrines which the English migrants had already found attractive. [13]

So it was that New England and New Netherland possessed people predisposed to Quaker beliefs, ready for conversion when the first Quaker missionaries arrived. There was also potential opposition to Quakers in Massachusetts from an already challenged leadership around Boston. These men recognized the threat of Quakers as similar to that of earlier Antinomians. Their frenzied reaction to the Quaker invasion had been conditioned by an already hardened position vis-à-vis those people who had settled in Rhode Island and, to a lesser extent, Plymouth and Long Island.

Massachusetts

The excitement of having found a faith, and the belief that their faith was in the vanguard of the Reformation, led Friends to attempt to convert everyone else. Quaker women and men set out on long journeys convinced of the need to convert the world to their doctrines. In the heady first five years (1652–57) after George Fox and others organized the North of England, it seemed to Quakers and their opponents as though Friends might indeed conquer the world, for their numbers doubled and redoubled after their initial organization in 1652. Thereafter the rate of increase slowed as Friends confronted resistance in both England and the new world and as persecution mounted during the Stuart Restoration. By the year 1660, however, when Charles II returned from his travels, Quakers had established a foothold in both New England and New York and had converted substantial numbers of receptive persons, especially in Long Island, Plymouth, and Rhode Island.

Two groups of Quakers arrived in 1656. The first, led by Anne Austin and Mary Fisher, came to Boston in July. The Massachusetts government promptly imprisoned them for five weeks; after checking them for marks of witchcraft, they expelled them in August. A second group of eight Quaker missionaries came to Boston two days after their expulsion. Massachusetts imprisoned this group for eleven weeks and expelled them also, after the clergy had examined and debated with them. The General Court of Massachusetts passed its first anti-Quaker law, intent on preventing both Friends and their books from entering the colony. Under it any shipmaster bringing in Friends knowingly was subject to a hundred-pound fine. Anyone who imported or possessed a Quaker book was to be fined 5 pounds.[14]

Despite the fact that the colony's leaders sought to keep the eight Friends incommunicado and the colony thereby free of infection, one old man, Nicholas Upshall, was so eager to speak to them that he agreed to pay the jailer five shillings a week for their board. A small group in Salem Woods, disaffected from that town's church and the community in general, must have secretly sympathized with these missionaries and may have made contact with them through Upshall's good offices. For his sympathetic support of the eight Friends, Upshall was expelled to Plymouth.[15]

The major Quaker effort in Massachusetts began in 1657 with the arrival of Robert Fowler's ship *Woodhouse*. Of the eleven Quaker missionaries who left England with Fowler, six had already debarked to proselytize New Netherland and other colonies en route to Massachusetts. Five pressed on and were eventually joined by the others. These traveling Friends immediately sought out potential sympathizers in Salem and met with almost instantaneous success among residents unsympathetic with both the Salem community and the Massachusetts way. Several days later, on September 21, two of the Quaker missionaries, John Copeland and Christopher Holder, went to the meeting house. Holder attempted to speak, perhaps after the clergyman had finished speaking, perhaps even before that—subsequent accounts are not clear. When commanded to cease disturbing the meeting, he refused to be silent, had a glove stuffed in his mouth to gag him, and was hauled off to jail with Copeland. Before he was led away, a sympathetic Salem resident, Samuel Shattuck, drew suspicion on himself by removing the glove.[16]

Soon *Woodhouse* missionaries and at least some of their converts in Salem were incarcerated in the Boston jail. Shattuck may or may not have become a Friend before the church service at which his public act raised suspicions, but thereafter he was numbered among the first converts, as were Lawrence and Cassandra Southwick, also Salem residents. The 1656 anti-Quaker law had not prevented Quaker missionary activity, but it was apparent that there were few conversions in Massachusetts outside Salem. Had Massachusetts authorities only noted that fact and acted with restraint, many ensuing difficulties, to say nothing of several additional conversions to Quakerism, might have been avoided and Massachusetts spared the damaged reputation that followed its persecution of Quakers.[17]

Unhappily, Massachusetts leadership was not of the stature of previous years. Governor John Endecott, Lieutenant Governor Richard Bellingham, and Edward Rawson, the secretary of the colony, were not politically astute enough to sense the need for deft handling of this potentially explosive situation. They became convinced that Quakers were in fact such a menace that existing legislation was insufficient to control them and thereupon began to escalate the conflict. The new law of 1657 provided a fine of 100 pounds for importing Quakers and a fine of 40 shillings for each hour Massachusetts residents entertained Quakers knowingly, with imprisonment until payment. Each Quaker entering the colony after previous punishment was to have one ear cut off, a second ear on repeating the offense, and his tongue bored through with a hot iron for a third offense. The severity of the law, their limited success in Salem, and the well known political and economic importance of Massachusetts among the New England colonies (which in itself made Massachusetts important to Quaker missionaries) all served not to discourage Friends but to make them redouble their efforts.[18]

Additional Friends came to Massachusetts in 1658, challenging anti-Quaker laws and joining the *Woodhouse* passengers, who continued active. Two Rhode Island women—Catherine Scott, sister of Anne Hutchinson, and the adulterous Horod Gardner—John Rous from the Barbadoes, and Humphrey Norton from England were among the newcomers. They used Rhode Island as a base of operations for efforts in Massachusetts, where they spent most of the spring and summer imprisoned. During the summer three Friends already previously convicted—Christopher Holder, John Copeland, and John Rous—were rearrested, convicted of still being in the colony, and had their ears cropped. However severe the punishment, it remained uncertain whether ear-cropping was sufficient to deter Quaker activity.[19]

There was no opportunity to find out, for at the October 1658 sitting of the Massachusetts General Court many deputies were eager to pass even more drastic legislation. Egged on by several Massachusetts ministers, especially John Norton, minister of Boston's First Church, one assembly faction proposed that foreign (nonresident) Friends convicted of spreading Quaker tenets should be banished on pain of death should they return. One stipulation of the act was that Quakers should be tried by a special court of assistants. A part of the continuing struggle between assembly and assistants, this aspect of the act only narrowly passed the assembly and was roundly condemned by Friends as a violation of the right to be tried by one's peers. The General Court then set aside a day of public humiliation to ask for God's favor (to eliminate Quakers from their midst) and ordered John Norton to draw up a declaration on the need to suppress Quaker heresies. As its final anti-Quaker act of the year, it ordered that if Salem residents and Quaker converts Samuel Shattuck, Lawrence and Cassandra Southwick and their son Josiah, Nicholas Phelps, and Joshua Buffum would not retract their Quaker errors, they were to be banished on pain of death.[20]

Neither Friends nor Massachusetts authorities were prepared to retreat from their positions. Before and after the passage of the act, more Quaker missionaries had arrived. They and a growing number of converts were soon incarcerated in the Boston jail. If the law was not working, Massachusetts authorities nevertheless did not tire of attempting to enforce it. In May they sent the Salem residents into exile. The General Court demonstrated the extent to which it had lost control of the problem by ordering the sale of the Southwick children. No buyers were found. Two new English missionaries, William Robinson and Marmaduke Stevenson, and the onetime Antinomian and long-suffering opponent of the Massachusetts Standing Order, Mary Dyer, were arrested as Quakers in September 1659 and banished on pain of death. As yet more Friends flocked in, William Robinson and Marmaduke Stevenson were arrested again (they had not left Massachusetts) and were soon joined by Mary Dyer, who returned from Rhode Island to test the act. A special court of assistants sentenced all three to death on October 18. Robinson and Stevenson were hanged on October 27. Mary was reprieved the same day, officially because of pleas by her son William, but no doubt also because of the notoriety attendant on hanging a woman in such a case, especially one who had remained a member of the Boston church since her expulsion to Rhode Island two decades earlier. But when she returned the following May, the Massachusetts leaders determined that they had to act or face the collapse of their policy; so they hanged her.[21]

Meantime John Norton had written an elaborate statement of the Massachusetts position. Published in Cambridge in 1659, it was reprinted in England the next year, accompanied by a broadside that presented the case of the General Court. Norton's pamphlet delineated the fears of Puritan Massachusetts. Quaker beliefs, Norton argued, were a threat to New England's godly experiment. Friends were guilty of many heresies as old as Christianity, having rejected the sacraments, the historic Christ, the Trinity, and Scripture itself, and they looked suspiciously like the anabaptist Münster heretics of the previous century. Furthermore, he argued, they fully deserved expulsion, for New England was "a Plantation Religious, not a Plantation of Trade." It could not maintain religious purity by permitting heretics to remain within its borders, heretics who threatened not only the godly experiment but all civil order.[22]

It did not take long for Friends to reply; indeed they had already been publishing their case in pamphlet after pamphlet, most of them repetitious, drawing information almost verbatim from previous pamphlets and adding the most recent news. Francis Howgill's *Heart of New England Hardened* appeared in London in 1659. Howgill dismissed Norton's charges that Friends were anti-Scriptural ("I prefer it above and before all Ecclesiastical Histories . . ." was hardly the statement on Biblical authority desired by Puritan opponents) and the relationship of Friends to earlier heretical groups ("I shall not trouble the Reader with thy old *Heterodoxes*, as thou calls them . . ." without attempting to prove that beliefs were not similar to past heresies). He then proceeded to assert an anti-Trinitarian belief in three bearing record in heaven but not coexistent through eternity. Thus he could affirm the existence of the historic Christ and turn the tables to argue that by accepting an eternal Christ as part of the Trinity, Norton had denied the historic Christ. The pamphlet, like many of Friends writings in the prophetic period, was an attempt to have it every way. There could be continued revelation, hence the Bible was not the end of revelation; yet the Trinity was not mentioned specifically in the Bible, hence because it was unscriptural, it was invalid. Curiously, Howgill and other prophetic Friends could not accept the possibility that continued revelation itself could account for the Trinity.[23]

In Massachusetts, even before the execution of William Leddra in March 1661, authorities had started to draw back from further draconian measures, being content to fine and imprison Quakers both resident and missionary. As the Boston jail filled up, Massachusetts leaders must have had occasion to wonder at the wisdom of their actions. Friends seemed determined to suffer to justify their peculiar beliefs. Were these people dangerous heretics or mere cranks? Increasingly, it appeared that Friends were not so dangerous as Massachusetts legislators had thought, and perhaps needed much different treatment.

Some evidence for this necessary change of position is generally well known. Quakers filled the jails, and the colony had to face the very real likelihood that it was not only serving the martyrs' purposes but also obtaining an unwanted notoriety now that England was again politically chaotic following Oliver Cromwell's death. It was possible that Charles II could be restored, and it would do Massachusetts little good to hang Quakers if by so doing it was to enhance its record of harboring and sympathizing with regicides.

In addition to the Quakers' fairly well established characteristics, some married Friends—it is not certain how many or how far the practice spread outside Boston and Salem—had before and during their imprisonment in Boston jail determined to stop engaging in sexual intercourse. Whether their decision was temporary or permanent we do not know. The elder Southwick couple apparently started the practice, and it continued at least through 1660. According to Joseph Nicholson, all prisoners in Boston jail in 1660 had withdrawn from sexual intercourse. (For several of those who decided to abstain, nothing, in fact, was given up: they were single.) Among them were English missionaries Dorothy Waugh, Mary Clark, and William Brend. William Robinson, Marmaduke Stevenson, and Mary Dyer had also taken that position before their execution, residents of the jail claimed, as had a large number of other Friends. When Joseph Nicholson and his pregnant wife Jane arrived, the Friends in prison were appalled: clearly the Nicholsons had not abstained. Many Boston residents who were not Quakers were also surprised. Local expectation was that Friends would not reproduce. Yet when Joseph was arrested after having been banished on pain of death, it seems that Jane Nicholson's delivery of a child was instrumental in Joseph's release, although their agreement to leave the colony doubtless helped. Not only did a newborn babe soften the hearts of the magistrates, but, Nicholson thought, this demonstration of diversity within the sect also contributed to his release. Could so fragmented a group be dangerous to Massachusetts? Certainly Quakers were not wanted, but by 1660 authorities were apparently having second thoughts, even though they proceeded with the execution of Mary Dyer.[24]

Well they might have contemplated a change in policy. Quakers in England plied a restored Charles II with their version of events in Massachusetts. They gave Charles the recently published first volume of George Bishop's *New England Judged*. For the most part a repetition of earlier works, it included new information on Massachusetts persecutions, including the recent executions of Friends. Edward Burrough presented an address to Charles which informed him of William Leddra's sentence of death. Probably warned that the Restoration government could be expected to do something for Quakers, the Massachusetts magistrates released some twenty-eight Friends, one of whom, Wenlock Christian, had been under the sentence of death.[25]

Governor Endecott must not have expected so peremptory a command as he received from Charles II in 1661. Burrough and Bishop had done their work well, and Charles was certainly not restrained either by affection for or the need to preserve the Massachusetts Standing Order.

No doubt he relished the opportunity to strike at Massachusetts authorities as he commanded them to cease executing his Quaker subjects. To add insult to the command, he had it carried by Friends, principally the banished Samuel Shattuck, who, when he came before Governor Endecott to explain his return, went through a ritual refusal to render "hat honor." Discovering the King's letter, Endecott was forced into the humiliating act of having to remove his own hat before this unlikely royal ambassador.[26]

Perhaps Massachusetts authorities had anticipated the repeal of their law as they had anticipated being compelled to release imprisoned Quakers. The May session of the General Court had already solved the problem of how to control Quakers. If there was no effective precedent for executing Friends, there was ample precedent and considerable public sentiment in favor of expelling itinerant Quaker ministers—"vagabond Quakers," as Massachusetts put it. The Act of 1660 provided that foreign Quakers were to be whipped through each town at the tail of a cart until they reached the bounds of the colony. Whatever one might think of the barbarity, in effect it demonstrated that Massachusetts had attained a measure of control in response to Quaker inroads, a shift in position from which the colony moved first to a grudging toleration through the remainder of the seventeenth century, to a benign acceptance of the place of Quakers by the fourth decade of the eighteenth century.[27]

Plymouth

Although Friends established themselves in Massachusetts only with great difficulty, Plymouth Colony proved to be more receptive. One reason was the much more permissive religious attitude of Plymouth authorities. Plymouth was not a center of New England Puritanism, and the colony, with its thinly populated towns, had not been as concerned with establishing a church by legislative means and erecting a New Zion as had their counterparts in the Bay Colony, Connecticut, and New Haven. Indeed, the Plymouth General Court did not require until 1655 that all towns have a minister, which was not the consensual rigidity which recent studies indicate was typical of towns near Boston. The law of 1655 may indicate that Plymouth Colony was attempting, belatedly, to resist such groups as Quakers. If so, the effort came too late, for the colony found it impossible thereafter to establish an orthodox ministry in the town of Dartmouth. As in other areas where there was little competition from orthodox Puritans—the North of England, Long Island, and Rhode Island, for example—Quakers found it easy to make converts. Consequently, southern Plymouth provided many new members and remained a center of Quakerism throughout the colonial period.[28]

Although many residents found Quakerism attractive, Plymouth did resist the Quaker invasion. Governor William Bradford favored a mild policy that might have resulted in a subdued form of harassment; but Bradford died and was succeeded by Thomas Prence, who would have no people who sought to tear down Plymouth's churches. He and a majority of Plymouth's General Court found the same vices in Quakers as had Massachusetts authorities. The difference lay in the kind of persecution: Plymouth authorities, though ordering the occasional whipping, never indulged in corporal punishment to the same degree as did Massachusetts, did not banish its own people (although it encouraged their migration), did not execute Friends, and did not mutilate either Quaker missionaries or their converts. Plymouth also sought to use persuasion to bring Quaker converts back to an orthodox position.[29]

The first sign of difficulty came on February 3, 1657, when several complaints were made at the Court of Assistants. Jane Launder, wife of William, and Sarah Kerbey, daughter of Richard, had made a disturbance in the Sandwich Sunday meeting by criticizing and abusing the speaker, and were summoned; Richard Kerbey and the wife of John Newland, both of Sandwich, and the Massachusetts exile Nicholas Upshall had met at the house of William Allin on Sundays and other days and had criticized clergy and magistrates. Allin, John Newland's wife, and Richard Kerbey were summoned to the next Court. Nicholas Upshall, the apparent perpetrator of Sandwich difficulties, hence the first Quaker missionary to Plymouth Colony, had his license to stay in Sandwich terminated as of March 1. But meetings continued at John Newland's house, and on March 5 the Court of Assistants ordered a halt to them and also issued a second order expelling Upshall, who had not departed.[30]

As a consequence of the appearance of Quakers, Plymouth General Court passed the first of a series of anti-Quaker laws, legislation which would be abandoned, although not repealed, after Charles II's restoration. These laws, passed in June 1657, required all Plymouth residents to take an oath to the colony and Commonwealth before the following October, a stipulation clearly designed to smoke out any Quakers, who would not swear an oath. Anyone bringing in a "Quaker rantor or other Notoriouse heretiques" was to take them out within a week or pay a one-pound fine for each week such person or persons remained. In October the General Court passed further legislation, adding a fine of 5 pounds or whipping for entertaining any Quaker knowingly, and requiring residents to inform a magistrate of the presence of Friends. The General Court moved belatedly to put an end to Quaker meetings: speakers in meetings and owners of houses where Quakers met were each to be fined forty shillings; every head of a family attending the meeting was to be fined ten shillings.[31]

The legislation in the fall of 1657 was a result of the continued influx of "foreign" Quakers—a visitation from *Woodhouse* missionaries—and identifiable participation of other Plymouth residents: additional Sandwich inhabitants as well as those from Marshfield and Scituate. Humphrey Norton, a recent addition to the foreign missionaries, was examined, found guilty, and expelled, to meet with much more severe treatment in New Haven, his next point of confrontation with New England Puritan opponents. Robert Hodgson, rumored to be at Arthur Howland's house, escaped. For having frequently assisted Quakers, Sandwich residents William Newland and Ralph Allin were ordered to find sureties for their good behavior and when they refused were incarcerated, a mild punishment compared with Massachusetts treatment of resident Friends. The General Court ordered the Marshfield Howlands, Arthur, Henry, John Junior, and Zoeth to appear before it in March; but for all of Plymouth's efforts, foreign Quakers maintained their ministrations in the colony.[32]

On February 2, 1658, John Copeland was found guilty of speaking falsely about John Alden—he was whipped and again expelled. There followed another spate of confrontations as most resident converts refused to give in and Plymouth determined to make them. In 1658 the colony effectively disfranchised Friends: no Quaker, drunkard, or person who refused to take the oath could vote. Furthermore, in an effort to deal with foreign Quakers who had no means of visible support, the colony ordered the erection of a workhouse so that they would support themselves. Fourteen Sandwich Friends were fined in June, a procedure that continued semiannually until the Restoration brought an abandonment of this policy. Only one adherent, Arthur Howland, abjectly sought the Court's forgiveness of his "factiouse, seditious, and slanderouse" activities. Humphrey Norton appeared again, accompanied by John Rous, and behaved as "turbulently" as he had recently in New Haven. When they refused to take the requisite oath, both were whipped.[33]

Despite this repression, matters were out of control. Sandwich as a town was resisting Plymouth Colony's attempts to enforce policy within it—not the last time Plymouth and Massachusetts were to meet resistance on that basis. The colony ordered the appointment of a marshal to enforce its law as the Sandwich constable had not been able to do (or would not do). Never a respected position anyway, the post of constable did not draw men of talent in the colonial period. Nor was the appointed marshal, George Barlow, admired. Barlow endured a lengthy period of abuse from residents who probably resented the colony's heavy-handed tactics as well as ex post facto exclusion of nine Sandwich residents from participation in town meeting. The General Court acted, it is true, in response to a petition, but given the need for the colony to appoint a marshal, it is probable that the petition asking for a marshal represented only a minority view within the town. The struggle thereupon took on the character of a town-colony skirmish, not simply a colonial struggle with heterodoxical invaders.[34]

Defiance in Sandwich continued, and to a lesser extent in Scituate. In the latter town James Cudworth, a magistrate removed from office for disagreeing with Prence's policies in March 1658, had criticized colonial actions, had written a correspondent abroad about his views, and had those views published. The General Court disfranchised him. Paralleling George Barlow's efforts to coerce Sandwich residents, colonial leaders in June 1659 attempted to entice opponents to leave the colony. Friends who would "engage" to move from Plymouth could do so without fine, and a committee was to see if Friends could be persuaded to abandon their errors. The colony continued its efforts in 1660, passing a new act to incorporate provisions of old laws before the Restoration, and the following year maintained its campaign against itinerant Friends. But that the policy had failed was well demonstrated by Cudworth's resumption of colonial responsibilities and by reference in colony records to "a Constant monthly meeting" of Quakers. To meet that threat the best the General Court could do was send two men to convince Quakers of their errors. After 1661 it appears that major persecution ceased, although anti-Quaker laws remained on the books and some local harassment of Friends continued fitfully.[35]

Rhode Island

Rhode Island proved to be the most fruitful area for early Quaker missionary activity among the northern colonies. A tolerant leadership permitted virtually any belief to be propagated. More important, many residents had beliefs which for years had closely paralleled Friends. The one-time Antinomian supporters of Anne Hutchinson, most of whom lived on Aquidneck Island in the towns of Portsmouth and Newport, proved to be the earliest and most numerous converts. Probably because of Quaker successes and the lack of persecution, relatively little docu-

mentation survives on conversions in Rhode Island. Most Quaker literature of this period used Rhode Island as a happy contrast to less tolerant
neighboring colonies. Friends writing about New England were more
interested in persecutions than in recording conversions and thereby
helped cause significant distortion of the records.

Rhode Island had a certain notoriety before Quakerism appeared in
New England. Dutch pastors in New Amsterdam referred to it as a
cesspool, as noted, and English leaders outside Rhode Island had little
affection for either Roger Williams or the Antinomians. When in 1657
the United Colonies of New England, reflecting Massachusetts leadership and, no doubt, the enthusiasm of the other members of the confederation (Connecticut, New Haven, and Plymouth), sought Rhode
Island's support for their anti-Quaker policy, they could not have hoped
for a favorable reaction.[36]

Replies from the heterodox colony must have confirmed the worst
fears of the United Colonies and certainly signaled that there would be
no repressive policies. Benedict Arnold, president of the Court of Tryals
at Providence, sent them a letter on October 13, 1657. He reminded
commissioners that Rhode Island did not have laws abridging expression of anyone's political opinions and suggested that the menace seen
by commissioners would probably go away if only Quakers were ignored, for "they delight to be persecuted by civil powers." Further
confirmation of toleration came from John Sanford, clerk of the Rhode
Island assembly, when he informed Governor John Endecott of Massachusetts and the Commissioners of the United Colonies in March
1658 that Rhode Island intended to continue to comply with charter
provisions requiring freedom of conscience in the colony.[37]

Rhode Island was much more than a base of operations. First conversions in the colony in 1657 simply marked the beginning of a fifteen-
year process by which Quakers would eventually become the colony's
dominant political and religious faction. Prominent among early Quakers were Nicholas Easton and his two sons, John and Peter; William and
Anne Coddington; Catherine Scott (sister of Anne Hutchinson); and
Henry Bull. The impact of conversions surely must have gone beyond
these people, especially on Aquidneck Island; in any event, resident
Quakers were reinforced by English Friends traveling in the ministry who settled there: Robert Hodgson, Ann Clayton, and Joseph and
Jane Nicholson. It also became a haven for such refugees from Massachusetts as Joshua Buffum, and Eliakin Wardell and his wife, Lydia
—at least before the Wardells moved on to Newtown, Long Island.
The process of most conversions, early growth, and organization, how-

ever, went unrecorded as attention of Friends was focused on campaigns in Massachusetts which had little success. Despite this lack of atten tion, before 1670 and probably as early as 1660 Rhode Island was the most important Quaker northern colony.

New York

Quaker missionaries came to New Netherland within a year of Anne Austin's and Mary Fisher's arrival in Massachusetts. Unlike the United Colonies of New England, New Netherland for the most part did not actively seek to coerce local residents to abandon Quakerism. Nor did savage repressive legislation and a major English town like Boston serve as magnets. As indicated, there were residents in English towns on Long Island many of whom had migrated from Massachusetts and were favorably disposed toward the message of early Friends, much as there were former Antinomians in Rhode Island. Friends found no support for their activities in Dutch areas. Governor Peter Stuyvesant was primarily responsible for the reception given Friends. Although he wanted to maintain reformed churches, the Dutch West India Company forced him to accept a policy whereby the colony would not harass peaceable dissenters. There would be difficulties for Quakers, but not in degree like those in Massachusetts and Plymouth.[38]

First signs of a Quaker presence came to an unsuspecting New Amsterdam in 1657 when five of the *Woodhouse* Friends debarked. Two of them, Mary Wetherhead and Dorothy Waugh, felt constrained to proclaim "Truth" in the streets before startled Dutch residents. Unappreciative, the colony banished the two women for their outburst; joined by the other woman, Sarah Gibbons, and Richard Doudney, the four set out on a proselytizing trek to Boston, apparently via Rhode Island and Plymouth. One man, Robert Hodgson, stayed behind; he was apprehended in Hempstead and carried back to New Amsterdam. While Governor Stuyvesant would probably have been content to expel him, he was also bent on having the proprieties due his rank and office observed. When Hodgson refused to doff his hat, Stuyvesant had him imprisoned and ordered him to do manual labor beside African slaves. Hodgson refused. His imprisonment was unjust, he claimed, and moreover, he was not used to such work—a reflection not merely of his social status but perhaps of his view of Africans. There followed such a savage series of beatings that some residents thought he would die. Dutch efforts to wring compliance from him proved unavailing, and eventually he was expelled. Yet not, it seems, before he and other Friends had spread the Quaker message to English towns where inhabitants set up Quaker meetings—an easy task, since most of these towns did not have resident clergy, and, like Sandwich in Plymouth colony, proved vulnerable to Quaker efforts.[39]

New Netherland belatedly established legal defenses against foreign Quakers. A new law set a 50-pound fine for any resident who entertained them. It was soon tested by Friends in the town of Flushing, where Henry Townsend was the first to suffer its penalty. Many town residents, rallying to his support, presented a petition to Stuyvesant. The action has been known since as the Flushing Remonstrance and was an early instance of demand for religious toleration. Thirty-one residents signed the petition, including the town clerk, Edward Hunt; Tobias Feeke, the schute or sheriff; and Edward Farrington and William Noble, magistrates. Stuyvesant and his Council soon discovered that the originator of the petition was Tobias Feeke, who had talked clerk Hart into drawing it up and the magistrates into signing it: all except Feeke offered abject apologies and remained in office, although the magistrates were suspended from acting in office. Aside from this action, essentially directed against foreign Friends, there seem to have been no immediate steps taken against native Quaker converts, who appear to have been numerous, particularly in Flushing, Oyster Bay, and Cow Neck, all part of the Dutch Long Island jurisdiction.[40]

Not until 1662 did occasion for confrontation arise again. This time Stuyvesant had John Bowne, a well-to-do resident of Flushing, hailed before the Council in New Amsterdam on September 1 for entertaining Quakers in his house and for permitting Quaker meetings there. The Council fined Bowne 25 pounds and costs, with the threat of a double fine for a second offense and banishment for a third. Bowne refused to recognize the decision and for his recalcitrance was imprisoned for three months. The Council then ordered him transported, and on December 31 he sailed, intent on appealing to the company in Amsterdam. After Bowne presented his case there, the governors of the West India Company sent a reprimand to Stuyvesant in 1663 ordering him to cease his harassment of Quakers. There the matter rested insofar as the Dutch were concerned, for the following year the English captured New Amsterdam.[41]

New Haven

Most of New Haven colony was not exposed to Quaker ministrations. Its communities on the mainland were served effectively by its clergy, and the residents resisted Quaker preachings. There had not been an Antinomian schism. Mainland towns of New Haven were safely orthodox. There was, however, the town of Southold on Eastern Long Island, at this time under New Haven's jurisdiction, where there was no clergyman and which as a consequence was potentially vulnerable to Quaker missionary activity. So too was Shelter Island, facing Southold, where Captain Nathaniel Sylvester was open to Quaker views. Some residents of Greenwich on the western mainland border with New Netherland also listened to Quaker missionaries and may have become Friends. [42]

Rather suddenly in March 1658, New Haven became aware that it had a problem on its hands. Authorities seized Humphrey Norton, recently banished from Plymouth, in Southold and took him to the town of New Haven for trial. The town convened a special court to try him, with special judges William Leefe of Guilford and Benjamin Fenn of Milford to assist the magistrates. Charged on the first day of trial with having attempted to seduce Southold residents with heretical beliefs and also disturbing the peace by interrupting a church service, Norton refused to answer the colony's charges, demanding that charges of his own be read. He remained silent for the remainder of the day as the court heard evidence against him alleging that his views were anti-sacramental, perfectionist, and anarchistic. When elders from Connecticut churches sought to debate with him, he refused to talk. The spirit did not move him, he said. To the consternation of authorities he did speak out the next day, in an outburst which the court, by this time preparing to sentence him, had no intention of hearing. Silenced, he was sentenced to be whipped, his hand was branded with an "h" (for heretic), and he was fined 10 pounds. A Dutchman, probably Andries de Haas of Manhattan, paid his fine. After being whipped and branded, Norton and three other Friends were sent out of the colony. [43]

It remained for New Haven to enact a law sustaining punishment already inflicted on Norton, a form of ex post facto legislation that seems to have escaped Quaker critics at the time and an action that made the colony's actions thoroughly reprehensible, for although Norton had behaved in a provocative manner, he had broken no law. In May the General Court first approved the sentence given Norton and then passed the law that was supportive of his sentence. The preamble contained the familiar rubric of anti-Quaker legislation: "Whereas there is a cursed sect of hereticks lately risen up in the world . . ." A fine of 50 pounds was provided for anyone knowingly bringing a Quaker to New Haven, and for Quakers coming to proselytize, a whipping, followed by expulsion. For a second offense men were to be branded on one hand with an "h"; for a third offense they were to be branded on the other hand; and for a fourth, their tongue was to be bored with a hot iron.

Women were to suffer whipping, not branding, for second and third offenses. Additional provisions provided fines of 5 pounds for importing Quaker books, 20 shillings for each hour one knowingly entertained Quakers, and for defending the Quaker position 2 pounds the first time and 4 for each additional time; and 5 pounds and a whipping for reviling the magistrates.[44]

New Haven found few victims for this law. Goodman Richard Crabb and his wife lived in Greenwich, a jurisdiction in dispute between New Haven and New Netherland. Crabb came before the court in May 1658, contrite and no longer asserting his previous defiance to New Haven authority (in part because of his claim that New Netherland had jurisdiction over Greenwich). He pleaded that he was unable to control his wife's outbursts against and abuses of authorities, or her preference for Quakers. Moreover, she had refused to accompany him to court. The court fined him 30 pounds and demanded security of 100 pounds. Other than Crabb, no one appeared before the courts in 1658. Perhaps neither Southold residents sympathetic to Friends nor Nathaniel Sylvester of Shelter Island had been caught yet.[45]

By the next year the situation in all of New England had changed. As alert now to a threat to authority from within as from without, New Haven turned on resident Quaker sympathizers. On May 23, 1659, Arthur Smith of Southold came before the General Court to answer for his apparent Quaker views. Asked how he came to be corrupted by Quaker beliefs, he answered that he did not think he was corrupted. Thereupon, New Haven authorities set out a list of his views (which to them were "errors"): he had urged attention to the Light Within; he had said there was no devil; he had said infants had no sin until they had sinned (denying evil inherited from Adam); and he had argued that God only (and not a hireling Presbyterian priest) could be his teacher. The Court found his behavior "p[ro]phaine, absurd, conceited and ridiculous." Demonstrating remarkable restraint compared to Massachusetts, the Court bound him over on 50 pounds for good behavior, to appear at the next session, unless, as New Haven leaders apparently wanted him to do, he had left their jurisdiction.[46]

Resistance gradually disappeared after this. Smith and other Southold Friends apparently left New Haven. By the end of the century visiting Friends would note that Quakerism was not to be found in eastern Long Island. New Haven reduced the severity of its law in May 1660, giving justices the alternatives of imposing fines for first and second offenses by Quaker missionaries. And the Court dealt with Nathaniel Sylvester's evident sympathy with Friends (he had made his views known in Southold, had written a letter to New Haven, and had sheltered Salem refugees) by ordering 100 pounds worth of his goods seized until he made satisfaction at the next Court. He did not appear the following October, nor in May 1661. There is no record that any of his goods were seized. In any event the case became moot after 1664 when Southold and Shelter Island were added to the jurisdiction of the recently conquered New York, although Connecticut authorities could not have been pleased by New York Governor Richard Nicolls' confirmation of Sylvester's claim to the island in 1666.[47]

Connecticut

The Connecticut relationship with Friends was confined to proscriptive legislation and to support for the United Colonies' efforts to eject and keep Quakers out. Connecticut had no cells of discontented people sympathetic to Friends; churches had clergy; and there was a capable and restrained leadership in the hands of John Winthrop, son of the former Massachusetts governor. Of course Winthrop did not have the considerable invasion of Quakers which Massachusetts faced, but even if he had, one suspects, the response would have been more restrained.

Connecticut acted to keep Quakerism out even before Massachusetts and without any Quaker harassment. On October 2, 1656, the General Court prohibited towns from permitting Quakers to reside in them for more than fourteen days, with a 5-pound penalty for each week in excess of that time. Townsmen were to inform magistrates of the presence of Quakers, and the law required those persons who brought Friends in to take them out again or pay a fine of 20 pounds. Two years later the Court passed a law to supplement the original legislation providing magistrates with the option of punishing Quaker missionaries by either fine or corporal punishment and providing a fine of up to 10 pounds for any Connecticut resident "instrumental" in bringing Quakers in. A final law followed in 1661 providing a penalty of 10 pounds for each conviction for having Quaker books or writings.[48]

Thus in the space of four years Quakers had come to New England and New Netherland. Particularly successful in Rhode Island among onetime Antinomians, they also enjoyed considerable success in Plymouth and in English settlements on the western end of Long Island. They did much less well in Massachusetts, where they seemed determined to fight the "Lamb's War"—as they put it—against antiChrist. They suffered imprisonment, whippings, ear-croppings, and execution at the hands of Massachusetts authorities in this expansive period when many Friends sought martyrdom. They might have stayed in Rhode Island, where they were safe, tolerated, and even welcomed by many people. As a consequence, attention then and since has focused on Massachusetts, the area of particularly sharp conflict, where there were few converts, rather than on sections where Quakers successfully proselytized the population.[49]

Chapter 2
Schism, Persecution, and Politics

BETWEEN 1661, WHEN A restored Charles
II effectively terminated the Massachusetts practice of executing Quakers, and 1684, when Massachusetts lost its charter in *quo warranto* proceedings, there were a host of developments which affected Friends.
Rhode Island received a charter in 1663, continuing its existence as a
corporate colony and thereby assuring Friends of the continuance of one
hospitable northern colony. Plymouth was not accorded similar recognition, but was permitted to continue without hindrance, whereas Massachusetts, still defiant of royal authority, found itself under the threat
of increasing control. New Netherland ceased to exist: after 1664 it was
an English colony renamed New York, under the proprietorship of the
Duke of York. Complementing imperial changes was the maturation of
the colonies themselves. The few founders still alive in the 1650's and
many of the second generation of New England leaders died, signaling a
change in colonial outlook. Old causes created new effects and sometimes reappeared as myth. In New York an entire leadership was replaced.

Set against this background, many of the developments of Quakerism become intelligible. In the 1660's the Quaker movement was much
the same as in 1656—still persecuted in Massachusetts, in part because
its prophetic excesses gave the leadership there an excuse to persecute—
nonexistent in Connecticut—but flourishing in Rhode Island and in
Sandwich, Dartmouth, and Tiverton in Plymouth. It increased in numbers, however, and after 1670 in Rhode Island it became a political
force to be reckoned with. On Long Island, Friends were permitted to
settle and were not harassed, save for occasional distraints to support
war-making, fortification-building, or other churches; and there were
several prosecutions to challenge marriages contracted in Quaker meetings. Gradually, however, Friends received better treatment in the hitherto hostile colonies, and in their turn became more conservative.

Massachusetts

In 1661 Charles II's letter prohibiting further execution of Quakers jolted Massachusetts, and the colony sent John Norton to London to argue its case. The following November it repealed, for a time, the Cart and Whip Act in obedience to Charles's command. The General Court noted that Charles certainly would not have undertaken this action if he had been better informed. Perhaps in response to this royal misunderstanding, the General Court declared that Massachusetts was to observe a day of humiliation, for heretics had been permitted to "ruin sincere servants of God."[1]

Because of Charles's letter, Friends perceived an opening (soon to be terminated) to proselytize in the colony. They turned from the vicinity of Boston to more fruitful regions under Massachusetts control north of Salem. Whether they had prior information about potentialities for conversions in northern Massachusetts, their penetration was successful, judging from the subsequent reaction of the Massachusetts General Court which a year later reenacted the Cart and Whip Act. Quakers, according to the Act's preamble, now abounded "especially in the eastern parts" (that is, the settlements north and east of Salem) and had attempted "to draw away others to that wicked opinion." In part, the General Court was responding to a petition from the town of Dover and in addition to the reenactment of the Cart and Whip Act ordered Captain Richard Waldern to execute anti-Quaker laws. No doubt the General Court had also responded to a second letter from Charles II, who had had a chance to reconsider. John Norton had just returned from his mission to England, for which the Court voted him payment of 66 pounds, and it is quite possible that he carried the letter, although the letter itself was not entered in General Court minutes until two years later. Charles had asserted on June 28, 1662, that he had not intended "to direct or wish that any indulgence should be granted to those persons commonly called Quakers." He had found it necessary to have Parliament pass laws against them, and Charles was "well contented that you doe the like there."[2]

Conflict followed the renewed attempt to deal with Quakers in Massachusetts. Defying the law, friends continued to disseminate their views north of Salem. Alice Ambrose, Mary Tomkins, and Ann Coleman outraged "Priest" Raymer of Dover. Raymer had charged that Friends did not believe in the Trinity of three persons. The women challenged him to prove the existence of those three, and, they said, he fled the debate, being unable to do so. The women were soon joined by Edward Wharton and George Preston of Salem. The enlarged group sought out old Hutchinsonians at Kittery, then returned to Dover to

suffer under the recently reenacted Cart and Whip Act. As before, physical punishment failed to deter them. Resident Friends, of course, remained subject to provisions of other laws requiring church attendance
and tax support, and they continued to be fined for breaking the laws.[3]

As indicated, many of the Salem converts were on the fringe of their
community—deviants, as Kai Erikson argues. They were probably
thought of as eccentrics even before their conversion to the Quaker
movement, which at this stage had decided millennial tendencies.
Moreover, early Quakerism, an offshoot of the Puritan left, developed
an astonishing number of schisms in England and America before
George Fox and his supporters brought the movement and particularly
the ministering Friends under control. Even before 1660 the new faith
had triggered an ascetic response principally, though not exclusively,
among Salem converts. Subsequently, Friends had been temporarily
freed from restraint and, so far as one can tell, abandoned their deviant
practices. Now the reenactment of the Cart and Whip Act not only
sparked a renewal of aspirations for martyrdom among Quaker missionaries and their converts, but also increased their bizarre behavior. Perhaps the frustration of Quaker expectations, which had attended the
revival of persecution, fueled this response.[4]

The first signs of Friends going beyond verbal denunciation of opponents in churches and streets and of their willingness, even eagerness, to
seek punishment came in 1663, in response to renewed persecution.
Catherine Chatham, an Englishwoman, went through the streets of
Boston in sackcloth and ashes "as a sign of the Indignation of the Lord
against that oppressing and tyrannical Spirit" of Massachusetts leaders.
The magistrates responded by imprisoning her. The same year Thomas
Newhouse, who had already received a whipping for his missionary
efforts, went into the Boston meeting house and broke two glass bottles
on the floor, telling the startled congregation "'*So shall you be dashed in
pieces.*'" He received another whipping.[5]

The whippings continued. Generally, they resulted when missionaries aroused the clergy by successful forays into the distant communities above Salem and from the strange behavior of those who either
appeared in sackcloth and ashes or went naked publicly as a sign to their
persecutors. Occasionally, they sprang from the authorities' attempts to
stop peaceable meetings, as when Secretary Edward Rawson exceeded
the bounds of the Cart and Whip Act by having Edward Wharton, a
resident of Salem, punished in May 1664 for being a vagabond Quaker.
In 1665 two women, excited by their faith and the persecution it had
attracted, went naked for a sign. After Eliakin Wardell of Hampton had
been fined for entertaining a Quaker missionary, Wenlock Christian,

and for not attending church services, Eliakin's wife Lydia went naked into the Newbury meeting house. She was, Joseph Besse tells us, testifying against the whipping of women stripped naked above the waist, a punishment that Ipswich magistrates inflicted on her also, and not an unusual punishment for disturbers of the peace, male and female, in all New England colonies at this time, including the Quaker haven of Rhode Island. Deborah Wilson of Salem had also gone naked in the streets of Salem and had also been whipped. Her mother, Thomasin Buffum, and her sister, Margaret Smith, who had accompanied her, were also lashed, but so leniently that magistrate William Hathorne and the Salem clergyman John Higginson saw to it that a more rigorous constable was elected at the next town election. To complete an untidy year, Elizabeth Hooten, an English Quaker missionary who had the added distinction of being George Fox's first convert, had actively and successfully sought converts north of Salem. She had already endured imprisonment and whipping in Massachusetts when she went to the funeral of John Endecott, the late Massachusetts governor, whom she denounced during the burial service, a breach of propriety for which she was again imprisoned.[6]

After 1665 Quaker hostilities apparently diminished as a new generation of rulers came to terms with Quakers who would not go away, and Friends thereby became less militant in spreading their gospel. For the balance of the decade, in fact, Friends in Massachusetts apparently were able to meet undisturbed, although they continued to be fined and to have their goods distrained for failing to attend church services. In Plymouth the practice of distraints seems to have disappeared, as towns worked out their own religious compromises. New York authorities left Friends free to worship in the little English towns on Long Island, where they formed at least a substantial minority in Hempstead and neighboring communities and probably a majority in Flushing.[7]

The Perrotonian Schism in New England and New York

One of the most serious disputes that rent Quakerism in its early years was the schism led by John Perrot. It raised questions that would surface again. As noted, Perrot was one of the early traveling ministers. In 1657 he had gone to the Italian peninsula to convert Catholics. Eventually he went to Rome and sought out the Pope. In that he was unsuccessful, and for several years he was imprisoned there. On his return to England in 1661 a separate movement began to grow up around him and by 1662 was fully developed.[8]

The point first at issue between him and George Fox, George Whitehead, and others of what came to be "orthodox" Quakerism centered on whether one should remove one's hat in times of public testimony in Quaker meetings. Eventually (by 1664) Perrot himself had reached the point of arguing against even scheduling meetings, although to what extent his movement followed him in that practice cannot be determined. The heart of the controversy centered on authority within Quakerism: was a central group of Fox, Whitehead, and others to impose regulations on all Friends? If so might they not frustrate the leadings of the Spirit? Could Perrot and his followers be sure that they followed the leadings of God, the spirit of Christ within? Should not individuals submit themselves to group judgment for fear that the devil, not Christ, was guiding them, or that their creaturely desires misled them? Non-Quaker critics had raised these questions before, charging that Friends, like the Antinomians and Ranters, were without restraint—were in fact anarchistic. Quakerism, initially a splinter of the Puritan Revolution, now began the long process of bringing its millennial expectations under control and as a consequence changing from a group of excited spirits to an orderly religious movement.[9]

Evidence is lacking of the reception given Perrotonian views by most Friends in New England and New York. It seems safe to assume, however, that because there was no reference to its existence, this schism had little effect on friends in the New England Quaker centers of Plymouth and Rhode Island, and it may not have affected Friends on Long Island, for there is no direct primary evidence that groups were under Perrot's influence, although Kenneth Carroll, the historian of the schism, convincingly argues that a group that opposed John Burnyeat in 1671 might have had Perrotonian tendencies. Only in Salem and Boston is there solid evidence of the schism and of its continuance for a number of years.[10]

As noted, Salem Quaker celibacy had caused disagreement among Friends. Of those who had turned to celibacy, Salem Friends Samuel Shattuck and Josiah Southwick and Boston's John Chamberlain had accepted Perrot's position by 1664. Perhaps Jane Stokes, one of Perrot's leading followers, had contacted them, as she may also have influenced residents of Nantucket. Whatever the source of their conversion, those onetime Salem celibates testified against the loyal supporters of George Fox, Elizabeth Hooten, and Ann (Borden) Richardson. When Elizabeth and Ann returned to Salem accompanied by Jane Nicholson, Shattuck opposed the reading of one of George Fox's papers against John Perrot. Thereupon Jane denounced Shattuck much as she would have a magistrate or clergyman of that area. Shattuck countered that she had "A ranters Spirit." Ann in turn told Shattuck he was a reprobate, for "he was not Ignorant of the power of God." Shattuck and supporters charged that Ann was "there greatest troubler" and that she had written papers which she made old Elizabeth Hooten sign. Not so, said Ann, she had simply written what Elizabeth (who was apparently unable to write) had told her. The upshot was that Ann Richardson and Jane Nicholson sent a letter of testimony against Southwick, and Ann sent another against Shattuck. None of this could have helped Friends in the eyes of local inhabitants. Furthermore, the Perrotonians seemed to be an entrenched group: John Chamberlain was disseminating Perrotonian views in Boston and Elizabeth Hooten was not able to do anything about it, for the authorities would not permit her to buy a house—a purchase, it would seem, which had as much to do with countering Perrot's views as testifying against recent persecutions. John Perrot's followers continued to maintain their position, and perhaps they passed for Quakers as far as Boston and Salem residents were concerned. Eight years later in 1671, when John Burnyeat, the Irish Friend, was in Salem, he encountered Friends still following Perrot. They also opposed the efforts by Burnyeat, Fox, and other Friends from England and Ireland to establish meetings for discipline.[11]

Thereafter, so far as the historian can tell, this schism disappeared. Those holding Perrotonian views who did not rejoin the Society may have joined later disaffected groups or simply left Quaker meetings completely. The schism had not had a great effect on major centers of Quakerism, where converts were more stable, more willing to accept organization, and more likely to have expectations of commanding a place in the world. In many ways the Perrotonian schism in New England was symptomatic of developments throughout Quakerism. Partly because of it, before the termination of the Massachusetts charter made Quaker missionary activity again successful in the 1680's, Friends were centered in Plymouth and Rhode Island, not in the symbolic centers of early New England Quakerism—Boston and the neighboring town of Salem.

Rhode Island Politics

The debate between Friends and Roger Williams in 1672 ranks high in early New England Quaker history. Missing from the accounts of this confrontation, however, are the circumstances behind both the date and the ultimate publication of Williams' version of it. The occasion for the debate lay in an attempt by Williams to refurbish his political faction's tarnished image and to unseat the dominant Quaker group in forthcoming elections. The attempt failed, however, for Friends solidified their political power and probably would have continued to dominate Rhode Island politics had it not been for King Philip's War. The war not only enabled a temporary comeback of the Williams faction in Rhode Island, but also brought about renewed persecution of Quakers in Massachusetts. That persecution in turn led to an exchange of pamphlets which finally gave Roger Williams the opportunity to publish his account of his debate with Friends four years earlier. Historians have too easily accepted Williams' apologia, however, thus failing to appreciate the ambiguities in the affair.

For over a decade after their arrival in 1656, Quakers in Rhode Island were free from controversy and persecution. All elements of that factious colony united to defend the right of Friends to convert Rhode Islanders and to use the colony as a base of operations against other New England colonies. Rhode Island's leaders favored this tolerant policy. Previous and current attempts of Connecticut and Massachusetts to take territory claimed by Rhode Island may also have encouraged toleration. As a consequence, Quaker successes in making converts in the colony attested to Rhode Island's continued acceptance of resident Friends and reception of Quaker immigrants. Though Friends as a group avoided political disputes before 1672, their increasing numbers, the prominence of several of them in colonial politics, and factional disputes within the colony brought them into prominence—if not as a party, at least as a group which for the moment dominated Rhode Island politics.[12]

Elections in May 1671 had returned Governor Benedict Arnold and replaced Deputy Governor Nicholas Easton, a Friend, with John Clarke, a Newport Baptist. One of the issues confronting the Rhode Island Assembly that May resulted from the refusal of a number of towns, among them Providence and Warwick, to pay 1670 taxes—neither the first nor the last time those and other Rhode Island towns would refuse to do so. The Assembly, to secure payment of taxes from the recalcitrant towns, empowered the Governor and any two assistants to appoint assessors if town assessors refused to act. If towns failed to name assessors, the legislation authorized the commissioners themselves to make the assessment. One of the commissioners was the elder statesman of the colony and a Providence resident, Roger Williams. He and the other commissioners apparently encountered so much resistance that they returned the matter to the Assembly, which during its September sitting nominated rate-makers and ordered a doubling of rates for persons failing to pay.[13]

The other long-standing difficulty confronting the Assembly in 1671 concerned title to the Narragansett and Pawtuxet lands—essentially to the west of Narragansett Bay. Speculation in these lands by residents of Massachusetts, Connecticut, and Rhode Island formed one aspect of the problem; another involved a claim by the colony of Connecticut to the Narragansett lands; a third centered on the dispute over Pawtuxet lands among Providence residents. In the Pawtuxet case, Roger Williams opposed claims advanced by older settlers led by William Harris, also of Providence. To deal with Connecticut's claims, the Assembly voted 200 pounds so that Deputy Governor John Clarke could present Rhode Island's position to the crown. To break up the control of Narragansett speculators, the Assembly recommended that the next assembly authorize the division of speculators' lands.[14]

William Harris, an opponent of these measures, thereupon entered into negotiations with Connecticut. To secure his own claims and probably those of others, he offered to accept the Connecticut claim. Roger Williams, hearing of Harris' activities, accused Harris of disloyalty. Harris, taken before the Rhode Island council on February 4, was arrested and imprisoned, awaiting trial "for speaking and writing against his Majesties gracious Charter . . . and in subverting the Government there established."[15]

Several issues converged to cause a crisis in the young colony in April 1672. Trouble continued with Providence. In March the refusal of deputies from that town to attend the Assembly had forced it to dissolve for lack of a quorum. Now, in April, two rival delegations claimed seats in the Assembly. Why the first group of delegates refused to attend in March (or whether they refused at all) is uncertain. In any event, the Assembly voted to seat the second group. Although these delegates had in the past supported William Harris and may have continued to do so, within a year two of them, Thomas Olney, Jr., and John Whipple, Jr., opposed Harris and his Quaker allies. Having resolved the delegate issue, the Assembly refused to accept a paper from William Harris presented by Friend Walter Clarke (probably at this stage a leader of an emerging Quaker-Harris faction and later governor). The majority rejected it on the flimsy excuse that Harris had failed to address the Assembly in the terms used in the colony's charter. Then, after passing a law to permit Providence and Warwick to decide how to raise funds, including the financing of John Clarke's trip to England, the Assembly faction with which Roger Williams was associated proceeded to pass another law, probably directed against Harris and his supporters, which muzzled debate, abridged free speech, and consequently placed a blemish on the record of that apostle of freedom as well as the faction as a whole. The Assembly acted, it said, against "covetous . . . Factions and mallicious spirit . . . in sundry townes." These groups, according to the act, had opposed "all or any rates," thereby putting Rhode Island in dangerous financial circumstances. In the future "if any person or persons in any town or place . . . more especially in any town meeting or other publique assembly" should oppose rates set by the Assembly or its "Acts and Orders" by speaking against them or urging their rejection, "all and every such person shall be questioned and proceeded against as for high contempt and sedition." The penalty stipulated thirty lashes, or imprisonment for twelve months, or a fine of 20 pounds. In actions related to its anti-Harris measures, the Assembly provided for the ejection of any residents of Stonington, Connecticut, who invaded Westerly, Rhode Island, and the expropriation of land belonging to Westerly residents who had submitted to Connecticut authority. It also established a committee to survey Narragansett lands, to prepare for the settlement of new towns, and to treat with the Indians and English colonists to extinguish their claims by May, when a new Assembly would meet. Finally, the Assembly raised the salaries of the governor, deputy governor, assistants, and deputies.[16]

The new law, which muzzled criticism, enraged Rhode Islanders, who promptly voted most of its perpetrators out of office in May 1672. After former governor William Brenton (a land speculator himself) refused the governorship, the assembly chose Quaker Nicholas Easton. The new Assembly, all the Newport deputies of which were Friends, repealed the "muzzling" act, the legislation sending John Clarke to England, and the provision increasing the pay of public officials. It considered the complaint of Providence resident Arthur Fenner, one of the recently elected assistants, that the previous Assembly had seated an improperly selected delegation from Providence. The May Assembly forbade such actions in the future "as being innovations in law and government and contrary to law and equity." It also sent conciliatory letters to Connecticut, thus disavowing the Williams faction.[17]

In November the Assembly continued earlier policies. As Providence deputies and assistants had again absented themselves in October, forcing an adjournment, the Assembly passed an act permitting as many magistrates and deputies as could assemble to legislate in all matters except taxation, and fining those absent without excuse. With Providence absenteeism controlled, the Assembly revoked previous forfeiture legislation concerning land claims in the Narragansett, thereby relieving several Rhode Islanders, some of whom were Friends, from the threat of expropriation. It reimbursed William Harris, now one of the deputies elected from Providence and recently imprisoned as a traitor by the Assembly dominated by Roger Williams and his friends.[18]

Friends had now gained control of Rhode Island government. Associated with land speculators as they were, their motives must have extended beyond a concern to protect free speech. Most important, however, the behavior of the Williams faction had provided the impetus for the Quaker electoral victory. Under the circumstances the identifiable entrance of a Quaker party to government was not as antidemocratic as some historians have suggested. Although in retrospect the actions of land speculators—ranging from the notorious purchases by the Atherton group to William Harris' negotiations with Connecticut—seem reprehensible, the activities of the Williams faction appear in their own right as both arbitrary and oligarchic. The clash brought Friends and Roger Williams into open conflict, and one must interpret in this context the doctrinal debates that ensued.[19]

Sixteen hundred and seventy-two was also the year that the leading English Friend, George Fox, visited the North American colonies. He came primarily to organize Quaker business meetings in America, like those established in England. He set about doing so as he moved north from Barbadoes, confirming in some instances work already started the previous year by the Irish Friend John Burnyeat. Fox arrived in Rhode Island shortly after Friends, in alliance with William Harris' supporters, had taken control of the colony government. The chances are high that he would have been well received anyway, but the recent election of a Quaker government enhanced his reception. It was also a virtual certainty that Williams would not be favorably disposed, and his sudden public opposition to Friends (he claimed later that he had sought to debate Friends in 1671), after they had been present in the colony for at least fifteen years was hardly accidental.[20]

Williams challenged Fox to a debate after Fox's visit to Providence. Fox later claimed that he had left Rhode Island before Williams' challenge reached him. Williams argued that Fox had fled from his challenge—a highly unlikely circumstance, for Fox was not one to avoid disputation. It is possible, however, that word of the challenge failed to reach Fox. Why Williams did not challenge him when he visited Providence remains unclear. If Williams was indeed intent upon attacking Friends on theological grounds, he had had ample opportunity to prepare ever since Friends first arrived in the colony. In the absence of compelling evidence to the contrary, it is best to place Williams' challenge in the context of current Rhode Island politics. His challenge had as much to do with an attempt to refurbish his group's political fortunes as with publicizing Quaker heresies. If he could exploit his charge of Quaker heresy and potential anarchism, he might restore his faction in the upcoming autumn elections of Rhode Island assemblymen. Whether he debated Fox was not a crucial matter. What he needed that

August 9 was a forum, and to have it as close as possible to the forthcoming elections.[21]

Williams had to make do with three stand-ins: the traveling Friends
John Burnyeat and William Edmundson from Ireland and John Stubbs
from England. They agreed to discuss fourteen propositions which
Williams had suggested, the first seven of them in Newport and the
others in Providence. As Williams subsequently wrote in *George Fox
Digg'd Out of His Burrowes*, he charged the Quakers with heresy on a
number of grounds all of which had been essentially put forward previously by other Quaker critics.[22]

Central to his objections was his belief that Quakers assumed infalli-
bility and perfection. Their assumption, he said, smacked of popery.
Quakers knew they were saved. They claimed knowledge of the only
means by which man could understand Scripture and the process of
salvation—the Inward Light. Their self-righteous assertiveness of-
fended him, as did their rejection of the Bible as the final authority for
Christian knowledge and their making a Christ within (the Inward
Light) the equal of the historic Christ. For Williams the Inward Light
was the Quakers' own conceit. Their faith was not based on the Holy
Scriptures, and it incorporated the worst of other heresies. The result of
Quaker perfectionism, Williams wrote, would be a reversion to barbar-
ism, anarchy, arbitrary government, and the greatest of persecutions
the world had known—the consequence of a complete breakdown of
civil authority.[23]

Although debate centered on these points, Williams, according to
his version, had little chance of having his views heard during the first
half of the debates at Newport. Quakers, some of them identifiable
political opponents, heckled, sighed, and sang when he tried to talk;
William Edmundson interrupted constantly, forcing him to shout; he
had caught cold rowing to the debate from Providence and was hoarse;
and some Quakers in the audience whispered that he was drunk. He
fared better in Providence, where he had a more sympathetic audience.[24]

No contemporary Quaker account of the debate exists. George Fox
and John Burnyeat did not reply to Williams until 1678 (two years
after Williams' version appeared) in *A New England Firebrand Quenched*.
Fox's and Burnyeat's position paralleled similar seventeenth-century
Quaker apologies written before and after 1678. According to the
Quaker account, Burnyeat, Edmundson, and Stubbs argued that Quakers did believe in the historic Christ and His atonement. Nor, they said,
were Friends papists, Manichaeans, Ranters, and Arians, as Williams
had charged. Moreover, since he had been unable to prove that Scrip-

ture was the word of God, his charge that Quakers believed in a crucified Christ within them was untrue.[25]

Williams' efforts failed politically. The Providence delegation (which
did not attend the October Assembly, although it attended in November) consisted of Harris partisans and, as noted, included William Harris himself. That Williams' efforts had come to naught was even more
fully demonstrated in the May 1673 elections, in which the Governor,
Deputy Governor, and several assistants were Friends. Quaker allies like
William Harris, an assistant for the first time since 1669, and his
Providence supporter, John Throckmorton, a deputy, were also returned.[26]

Once elected, Friends in government faced the possibility of intercolonial war, foreshadowing their difficulties two years later in King
Philip's War. When the Dutch recaptured New York on July 30, the
colony had to mobilize. In August the Assembly empowered the Governor or Deputy Governor and a majority of assistants to nominate
commanders. Some Friends were thus forced to participate in warfare to
the extent of nominating commanders and disbursing funds. John
Cranston, happily not a Quaker, accepted appointment as commander,
thereby easing leadership problems. Friends in positions of authority on
Aquidneck Island were to remain in the vicinity in the event of enemy
invasion. Similarly, Friend Peter Easton, the colonial treasurer, was to
pay for troops, any Rhode Island soldiers injured in combat, and families of any soldiers killed in line of duty.[27]

Perhaps to ease the consciences of Quaker members of government
and certainly to confirm Quaker principles, the Assembly also passed
the most favorable law for pacifists in seventeenth-century New England. Its preamble stressed the need to put an end to war, pointed out
that Rhode Island required no oath because to do so would be contrary
to the religious principles of some residents, and adopted a biblical
justification for pacifism. The act itself provided that none who opposed
war for conscience be required to train or serve in the armed forces. It
did require able-bodied male noncombatants to help safeguard property
and remove women, children, and cattle from the area of contention
when an enemy invaded. In September the assembly reaffirmed the act,
which, fortunately for Friends at this stage, was not tested because the
Dutch did not invade.[28]

Quaker government in Rhode Island signified a change in Quakerism
in the northern North American colonies. Clearly, Rhode Island
Friends could no longer be confused with the early prophets of Quakerism. Their acceptance of political responsibility forced that Rhode Island apostle of soul liberty and onetime champion of freedom of con-

science, Roger Williams, to launch a doctrinal attack which paralleled his faction's stillborn attempt to muzzle opposition. Not that prophetic Friends had disappeared, for, as we shall see, they reappeared in reaction to persecution in King Philip's War. It was, however, becoming increasingly irrelevant for Quaker opponents like Williams, Increase and Cotton Mather, and Nathaniel Morton to report old tales of Quaker heresies and improprieties. Events in Rhode Island heralded the coming era of Quaker respectability.[29]

King Philip's War

When King Philip, sachem of the Wampanoags, in 1675 led most of the New England Indians on the warpath against English settlements, Friends could not avoid the holocaust. Rhode Island Friends faced the dilemma of being either pacifist members or supporters of a government at war. Suddenly thrust into war, Rhode Island's Quaker leaders had to participate at least indirectly to the extent of placing the colony on a defensive footing while seeking to mitigate the horrors of the conflict for noncombatants. Outside Rhode Island, Friends saw their expectations of God's revenge on New England persecutors fulfilled—Philip was the instrument of God's vengeance on New Englanders who had persecuted Friends. The common Quaker position was that New England had brought the conflict on itself and only in time would God's desire for revenge abate. Friends also had to face the New England Puritan version of God's wrath—God would punish New England for permitting Quaker heretics to live in or near the New Zion.[30]

Trouble had been brewing between the Indians and the English for some time. Many factors were involved. Some colonists consummated sharp land deals, causing many Indians to think that the English had taken Indian lands, if not fraudulently at least without generosity. Because many Indians had settled in towns established for them and had converted to Christianity, traditionally oriented Indians felt that their culture and leadership were threatened. In June 1675, despite attempts to settle the dispute by both Roger Williams and Friend John Easton, war broke out near the Mount Hope Peninsula, then a part of Plymouth Colony. Conflict became general as other tribes joined the fray and drove the English out of exposed settlements in a series of quick and surprisingly easy victories. By November the English had stunning losses, especially in Plymouth and western Massachusetts. How could God have turned on His chosen people? To explain that problem, hysterical colonists looked for scapegoats. Indians were an obvious choice—imps of Satan—and it became virtually impossible to defend even friendly Indians during wartime hysteria. Quakers in the midst, if not under the bed, were also a promising target.[31]

Even the grudging toleration that Massachusetts had given Friends since 1662 now looked like excess, as did the permissive society which allowed new and frivolous fashions. Surely God was punishing Massachusetts for permitting both heretical beliefs and loose behavior to go unchallenged. On November 3 during the darkest moment of the war, the Massachusetts General Court met and catalogued a long series of missteps that had brought God's visitation: some male residents were wearing their hair long; others hid their natural growth with periwigs; some residents indulged in excessive apparel (bright ribbons and other gaudy things). The Court provided fines for these errors. Then it turned to the Quaker problem. Friends had been permitted to meet openly and to spread their "damnable heresies, [and] abominable idolatries . . . to the scandall of religion, hazard of souls, and provocation of divine jealousie against this people." As a consequence, each person attending a Quaker meeting was to be apprehended, taken to the house of correction, and either imprisoned or fined 5 pounds. Town constables had been lax in enforcing anti-Quaker laws; now they were to be fined 4 pounds if they failed to act. Fellow townsmen informing on non-complying constables were to receive one third of the fine.[32]

Three Friends, led by either Edward Wharton of Salem or Edward Wanton of Scituate in Plymouth, responded in January 1675/76 by placing an edifice over the unmarked graves of Quaker martyrs William Robinson and Marmaduke Stevenson. They sneaked the contraption up to the graves, coming close to a military watch while doing so. Next morning, a market day, startled Boston residents and many visitors discovered the Quaker version of God's controversy with New England. On the front of the memorial was the verse

Although our Bodyes here
   in silent Earth do lie,
Yet are our Righteous Souls at Rest
   our Blood for Vengeance cry.

The message was clear: Indian war came as a result of previous persecutions. The recently enacted law would bring yet more vengeance down on the persecutors. They should take heed. They did, to the extent of having the memorial contraption torn down, but not before many people had seen it. The war, as the verse and edifice indicated, made it as possible for Quakers to view themselves as victims as for Puritans to view them as dangerous fanatics. No further legislation was enacted, however, nor was the anti-Quaker law enforced.[33]

Anti-Quaker activity did occasion an outburst of pamphleteering for and against Quakers and Massachusetts, showing that Quaker relations remained hostile, and that Massachusetts law was enforced just enough to justify English Friends writing against it. Between 1675 and 1677 George Fox wrote two pamphlets pertaining to Massachusetts, Samuel Groom had one, and English Friends printed the letters that detailed the market-day prank. Friend Edward Perry of Sandwich attempted to have Massachusetts publish his view that Puritan persecution lay behind the war. The General Court was not tempted. Massachusetts clergy and officials were spared the task of having to defend themselves in print. Roger Williams' manuscript concerning his debate with Friends four years earlier served well, and if George Fox and John Burnyeat were correct, the Massachusetts Governor, John Leverett, contributed 20 pounds to its publication in Cambridge. Surely *George Fox Digg'd Out of His Burrowes* would establish the validity of the Massachusetts case against Quakers as both heretics and anarchists.[34]

The war soon ended, but tension in Massachusetts declined slowly. For one thing, as in the times of persecution in the sixties, some Friends resorted to bizarre behavior. A Quaker appeared in the streets of Boston in 1676 and called on the town to repent—without notable success. The next year Friend Margaret Brewster with two companions went into the Boston meetinghouse in sackcloth and ashes as a sign to Massachusetts to repeal a recent act requiring an oath of fidelity. The act was part of yet another bundle of legislation designed to suppress dissenters. Eventually, the attorney general in England ordered its repeal.[35]

The dominant political position of Rhode Island Friends provided quite another test. With the outbreak of war in 1675, Friends in Rhode Island government found themselves participating indirectly in hostilities. That summer and fall as Indians attacked communities in Plymouth and mainland Rhode Island, refugees began to appear on Aquidneck. Preparations on that island were essentially defensive, and Quakers in Rhode Island government had to participate in these mild measures. Quaker governor William Coddington signed John Cranston's commission as major of the colony's forces. Deputy Governor John Easton, Walter Clarke, and John Coggeshall, all Friends, were members of a committee appointed in April 1676 to command Newport's defensive fleet. Walter Clarke became Governor in May 1676, and he, too, signed a commission—for Captain Arthur Fenner.[36]

Despite this modest participation, Friends were unable to retain the law exempting men from service in the militia on the grounds of conscience. In June 1676 the Assembly repealed that provision: too many without conscientious objection to war used the law as an excuse to avoid service. But the next Assembly, sitting after peace had been restored, reinstated the clause. Political fortunes, in part at least because of the war, were changing. The anti-Quaker faction returned to power in May 1677 and repealed the provision once again, protesting all the while that no one should "be in any wise molested, punished, disquieted, or called in question for any differences of opinion in matters of religion, who doe not actually disturbe the civil peace of the Collony." With the exception of pacifists, one might add.[37]

King Philip's War in many ways had interrupted a gradual process of reconciliation between Friends and others in Massachusetts and weakened Friends as the key political group in Rhode Island. Dormant for a number of years, persecution was resumed, to be answered by a spate of anti-Massachusetts pamphlets, pranks, and testimonies. If Friends were a cause of the war so far as Massachusetts law was concerned, divine revenge for persecuted Quakers was the first cause, as Friends saw it. Whatever the reason, among the war's casualties was Rhode Island's law for conscientious objectors and, in a sense, Roger Williams. His *George Fox Digg'd Out of His Burrowes* might never have appeared had not the war and the resultant recriminations between Quakers and Massachusetts occurred, making his ill-tempered self-justification possible. Nor for that matter would his debate with Friends in 1672 ever have attracted the attention it ultimately did.

Reduced Hostility to Friends

Massachusetts and Rhode Island Quakers had suffered temporary setbacks in their colonies, but elsewhere in New England and New York accommodation continued. This was especially true in Plymouth; though destruction in King Philip's War was severe, that government did not persecute dissenters, as did Massachusetts. Quakers and their neighbors had worked out a compromise as a result of which Friends were permitted to worship without hindrance. Many Quakers resided in the towns of Sandwich, Falmouth, Dartmouth, Tiverton, Scituate, and Duxbury with little molestation from the colony other than occasional challenges over the legality of marriages. Even better was the situation in Sandwich: there Quakers had their political rights in the town restored in 1681 after petitioning for them for years. The policy of toleration which would later frustrate Massachusetts was well advanced in these dissenting towns.[38]

New York Quakers were also getting along well with non-Quakers and with that colony's government. Worshiping freely in their little meetings, they had already managed to construct meeting houses and had plans for more. In the seventies they were only rarely subjected to church taxes. New York authorities apparently did not regard them as a threat. In only two areas did they encounter substantial difficulties: their refusal to participate in or pay for military activities and the reluctance of the New York government to accept marriages performed in Quaker meetings. Their sufferings, as they referred to penalties inflicted on them for matters of conscience, were especially great in 1672 and 1675, when they refused to help build a fort at New York or to participate in occasional military training. Their refusal in 1672 came at the outbreak of the Dutch War. Three years later they and their government could look back on the recent conquest of New York by the Dutch in 1674 and the outbreak of King Philip's War in New England. Under these circumstances confrontation with civil authority was unavoidable. It is noteworthy that the actions of authorities were restrained, indicating a development of mutual trust and tolerance unequaled in this region with the exception of Rhode Island.[39]

Gradually hostility between Friends and others from Long Island north was cooling. In New York and Plymouth prior difficulties were disappearing. Even Connecticut, in response to the Quakers' good offices with Indians in 1675, had temporarily set aside its heretic law as it applied to Friends, an action notably different from contemporary enactments in Massachusetts. Revival of old animosities in Massachusetts was due to Indian warfare, which unhinged some Massachusetts leaders; in fact the war delayed the growth of toleration in Massachusetts. It was a frustration matched in Rhode Island, where a political alliance between Quakers and others was temporarily sundered. But clearly the period of Perrotonian and similarly deviant disturbances was at an end.[40]

Chapter 3
Decline of the Quaker Menace

AS THE SOCIETY OF FRIENDS emerged from the prophetic period of confrontation and suffering, Quaker relations with leaders of other faiths and with the community at large began to improve. The change was barely noticeable at first: Massachusetts clergy in particular retained a distaste for Friends which for a time was suggestive of their attitude toward witches. Gradually, however, the running debate between Quakers and their critics softened. By 1730 Friends had for the most part been accepted as a benign if sometimes heretical sect, milder than other groups on the left wing of the Puritan Revolution, like Ranters and Gortonists, which had disappeared or would soon disappear.[1]

The changing climate vis-à-vis Quakers was apparent in several areas: in their exercise of the franchise; in the partial recognition of Quaker testimonies on oaths, pacifism, and church taxes; and in the diminution of bitter pamphlet exchanges. The present chapter focuses on this changed Quaker status by examining pamphlet literature and the events that lay behind it.

The severity of debates reflected in the literature declined. By the 1720's one-time opponents were treating Friends with measured respect. Accompanying this change was development of a Quaker view of the Society's past. Hardened into virtual canon, this version of the sufferings of prophetic Friends provided a standard to which not even the faithful remnant among eighteenth-century Quakers could measure up.[2]

Anti-Quakerism and the Quaker Canon
Before 1690 when Massachusetts clergy wrote about Friends, they retained their earlier suspicions. These hard views were eventually softened by Quaker attacks, changes in Massachusetts society after 1690,

and simply the passage of time, as the combative generation of the late
seventeenth century died away. Until then, however, leading New
England figures like Increase Mather and Nathaniel Morton remained
steadfast. They had wholeheartedly supported the publication of Roger
Williams' *George Fox Digg'd Out of His Burrowes*, although they could
hardly have agreed with many of Williams' Baptist views, or he with
theirs. Williams' position had a parallel in at least one of the histories of
New England written before 1690, although it was not directed specifically against Quakers.

When Nathaniel Morton wrote his *New Englands Memorial* in 1669,
he told a familiar tale. First there had been the Antinomian schism,
which Morton enlivened with tales of Anne Hutchinson's and Mary
Dyer's miscarriages, viewed as "monstrous births"—evidence, perhaps,
of a pact with the devil. The Gortonists followed, "belching out [famil-
ist] errours." Of the same ilk, he thought, were Quakers, whose beliefs
were riddled with heresy and who brought great disturbance to church
and state. Morton charged Quakers with the old bill of heresies: they
denigrated Scripture, denied the historic Christ, and rejected the doctrine of the Trinity.[3]

Meanwhile, Friends maintained their charges against Massachusetts—charges that functioned for them virtually as holy writ. Their
version of New England Quaker history continued to focus on Friends
activities near Boston and away from the greatest Quaker successes in
Long Island, Plymouth, and Rhode Island. Their major concern was
not balanced historical writing, either geographically or in terms of
objectivity. Rather, they sought the development of usable tradition
patterned on Pauline epistles, on other post-Gospel sections of the New
Testament, and on martyrologies like John Foxe's *Acts and Monuments*
and the Mennonite *Martyr's Mirror*. They created their own martyrol-
ogy, which became a part of New England's black legend. It continued
to be set forth in the eighteenth century in accounts that repeated earlier instances of persecution and added new ones.

The second volume of George Bishop's *New England Judged*, which
appeared in 1667, carried the tale of persecutions from William Leddra's execution to 1665. It also told of God's vengeance on John Endecott and John Norton. Each had died of natural causes, John Norton
of a stroke and John Endecott probably of cancer. To Bishop their
deaths were a result of God's striking them down for their part in the
execution of four Friends and the persecution of others. As Bishop put it
in Endecott's case: "the hand of the Lord struck *him* off, *he* stunk *alive*,
and *his* name doth rot, and for *his* works *he* knows *his* reward from the
Hand of the Lord."[4]

Other publications followed in the years before King Philip's War, all looking back at initial and post-Restoration persecutions. Writings of William Robinson and William Leddra came out the same year as Nathaniel Morton's history and may have been the initial response to it. Shortly afterward Quakers published Christopher Holder's *Faith and Testimony of the Martyrs* as a direct response to Morton. To defend the Quaker position, Holder argued that Friends valued Holy Scripture, but it was only Jesus Christ who could provide a rule, not Scriptures. Then, having denied primacy of Scripture, Holder quoted it to sustain the doctrines of Friends. He, like other early Friends, would have it both ways.[5]

For a time, disagreement was merely petty. In 1674 English Friends published William Coddington's *Demonstration of True Love*. Repeated were accounts of executions and persecutions which must have been familiar. In addition, Coddington alleged, Massachusetts Governor Richard Bellingham had once sheltered sentiments congenial to Friends but had since abandoned them. He had also recently abused one Nicholas Moulder of Boston, who had delivered a letter that Bellingham burned, and he seized and burned books that had been sent to Coddington. In a second letter Coddington told Bellingham: "thou shewest what Spirit thou art of, by thy Untrustiness and Wickedness in burning a Letter." Moreover, said Coddington, Bellingham was nothing but a common thief for taking Coddington's books. Coddington, long since expelled from Massachusetts with other Antinomians, took considerable delight in reporting that shortly after Bellingham read his second letter he died, the victim of God's wrath. He had been warned by Coddington but "the Hand of the Lord cuts him off, not giving him Repentance to Life, that other Sons of Belial of his persecuting Spirit might be warned not to put the Evil Day far from them."[6]

Far from being warned after the outbreak in 1675 of King Philip's War, Massachusetts had passed more anti-Quaker legislation, the effect of which, for Friends, was to reinforce further the Quaker view of godless Massachusetts and to inspire more pamphlets. George Fox responded to these emergency measures by contending that the Indian war was yet another instance of divine displeasure with Massachusetts. Moreover, said Fox, the law of November 3, 1675, had so aroused God's wrath that four officers and 121 men had fallen to an Indian attack. Fox's position was complemented by Samuel Groom's *A Glass for New England* (1676), which reiterated the history of Massachusetts persecution. Rounding off this decade's debate, Fox attacked new Massachusetts anti-Quaker legislation, and, as noted above, he and John Burnyeat defended Friends from the strictures of Roger Williams.[7]

After 1680 debate flagged; for a time no new Quaker pamphlets on Massachusetts intolerance appeared, although the reply of Fox and Burnyeat to Roger Williams continued to circulate from Long Island to Massachusetts. There matters would probably have rested, except for occasional repetition of old issues, had it not been for a heightened Massachusetts concern with witchcraft which coincided with the uncertainties accompanying the loss of its charter, the brief existence of the Dominion of New England, and the resumption of self-government after the Glorious Revolution.[8]

If Quakers were quiet, insecure Massachusetts clergy were not. In 1684 Increase Mather's *Essay for the Recording of Illustrious Providences* appeared. Mather added to former charges against Friends by linking Quakers to a group of Ranters ("Case's crew") in Long Island who, Mather thought, had bewitched people. For the moment no serious rejection of Mather's charges developed. Perhaps copies of the book did not immediately find their way to London and Philadelphia, where most published defenses of Friends originated. At this stage Mather's work was simply a hint of the pending witchcraft frenzy, although its suggestion of a link between Antinomian forerunners of Quakers, Friends, and witches was not new. Massachusetts authorities had midwives search Anne Austin and Mary Fisher for witches' marks. In the mounting unease of the late 1680's, suspicions of relationships between Friends and witches lingered. It was not until 1688, when George Keith, the disputatious Scotch Quaker immigrant to Pennsylvania, visited New England, that Friends developed an answer to Mather's charges.[9]

For over a decade before he left England in 1685, Keith had defended Quakerism in print. He visited New England in 1688 and, after taking part in the yearly meeting at Newport, went to Boston. No doubt emboldened by the greater freedom given Friends under the Dominion of New England by the Anglican Governor Edmund Andros, he preached in the streets and called on the people to repent. In July he challenged four Boston clergy, James Allin, Joshua Moody, Samuel Willard, and Cotton Mather, to discuss publicly the charges he made. They refused the same day. How could they possibly benefit from a debate that would have focused on Puritan mistreatment of Quakers when they already had problems enough with an Anglican governor friendly to Quakers? Keith had to content himself with excoriating them in a pamphlet, a medium in which he had already demonstrated considerable prowess.[10]

In *Presbyterian and Independent Churches in New-England and Else-where, Brought to a Test*, Keith outlined a defense of Quaker orthodoxy. Like his earlier pamphlets, this one showed the systematic bent of his mind, and reflected his Scotch Presbyterian background and his academic training. For Keith, Puritans preached and worshiped an absent Christ. Their religion was sterile and failed to give sufficient attention to the work of the Holy Spirit in man and the possibility of continued revelation. It was not that Quakers disbelieved credal statements of Congregationalists. Rather, Congregationalists had mistaken the nature of God, their error being the assumption that God is vengeful when in fact He is a God of love who infuses righteousness into all men. He concluded by referring to Increase Mather's linking of Quakers and Ranters. Mather's statements were a pack of lies, Keith stated. Instead of seeking to press calumnous charges against Quakers, he continued, Boston ministers would do well to look to their persecutions of Quakers for over thirty years as the real reason for the loss in 1684 of the Massachusetts charter.[11]

Boston clergy were quick to dispute Keith's statements. Cotton Mather responded the same year (1689) in *Memorable Providences Relating to Witchcraft*. The pamphlet contained Cotton's fourteen-page appendix defending his father. Because in earlier sections of the work he had mentioned Quakers, he foresaw that "(those usually no less *Absurd* than Angry people), the Quakers will *come upon me with great wrath*, for my writing" as they had "lately shown to my Father for a piece of one Chapter in his Book of *Remarkable Providences*, by one Keith . . . have made it necessary not only for me to explain myself, but to defend him." According to Mather, Keith had preached heresies against the Protestant religion in New England, and his recent book had repeated those heresies. Furthermore, Mather was as sure as his father that Quakers were no different than Ranters and that only a "Diabolical Possession . . . did *dispose* and *encline* men unto Quakerism." Concluding the Standing Order's side of the debate two years later after the overthrow of the Dominion of New England, Mather joined with the three other Boston clergy Keith had challenged in a more detailed reply to the offending pamphlet. Their *Principles of the Protestant Religion Maintained* (1690) simply repeated the usual arguments that Quakers denied the historic Christ, the final authority of Scripture, and the Trinity.[12]

The Keith-Mather exchange had an unanticipated, immediate, and divisive effect on Quakerdom. First signs of it came when the German-born, university-trained, convinced Quaker schoolmaster in Newport, Christian Lodowick, began to have second thoughts about Quaker beliefs. Unhappily for Newport Friends, Lodowick had been trained in theology and was concerned by their seeming departure from orthodox

Christianity and general lack of concern for defining essentials of their
faith. Probably the Keith-Mather controversy had aroused some doubts
Lodowick had entertained about Quaker beliefs. In 1690 he asked for a
discussion. Newport Quakers selected George Keith, who had come
north again to visit the New England Yearly Meeting, to defend their
Christianity. Temporarily, the discussion satisfied all parties, for Keith
returned to Pennsylvania and Lodowick caused no further trouble that
year; but by 1691 Lodowick had concluded that Quakers were not
Christians, and he had apostatized.[13]

Lodowick did not leave the Society quietly. First, he sought to have
Edmund Wright in the Barbadoes publish his account of the confron-
tation with Keith. When Wright refused, Lodowick wrote Cotton
Mather in February 1692 a letter that Mather had published, suggest-
ing reasons for his rejection of Quakerism and making some rather
sharp comments on the position of Keith. Lodowick quoted freely from
Keith's publications and ridiculed Quaker belief of the seed of Christ
within. He also drew a distinction between Quakers like Keith and
William Penn, who sought to accommodate Fox's faith in the Inward
Light with the Bible and traditional Christian orthodoxy, and Fox, who
stressed the primacy of spiritual revelations. As he put it, there were
Foxians, those who followed George Fox's beliefs closely, and "semi-
Foxians," like Keith and Penn, who found "some things to hard for
them [to accept]."[14]

Attacks from without along with Lodowick's apostasy seem to have
moved Keith to take specific steps to demonstrate Quaker orthodoxy.
At the same time, he continued a running debate with critics. In 1690
he had replied to the Boston clergy in one pamphlet and criticized three
other New England clerical authors in another, and in 1692 set forth
Quaker beliefs in the form of a catechism. Both the catechism and reply
to the clergy sought to show critics that Friends were indeed Christians.
But Lodowick's criticism led Keith and Rhode Island Friends to assert
more forcefully than before their belief in biblical authority and the
atonement of the historic Christ. They succeeded to such an extent that
Pennsylvania Quakers thought they had degraded the superior inspiration of the Inward Light and censured the printer William Bradford for
printing the pamphlet. Apparently New England Friends did not want
to press the matter, for they made no efforts to follow up.[15]

George Keith was not satisfied, however, and urged Pennsylvania
Friends to adopt a catechism that would clearly demonstrate their
orthodoxy that year. Failing to have it adopted, he left the meeting and
established a schismatic body known as Christian Quakers. It was a
short-lived group and had virtually disappeared by 1700. Surprisingly,

the schism did not extend to New England, where Quakers apparently continued to emphasize the Inward Light and forgot their earlier efforts to appear to be orthodox.[16]

Though one cannot be certain, there was another probable dividend of the Keith-Mather controversy. During the witchcraft hysteria in Danvers, Salem, and other Massachusetts towns, Quakers were not singled out, as one might have expected. Even though the Mathers and others had long suggested a relationship of Quakers and witchcraft, Keith's assertion of Quaker Christian orthodoxy, the control by Quakers of government in neighboring Rhode Island and in Pennsylvania, and the certain danger to Massachusetts charter hopes and to the 1692 charter if more Quakers were hanged no doubt saved Friends from prosecution as witches. As Massachusetts recovered from the excesses, Friends may even have benefited by finding it easier to convert residents of Salem and Lynn, for there seem to have been many converts near Salem in the last decade of the seventeenth century. Numerical growth probably emboldened a Salem merchant, Thomas Maule, to criticize Massachusetts clergy and authorities publicly. Maule had moved to Salem as a young boy of twelve in 1657 and had become a convinced Quaker shortly after. In February 1689 he had contemplated publishing a pamphlet that would almost certainly have been critical of Massachusetts orthodoxy, but apparently he was dissuaded by the Rhode Island Monthly Meeting. One of the leading members of the meeting in Salem by the 1690's, he started to write another defense of Quakerism in 1692, about the time Keith established separate Quaker meetings in Philadelphia. He finished *Truth Held Forth* in 1695, and it was published in New York the same year.[17]

Truth Held Forth was, indeed, an apt title. Maule sought to reassert Quaker emphasis on the Inward Light and on continuing revelation because of the Light, perhaps something of a reaction to George Keith. He argued, as Fox and other early Friends had, that no one could prove that Scripture is the word of God; it was only man's interpretation of spiritual influence. He also stated that Friends believed in a Trinity (if it was understood that there was a unity of the Godhead). The pamphlet was aggressive and in no sense defensively apologetic, as Keith's efforts had been. Unhappily, Maule went beyond mere theological quibbling and attacked the Massachusetts clergy; he also made the error of letting his name appear on the pamphlet rather than using a pseudonym. Writing in the aftermath of the Salem witchcraft hysteria and continuing the Quaker tradition of a persecuting Massachusetts, Maule contended that witches in New England were the result of the anti-Christ's being abroad. No doubt the Boston clergy agreed. They took vigorous exception to his assertion that they were as guilty of being creatures of the devil as the persons they had seen charged with witchcraft and executed for it, and to his charge that New England's recent troubles with witches and Indian invasions resulted directly from their persecutions of Quakers.[18]

For these accusations the irrepressible Maule was brought to trial for slander and sentenced to prison. He was not silenced by this punishment, although he did learn to use a pseudonym—Philadelephes. His next pamphlet, *New England Persecutors Mauled,* did not result in prosecution, although charges and personalities in it were much the same as his earlier work. Nor did his subsequent publications obtain litigation, although they lacked nothing of the verve of that which had landed him in prison. So extreme was he that one proposed pamphlet caused the New England Yearly Meeting to dissociate itself from him in 1699. In 1701 Maule denounced Mather for relating Indian warfare to the continued presence of Friends, again turning the charge: "the righteous bloodshed upon the earth, a part of which hath defiled *New* England, and will not be purged while the evil one abideth in *Cotton Mather.*" Unfortunately some of Maule's statements proved an embarrassment to English Friends, and they rather lamely attempted to dissociate themselves from him. Perhaps their embarrassment and the probable disapproval within his own yearly meeting led him to refrain from further publication against Mather and other New England clergy.[19]

The Pamphlet War

After 1691 Quakers and other dissenters were as free to worship in their meetings in an expanded Massachusetts (Plymouth had been added to Massachusetts in 1691) as in Rhode Island and New York. Indeed they had been permitted to worship unmolested at least since 1680 in Massachusetts and in New Hampshire after its formation in 1679, as did those few Friends in Connecticut, provided they did not disturb the peace. Now, as the new Massachusetts charter guaranteed freedom of conscience, there could no longer be any question of the state's hindering Quaker meetings. This increasingly tolerant framework was in the background of Thomas Maule's attack on Massachusetts clergy and of conversions to Quakerism near Salem in the last decade of the seventeenth century and first decade of the eighteenth. Accompanying the recently acquired freedom of worship came the Massachusetts attempt to extend its ecclesiastical system into southeastern Massachusetts, a subject discussed below (pages 111–122). Here it is appropriate to point out that attempts to extend and maintain a state-supported church paralleled continuing debate with Friends, a debate which ended in a rapprochement in the 1720's at the same time that Massachusetts was in reluctant retreat from taxing its dissenters to support orthodox clergy.

In 1702 the publication of Cotton Mather's *Magnalia Christi Americana* signaled the renewal of the longstanding controversy with Quakers. Part of chapter 4 of the seventh book was given over to Mather's résumé of the Quaker record in New England. It marked a retreat from some Puritan histories of the Quakers in Massachusetts, although the retreat must have gone unnoticed in what was an essentially petulant attack on Friends. Titled *Ignes Fatui* ("flaming fools"), the fourth chapter followed Mather's discussion of the Antinomians, the obvious predecessors of Quakers. The clear implication of the title and subsequent argument was that these "fools" had been taken too seriously and merited scorn, not persecution. Even before the Quaker invasion, Mather claimed, Quakers had existed in Salem, and he repeated old gossip that they had died childless, affirming Joseph Nicholson's suggestions of celibacy among Salem Friends. One should not take Mather's words at face value. It is likely that the Massachusetts tradition on which Mather relied had exaggerated instances of celibacy among some Salem Quakers during 1657–60, applying the practice to the period before 1657. There is no contemporary evidence that would confirm his statement. He also repeated Christian Lodowick's earlier contentions that there were two kinds of Quakers: Foxians and Christian moderates. Early Quakers (Foxians) were uncontrolled zealots and should not be confused with the new generation of Friends exemplified by William Penn and, until recently, George Keith. According to Mather the Foxians were still dominant in New England and continued to deny the historical Jesus, the Trinity, and Scripture. It was because of these beliefs and the behavior of the first Friends that anti-Quaker laws were passed. Given the benefit of hindsight, Mather thought they were mistaken laws, but considering the zeal of Massachusetts rulers, there was no other way for the colony to act. Mather concluded this Quaker chapter with a lengthy section essentially copied from Increase Mather's *Illustrious Providences*, thereby perpetuating the link between Quakers and witchcraft. In general, despite Mather's dissociation from corporal punishment, his discussion of Friends in Massachusetts was a deliberate and bigoted attack on Quakerism.[20]

Friends countered this reassertion of the Puritan view. English Friend John Whiting replied in an appendix to the 1702 edition of George Bishop's *New England Judged*. Whiting's more detailed defense, *Truth and Innocency Defended* (1702) made liberal use of George Keith's earlier dissociation of Friends from "Case's Crew" and similar groups and pointed out correctly that both New England and New York Yearly Meetings had suffered from interruptions from Thomas Case's followers (see below, pages 65–66). Whiting also reviewed the seventeenth-century Massachusetts persecutions of Friends, borrowing largely from other Quaker writers. In conclusion he referred to examples of God's vengeance against New England, quoting Cotton Mather's own *Boston Ebenezer*. Clearly, God had singled out New England for difficult times, shown by the Indian wars and witchcraft hysteria, because of earlier New England Puritan persecution of Quakers.[21]

John Whiting's pamphlet, delivered to Cotton Mather by the Boston Quaker merchant Daniel Zachary, had had little effect on Mather's views of Quaker "heresies," as Mather's *Man of God Furnished* (1708) made clear. This time Mather used the medium of a detailed catechism. In the second section he focused on the points which most clearly differentiated Quakers and Puritans, a rationale to defend the Puritan faithful from incursions of Quaker missionaries and to sustain those who might have waivered at the thought of compulsory maintenance of Puritan clergy. Affirming the orthodox position of the Massachusetts Standing Order, Mather urged that the sacraments of baptism and the Lord's Supper were as essential as Quakers found them meaningless—to Friends they were merely outward actions having no redeeming effect. Furthermore, he argued against certain Quaker practices: women could not be preachers, for Scripture forbade them to be, and the Bible only forbade profane swearing, not oaths that engaged the swearer to observe the law or tell the truth. He also attacked the Quaker denigration of the historic Christ, their position on continued revelation, and, basic to their belief, the sign of God within. Clearly Friends did not follow the rule of most Christians. In a succeeding essay not directly dealing with Friends, he argued for the doctrine of the Trinity as received from the traditional western church. Mather was simply maintaining his Calvinism.[22]

The Quaker reply this time came from the Irish Friend Patrick Henderson: *Truth and Innocence the Armour and Defense of . . . Quakers . . .* (1709). Henderson had been traveling in the ministry in New England when *Man of God Furnished* appeared, but after he reached home he hastened to attack Mather. His pamphlet was first a defense of the doctrine of the Light Within, based on quotations from the Bible. There followed an exposition of the Quaker position on outward sacraments, a defense of women as preachers, and an attack on hireling ministers. Next year John Whiting's broadside *Just Reprehension* supple-

mented Henderson's pamphlet. Whiting alleged that Mather had continued to make false charges verbally and in print. He had told two
New England Friends, Samuel Collins and Thomas Richardson, that
Friends were no better than Egyptian rat worshipers, and that they were
blasphemous for their belief in the light of Christ in all humans. The
exchange, at least on the Quaker side, was part of an attempt to gain
relief from New England church taxes. Defending Puritan Massachusetts, Mather was not yet prepared to relent on his opposition to the
Quaker doctrine of the Light Within any more than he was probably
ever prepared to relent on tithes. Even though he no longer commanded
the political power he had before 1700, his pamphlet on Quaker hetero-
doxy shows the parallel between continued doctrinal disagreements and
the attempt to force Quakers, Baptists, and Anglicans outside Boston
to give financial support to the congregational establishment.[23]

Gradually, however, Mather's position on dissenters changed, and
more rapidly after 1715. Massachusetts was still intent on enforcing
tithes, and Mather continued to support that policy, but his fear of
Baptists and Quakers diminished as he viewed the growing number of
Anglicans in Massachusetts. The Anglicans had been making headway
in Boston since George Keith visited Massachusetts as the first missionary for the Anglican Society for the Propagation of the Gospel in
Foreign Parts (SPG) in 1702. Both Cotton and Increase Mather had
contemplated a union of non-Anglicans to help meet this threat (a considerable reversal of Cotton Mather's strictures in the *Magnalia* on Baptists, a few years earlier).[24]

Mather's change of position depended on several factors. First there
was a softening toward Boston's Baptists (in 1718 he preached at the
installation of the Reverend Elisha Callendar at the Boston Baptist
church). There was also pressure from English Friends to obtain relief
from church taxes for their coreligionists, which served to demonstrate
both the respectability of English Friends and their political power in
early Hanoverian England. Most important to the aging Mather, however, was the appearance of a unitarian faction among British congregational dissenters.[25]

Mather became involved publicly when the trinitarian faction in England published two of his and one of his father's letters. Cotton
Mather's letters were dated September 7, 1719, and July 1, 1720. In
the second, in which Mather made reference to Friends, he denounced
the English unitarians. Of significance to the student is his acceptance
of the doctrine of the Light Within as "A Notion of Christ, more eligi-
ble and defensible, than what some *Free-Thinkers* would now thrust

upon us!" Free thinking enemies within made Quakers seem attractive.[26]

British dissent further helped to soften Mather's views. The English dissenting minister, Daniel Neal, wrote of the mistreatment of early Quakers and the Salem witchcraft trials in considerable and embarrassing detail, in his *History of New England* (1720). Mather sent his copy to Judge Samuel Sewall, who was grieved to discover "New England's Nakedness laid open in the business of Quakers, Anabaptists, [and] Witchcraft." No doubt Mather echoed Sewall's prayer that "the Good and Gracious God be pleased to save New England." It is hardly surprising that the old and now congenial Mather should have modified his positions on Quakerism to the extent that he did in the pamphlets *Vital Christianity* (1625) and *Lampadarius* (1626).[27]

Vital Christianity was a far cry from sentiments expressed in the *Magnalia*. By 1725 Mather could write flatteringly of Quakers. Far from denigrating belief in the Inward Light he now said (inadvertently accepting Quaker canon) that Quakers had been "raised up . . . to chastise us for the vile Contempt and Affront which People generally cast of the Light of God within them." Moreover, he had become "one who unspeakably abhors and laments the abominable Persecution which you have suffered in former Days from an unadvised and unrighteous World." Hardly a man was he now to defend the zealous actions of a John Endecott, a Richard Bellingham, or a John Norton, or to compare Friends to Egyptian rat worshipers. In the balance of the pamphlet he argued, without abandoning his essential Calvinism, that the only way people could come to God was by Christ living in them. In *Lampadarius* he offered essentially the same position: no abandonment of Calvinism, but by the introduction of favorable comment on the Light Within a considerably changed Calvinism, conciliatory to Friends.[28]

Mather had written Quaker Thomas Chalkley of Philadelphia a courteous letter in 1725 and received an equally courteous reply in which Chalkley had commented critically, although generally favorably, on *Vital Christianity*, as Mather probably hoped he would when he had the pamphlet printed in Philadelphia rather than Boston. As Mather retained his essential Calvinism, so Chalkley criticized the outward sacraments of baptism and the Lord's Supper, but at least the Doctrine of the Inward Light no longer was thought of by Cotton Mather as idolatry. Whether this mutual admiration spilled over to effect a changed set of relations between New England Friends and Mather can be debated. It is certain, however, that by the end of the first quarter of the eighteenth century, as Mather's pamphlets and the correspondence between Mather and Chalkley indicate, Friends were not regarded as a threat to civil and

religious life, nor were they any longer intent on disturbing the peace
that had developed with great difficulty over the preceding half century.[29]

SPG Missionaries

Much as hostility between Quakers and Puritan New Englanders
cooled, so did friction elsewhere in northern colonies, especially with
Anglican missionaries. Relations were especially bitter in New York
where the efforts of both the government and Anglican missionaries of
the recently founded SPG coincided. Even in New England the SPG
was temporarily in league with the Standing Order's struggle with
Friends at the beginning of the century. The animosity did not endure
for long, however, for by 1730 SPG authorities in England had made
their peace with Friends, a position soon emulated by Anglican missionaries from New York north. Although these men had little affection
for Quakers, it became evident that Friends were no threat to Anglicans, or to anyone else in the northern colonies.

The first significant clash between Quakers and Anglicans in these
colonies came when the Quaker apostate, now SPG missionary, George
Keith reappeared in North America in 1702. A major part of his effort
was to attract Quakers to the Anglican church. He found support
among Massachusetts clergy, concerned about recent Quaker inroads,
especially Jeremiah Shepherd of Lynn, who escorted him to a Quaker
meeting. The alliance lasted only a short time, but it served to help
counter Quaker successes in the vicinity of Salem and Lynn—Keith was
as eager to demonstrate Quaker heresy as Cotton Mather and, as a
onetime leading Friend, was much more convincing. But he had to face
English Friend John Richardson, a member of a Quaker truth squad
that shadowed Keith's movements.[30]

Having visited many Quaker meetings from the vicinity of Boston
north through New Hampshire to Maine, Keith turned south to Newport in August 1702, where he faced capable opposition. To undermine
efforts of leading Rhode Island Quakers, he was happy to report on
commissions signed by Quaker governors enabling privateers to fight
the French. Rhode Island Friends were equal to his discrediting their
pacifism: they charged that he had connived in the misapplication of a
legacy. He had met his match in Lieutenant Governor Walter Clarke
and Rhode Island Quakers.[31]

When he moved south to Long Island, Keith encountered similar
Quaker opposition. Here Friends were not members of the government;
indeed, recent appointments of justices of the peace had put in office

men hostile to Friends. Keith obtained a letter of support from the Governor of New York, Edward Hyde, Lord Cornbury. An old ally from combat with Pennsylvania Friends, printer William Bradford, was on hand to lend assistance. Together they went to Quaker meetings to see what they could do to undermine New York Quakers.[32]

At those meetings Keith again encountered allegations of his misapplication of a legacy. More important, he sought to silence an outspoken English Quaker minister, Samuel Bownas. It was November 21, 1702, and as Bownas spoke in a meeting for worship, Bradford took notes. Shortly afterward as a result of charges based on those notes, Bownas was arrested and imprisoned for what proved to be a stay of almost a year. According to Bradford's deposition, Bownas had spoken slightingly of baptism, of godmothers and godfathers, and of communion (the Lord's Supper). Eight days later, on November 29, the sheriff went to a meeting for worship to arrest Bownas, but as the name on the warrant was Bowne not Bownas, Bownas temporarily went free. When hailed before four magistrates sometime later, Bownas refused to make bail in the outrageous sum of 2,000 pounds and also refused to let one of the justices, Jonathan Whitehead, make bail for him. As a result Bownas was bound over to the grand jury, which met on February 28, 1703. Despite the fact that the jury refused to find a bill both then and on March 1, Bownas was kept in prison without an indictment until October 31, 1703, when another grand jury also failed to find a true bill, and the court set Bownas free.[33]

Bownas was not the only visiting Friend imprisoned. In 1707, still in the troubled period of Lord Cornbury's governorship, Irish Friend Patrick Henderson was jailed for approximately seven months "for Preaching in a Meet not Lycensed." The occasion may have been similar to Bownas' arrest: an unfriendly group of justices encouraged by Cornbury to promote the Anglican Church arranged for Henderson's arrest. But not all visiting British Friends received similar treatment. John Richardson and John Fothergill both passed through New York in this decade without apparent harassment. Perhaps they were less outspoken than Bownas and Henderson; perhaps they were simply lucky; it is clear, however, that the arrival of the SPG coincided with attacks on Friends which paralleled similar hostility in New England and exceeded it to the extent that visiting British Friends critical of Anglicans were imprisoned.[34]

The hostility on an official level was not to last. While SPG missionaries in New York continued to complain about the influence of Quakers, officials at home suggested restraint. SPG advice given between

1730 and 1732 to James Wetmore, an SPG missionary in Rye and recent convert from the Congregational ministry, signaled a shift away from the attack on Quakers.

SPG missionaries had alternated complaints about Quaker activities and reports of their own successes in making converts for their three decades in New York. James Wetmore reaffirmed the Quaker problem in his report to the SPG in 1730. Quakers were the "greatest troublers," as "they spare no pains to infect their neighborhood." In particular, Wetmore had been angered by Quaker revival meetings, the "great and general meetings, which I think are of pernicious consequence to religion and ought to be suppressed." He informed the Society that he intended to print a pamphlet as soon as he could obtain financial support.[35]

Wetmore had already incensed Quakers in his short pamphlet *A Letter from a Minister of the Church of England to His Dissenting Parishioners* (1730). He made exclusive claims for Anglican orders compared to ordination of dissenting clergy. In only a brief reference to Quakers, he suggested that they could not be certain that they were inspired by the Holy Spirit, as they claimed. Quaker James Mott replied in an apparently critical pamphlet that is not extant, *The Great Work of Christ's Spirit*.[36]

Mott's pamphlet provoked Wetmore to a direct attack on Friends in *Quakerism: A Judicial Infatuation* (1731). The pamphlet consists of a dialogue between a potential convert to Quakerism, one Tremulus, and a defender of the Church of England, Eusebius. Wetmore was outspoken in his statements about Quakers; they were "drunken, lying, cheating, [and] demure." He stated that the "Devil's School of Debauchery, Lewdness and Impiety" served as inspiration to them, and their "Teachers are generally Men that have been excessively wicked, irreligious, and debauched." No honest persons could become Quakers. In the balance of the pamphlet Eusebius (Wetmore) argued that the extent of this Quaker debauchery consisted of a denial of the sacraments of Baptism and the Lord's Supper. Eusebius won, of course. Tremulus abandoned Quakerism. And Wetmore probably thought he would impress the SPG, although it is unlikely that he impressed many New England and New York residents.[37]

He was soon disabused of that idea when the SPG informed him that it wanted no running battle with Quakers. The days of open hostility toward Friends were at an end, although SPG missionaries for at least another generation continued to complain about Quaker influence. Much as Cotton Mather had made his peace with Quakers, so too did

the SPG. The major enemies for the Anglican Society were the Congregational and Presbyterian churches in these colonies, not minority
Friends; at any rate, it was not wise to abuse colonial Quakers when
English Friends were well placed politically during Robert Walpole's
ministry. Not only were Friends now free from arrest for what they said
in their meetings—they were also free from molestation in print.[38]

PART II
Institutions, Growth, and Worship

INITIALLY, QUAKERISM WAS a formless religious movement, noteworthy for its high degree of individualism and rejection of authority. Headed by peripatetic ministers, the movement exercised little control over either ministers or their auditors. This potentially anarchic scheme did not last long. In the late 1660's in England and Ireland, acting under the twin pressures of persecution and a self-identified need to bring the unruly flock under control, George Fox and his ministerial allies established a series of business meetings capped by a central authority, the London Yearly Meeting. This organization effectively brought English and Irish Friends under central control not to be found among other dissenters in the British Isles. Having secured these meetings at home, Fox and his allies turned their attention to America and in 1671 and 1672 founded there a structure of business meetings patterned on that in the British Isles. They thereby initiated the institutional apparatus that would profoundly shape American Quakerism.[1]

For Quakers in the northern American colonies there were three broad periods of institutional development beginning with Fox's visit, periods that served to define what Quakers meant both to themselves and to outsiders. The time spans were roughly from 1672 to 1710, 1710 to 1755, and 1755 until well into the nineteenth century, a terminal date beyond our consideration here. In the first of these periods Friends set up a basic meeting structure and created precedents. The second was noteworthy for control of the institutional mechanism by a benign oligarchy. In both these periods the number of Quakers increased by the addition of children, rather than by those who voluntarily joined, although there were some mass conversions. This growth was unequaled by Quakers in Britain, where numerical decline set in early in the eighteenth century. But in the third period, after 1755, American Quaker institutional practices came to resemble the English and Irish. In this period of self-identified reform, the number of American Quakers stopped growing. At first merely rhetorical in the northern yearly meetings, reform developed disownment practices similar to the British counterparts in 1770. Thereafter a numerical decline set in which did not end until the nineteenth century, when Friends gave up their misguided attempt to recreate practices rarely if ever engaged in by their founders.[2]

Such periodization contradicts the usual estimates of Quaker history concerning both institutional and demographic developments. Usually, historians have dated major boundaries with the death of George Fox in 1691 and the onset of doctrinal splits in the late eighteenth and early nineteenth centuries. Others have described a flat institutional structure until the "reform" of the Society in 1755. As for when reform really took hold in the northern yearly meetings, there has been silence, or an assumption that northern American Friends followed Philadelphia, or contradictory dates (1760, 1764, 1767, 1770), caused by attention to disciplinary rhetoric rather than disciplinary action. This section seeks to clarify these matters and to place the practices of worship in an historical context.[3]

Chapter 4
Organization and Growth Before 1755

DURING QUAKERISM'S FIRST DECADE and a half there was little time or concern for organizing a church government. The enthusiasm of converts and the magnetic personalities of Quaker ministers like George Fox sufficed to keep Quakerism vital and expanding. Unhappily for Friends in England, the Restoration brought a persecution of nonconformists which was particularly severe for Quakers. Trouble from the outside was matched by apostasy and dissension within the Society. To meet such problems, English Friends set about creating a church government. They began to build an organization after 1667 and continued their efforts into the eighteenth century. Friends hoped that the organizational structure developed in that period would help subdue internal wrangling, provide defense against attacks from hostile civil authorities, and retain the essential features of the faith.

Quakers in the northern American colonies were slow to follow the example of English Friends. Although there may have been a need for stronger control in these colonies, institutional growth lagged behind English and Irish efforts. Part of the reason was that persecution in Massachusetts and Plymouth diminished after 1662. And though schisms caused problems, these problems of themselves were not sufficient to compel organizational growth. Indeed some of the schisms seem to have derived from institutional expansion. Although there may have been meetings which conducted business earlier, it was not until 1671—when John Burnyeat, seconded by George Fox and others in 1672, visited New York and New England—that meetings to conduct business started. These meetings for business assumed the decision-making responsibility throughout Quakerism. They helped Friends eliminate hitherto uncontrolled enthusiasts (called Ranters by Puritan critics and deliberately confused by them with Quakers). By the second decade of the eighteenth century Quakers in the northern colonies had developed and recognized their structure and authority.[1]

Quaker numbers grew, paralleling institutional growth. As already indicated, there were apparently enough conversions to worry clergy around Salem at the turn of the eighteenth century, and after several years of proselytizing, Friends became the dominant religious group on the island of Nantucket. Natural increase seems to have accounted for numerical gains of the Society in southeastern Massachusetts and Rhode Island. In New York, migration in the third decade of the century to newly opened lands in the Hudson Valley and to Westchester County earlier led to the growth of Quakerism in a colony where the Society of Friends was still only a tiny fraction of the population.

Establishment of Business Meetings

In August 1671, when persecution of English Quakers seemed to be slackening, George Fox sailed for America. With him were twelve other Quaker missionaries, and, as Frederick Tolles observes, "the number was surely not accidental." Fox's purposes in making the trip were threefold: to establish meetings for business among colonial Friends in the same pattern of church government as that developed by English Quakers, to encourage the growth of Quakerism in already settled areas, and to investigate possibilities of Quaker settlement in the wilderness that later became Pennsylvania. His mission thus went beyond the hortatory venture of a missionary. For New England Quakers it meant organizing their hitherto disorganized collection of meetings for worship.[2]

John Burnyeat had already been working to control Friends who opposed George Fox. In 1671, on his second trip to North America, Burnyeat had visited meetings in New England and New York. In New York, as noted in Chapter 2, he debated with Friends who may have been followers of John Perrot and who also opposed the establishment of business meetings. Burnyeat defended George Fox's papers—to the point, he said, that opponents went away. He also organized the first truly local meeting for business in the northern colonies—Flushing Monthly Meeting. There had not been similar opposition to him at the general meeting in Newport, a meeting that may have conducted business for all of New England and New York in 1671, although the extent of its activities and their nature is far from clear, for within a year Fox had made a clear impact on the nature and organization of meetings in the New England and New York region.[3]

Fox landed in the Barbadoes in October 1671 and gradually worked his way north, until by the spring of 1672 he had reached New York and joined Burnyeat in time for the Oyster Bay Half Yearly Meeting. Happily, he did not have the difficulties in New York which John Burnyeat had encountered the previous autumn. To avoid confrontation at the beginning of the meeting, he insisted on having meetings for worship the first two days; the third day he led business meetings; and only on the fourth day did he meet with dissidents. The delaying tactic worked well: by the fourth day the ringleaders of the opposition, "George Dennis . . . and his wife, not being well owned there by Friends now began to disown the matter and would have cast it upon others." Thereupon, John Burnyeat noted with some satisfaction that he proved Dennis to have been at fault. Fox and Burnyeat had defeated their opponents. Business meetings were now to determine the course of events for New York Quakers.[4]

From the Oyster Bay Meeting the band of English Friends went to Newport, reaching that town in time for the annual general meeting in June. Newport was little more than a small village in 1672, with only the promise of growing to be the urban center it became in the eighteenth century. It was, however, the capital of the colony of Rhode Island. It was also the unrecognized center of Quakerism in the American colonies in the 1670's and was not displaced until the next decade, when William Penn founded Philadelphia.

Consequently, Newport's general meeting (an annual worship meeting for southern New England Friends) was the obvious place to establish Quaker church government in New England. In 1672, as noted, Friends and their allies had just gained control of the Rhode Island government. The general meeting also seems to have been attended for several years before 1672 by many Massachusetts and Plymouth Friends, much as Sandwich Yearly Meeting, another general meeting, had had the attendance of Rhode Island Friends. Although the Rhode Island General Meeting may already have started caring for the poor and carrying on other types of church business in the vicinity of Newport, typical of later Quaker business meetings, it does not seem to have had any authority over Quakers elsewhere before 1672 and, as shown below, not always immediately afterward. Probably it was only an annual evangelistic gathering. Whatever role it had before Fox came, he used this meeting to organize meetings for business in New England and Long Island, "to take care of the poor, and other affairs of the Church, and to see that all who profess truth walk according to the gospel of God." By the time Fox left America, he had helped, by his account, to establish local meetings for business, called monthly meetings, at Dover in New Hampshire, Salem in Massachusetts, Scituate and Sandwich in Plymouth Colony, and in the colony of Rhode Island. It is likely that his visit confirmed the establishment of the monthly meeting at Oyster Bay on Long Island by John Bur-

nyeat in 1671. And apparently as a result of his visit, the Rhode Island
General Meeting had had its first session as the New England Yearly
Meeting for Business. Although many of the rules of this meeting had to
be worked out, most but by no means all Friends seem to have recognized
the Rhode Island Yearly Meeting as a representative meeting for all New
England and New York, with rule-making capabilities.[5]

Opposition to Organization

The establishment of meetings for business soon aroused opposition.
Many of the fiery spirits in New England and New York who had found
Quaker beliefs congenial did not take well to organization and authority.
Some opposition centered on English Friends who had come to convert
New Englanders and then settled in Rhode Island. Their opposition was
mild and free of the notoriety of a group on Long Island led by Thomas
Case, and after a few years of meeting in separation they became recon-
ciled to the majority. But Rhode Island difficulties were nonetheless se-
rious, occurring so soon after establishment of meetings for business and
joined by so many prominent Friends in the seat of northern Quakerism.

One is not sure of the occasion for opposition in Rhode Island. It may
have been lingering since Fox's visit in 1672; it may have been exacerbated by the tensions arising from King Philip's War; there were also possible ties to the contemporary Wilkinson-Story separation (in England,
inspired by the growth of business meeting authority). No doubt old
grudges among leading Friends also played their part.

Henry and Ann Bull were two of these apparently antagonistic and
prominent Friends who harbored long-standing grudges. Born Ann
Clayton, she came from Swarthmore in the north of England. One of the
early English Quaker missionaries to New England, she had married
Governor Nicholas Easton and, following his death, the old Antinomian,
now Quaker and subsequent Governor of Rhode Island, Henry Bull. Apparently some people had pastured their horses on the Bull land in 1676
(whether they were allies of Roger Williams or merely refugees from
King Philip's War we do not know), and the Bulls had shot the animals.
The horses may have belonged to other Friends, for Rhode Island Quakers
sought to adjudicate the case. But it was too difficult for them, and they
turned to George Fox for help. He decided that Henry Bull should not
have shot the horses, should have used arbitration or civil procedures,
and should make restitution to the owners. Eventually the dispute was
smoothed over when Bull acknowledged his errors, but it is likely that
the rancor lingered.[6]

The Bull affair was probably an indirect cause of troubles within Rhode Island Monthly Meeting two years later. Serious difficulties began in 1678 when one of the original Friends who had come from England on the *Woodhouse*, Robert Hodgson, had to acknowledge hasty words. His acknowledgment proved to be temporary, since the following year he accused Friends falsely (at least so the monthly meeting decided) of an unidentified slight. He headed a separate meeting in 1679 and probably was at the center of a controversy in March of 1680 over wearing one's hat when another was at prayer—a possible extension of the Wilkinson-Story schism in New England. He may also have been one of the Rhode Island Friends who opposed monthly meeting authority four years earlier when William Edmundson met opposition. By early April 1680, however, Ann Bull had joined him in opposing meeting authority; in August he still refused to satisfy the monthly meeting's demands. In March 1681 the monthly meeting discovered that Ann Bull had written someone in Lancashire setting out her case. Separate meetings continued. When Ann Bull attended the monthly meeting in June 1681, she had Peter Easton, Nicholas' son, take notes surreptitiously. The meeting disapproved. It attempted and failed to get Peter Easton's apology. The Easton family split. Peter and his wife sided with his stepmother and went with the separatists; John, his elder brother, remained with the official group. The schismatics established their own meeting for worship, a source of much concern to the official group. Separation continued through 1784, by which time Hodgson and most of the other separatists returned somewhat contritely to the meeting. Ann Bull had read a paper of self-condemnation in September 1683 leading the procession of separatists back to the monthly meeting. At most, opposition had flared openly for only five years. It disintegrated rather quickly and thereafter for almost a century church government was rarely challenged from within New England Quakerism.[7]

Opposition from the disreputable "Case's Crew" on Long Island lasted longer and did much more damage to the Society than had the brief separation in the 1680's in Rhode Island. Opponents of Quakers like the Mathers focused on Thomas Case and his followers, at best a fringe group. Deliberately or otherwise, the Mathers confused them with Quakers. Friends were not able, despite published disownments, to dissociate themselves from Case. There was yet another difficulty with Case and his followers: they had a disturbing tendency not simply to separate but to return again and again to meetings, particularly the large yearly meetings for business or worship where their hectorings, singing, and physical demonstrations made it virtually impossible to carry on either worship or business. Indeed, opponents may have had an excuse for confusing Case with Quakers, for Case and his followers attended Quaker meetings and must have regarded themselves as Friends. Nor did Friends resort to civil authority to have them expelled, as they usually did in the eighteenth and nineteenth centuries when obstreperous outsiders prevented quiet worship.

Many practices set Case and his group apart from Friends. In terms of doctrine and discipline, Case and company like early Ranters probably believed in individual perfectionism focusing on the individual's own conviction of conversion. Such control as there was came through Case, who held the group in an hypnotic state, if the Mathers can be believed. For outward manifestations, as in doctrine, the historian has only the accounts of critics and our picture may therefore be distorted. Case's Crew sang (no doubt they were the singing Quakers identified by governors of New York), danced, and, like the Ranters of the Puritan Revolution, did not subscribe to the usual standard of personal sexual morality (one unfortunate young man readmitted to Flushing Monthly Meeting had contracted the "French pox" while participating in Case's revels). The Mathers were happy to report that Case's followers danced in the moonlight, sacrificed animals, and consorted with the devil. The possibility that opponents might use the behavior of Case's Crew to link Friends to witchcraft made it necessary for the new business meetings to place Case and his followers at a distance.[8]

New York Friends bore the brunt of the Case problem. William Edmundson tangled with them in 1676. At various times, meetings, chiefly on Long Island, reported the loss of a member of these "ranters," or noted the reclamation of one of them. They were still a serious problem when Joan Vokins, an English traveling Friend, visited the Oyster Bay Half-Year's Meeting in 1681. The scene must have resembled bedlam, for Case "was bawling very loud," and his followers occasionally broke into song and dance. Joan Vokins tried to speak. She was happy to record in her journal that "God's living Power did most wonderfully arise," probably meaning that she was able to continue her remarks despite continued heckling. Thereafter the Case problem seems to have diminished. Although his group had expanded beyond New York, its base remained in Newtown, Long Island. The group existed late in the seventeenth century, as traveling Friend Thomas Chalkley reported. Shortly after the turn of the century "ranters" (presumably people in Case's tradition) disappeared from view in New York, and in 1712 the New England Yearly Meeting reported, with evident relief, that there had been no interruptions by ranters that year.[9]

New England and New York to 1710

The business meetings started by John Burnyeat, George Fox, and
other English and Irish traveling Friends in New England and New York
bore little resemblance to business meetings of the mid-eighteenth century. At first these rudimentary, basically local organizations had oversight of marriages, recorded births and deaths, and dealt with (that is,
sought to reform) Friends who did not observe Quaker testimonies to
marry within the meeting, to uphold business honesty, and to keep up
attendance at meetings for worship, or who violated the community's
moral standards. They also attempted either to bring potential schismatics back into the fold, as with the Bull-Hodgson group, or to get rid of
them by disownment, as with Thomas Case and his followers. There were
only a few instances of rule-making before the eighteenth century, for
rules made by George Fox and other prominent English and Irish Friends
in letters sufficed. These meetings differed substantially from their English and Irish counterparts and from each other, a situation often ignored
when scholars rightly point out the many unifying factors of eighteenth-
century "transatlantic" Quakerism.[10]

Fox had left the Quakers in New England and New York organized on
two basic strata. At the top was the general annual meeting in Newport
which came to be known as the Yearly Meeting of Rhode Island and later
as New England Yearly Meeting. It had a very loose authority over
Friends in New England and New York in the seventeenth century. On a
lower level were monthly meetings, which were local meetings for business, against which schisms were directed, and which at first, before organization developed in the late seventeenth and early eighteenth centuries, were the most important of the business meetings.

There were several of these basic meetings in 1672. Rhode Island's was
the largest: its control extended from the Narragansett country of western Rhode Island approximately to the contemporary city of New Bedford, Massachusetts. Nearby were the monthly meetings at Sandwich
and Scituate in Plymouth. To the north in Massachusetts and New
Hampshire were Dover and Salem monthly meetings. The southern extremes of the early yearly meeting until 1695 comprised the Long Island
Monthly Meeting, which had oversight of the many Friends on Long Island, and the few in the town of New York and on the mainland. Each
monthly meeting had within it one or more meetings for worship of varying sizes. In New England there were also representative preparative
meetings which might have one or more meetings for worship under
them. The preparative meeting organized business to be passed up to the
superior monthly meeting for action. It was to their monthly meeting

that Friends applied for permission to marry and to have births and deaths recorded. The monthly meetings raised funds, administered charity to members, oversaw the building of meeting houses, and corresponded with one another—functions as active after 1708 as before. They were, however, substantially more independent of superior meetings before 1700 than they were by the mid-eighteenth century. Lines of authority were just developing in the earlier period.[11]

As firm priorities were not established, there was much flexibility for actions in the four decades after 1672. On occasion Rhode Island Monthly Meeting functioned as an executive committee for the yearly meeting. It passed along suggestions and made decisions which ordinarily later would not be its to make, as when it, not a yearly meeting committee, wrote Queen Anne in 1708 on behalf of some of its members. Sometimes monthly meetings undertook correspondence with public officials on matters concerning Friends beyond their jurisdiction, as did Rhode Island Monthly Meeting in 1708, when it wrote Governor Joseph Dudley of Massachusetts soliciting repeal of Massachusetts church taxes. Similarly, Flushing Quarterly Meeting went outside the bounds of New York Yearly Meeting when it deferred to the judgment of the Meeting of Ministers and Elders in Philadelphia in 1708. So did Salem Monthly Meeting when it wrote directly to London Yearly Meeting in 1707. It was not unusual for individual Friends to appeal to George Fox when he was still alive, as William Edwards did from Rhode Island in 1680 and Ann Bull may have done, though she may have appealed to the Wilkinson-Story faction. Individual appeals to England clearly demonstrated the inferiority of American meetings to the English in the seventeenth century. That view of New England gradually changed after Friends stopped the practice in the eighteenth century, a circumstance frequently ignored by historians of eighteenth-century Quakerism.[12]

Eventually, Friends established yearly meeting authority at the expense of monthly meetings. In the seventeenth century, just as the yearly meeting and subordinate monthly meetings depended on rules derived from George Fox's epistles or from London Yearly Meeting decisions, so was decision-making by the yearly meeting limited. Between 1700 and 1710, however, New England Yearly Meeting took several steps that firmly established its authority over subordinate monthly meetings and placed them at some distance from yearly meeting functions.

The occasion for the addition to the yearly meeting's powers is impossible to pin down, but it is clear that English traveling Friend John Richardson had a hand in advising on its subsequent development. The yearly meeting leaders may have felt it was best to place power in the hands of a few trustworthy Friends. Other factors may have been the recent and continuing conversions of many people in the vicinity of Salem who needed guidance of older Friends, the long-standing war with French and Indians which had broken out again, the arrival of George Keith as an SPG missionary, and the attempts of Massachusetts to expand its ecclesiastical system to Quaker and Baptist towns in southeast Massachusetts. John Richardson was eager to see a tighter organization more closely resembling the English, at least in performance. In 1702 Richardson gave advice on "select meetings," established in 1701. Known Friends of stability and piety were appointed elders in these meetings to help direct and control the activities of ministers, also members, and by extension to establish in the select meetings the basic direction of all meetings for business. These meetings of ministers and elders were probably designed in part to emulate the executive committee functions and control of the London Meeting for Sufferings in addition to restraining some ministering Friends. English Friends had found raw, recently converted American ministering Friends near Salem in need of guidance. Similar select meetings were not generally established in England until over fifty years later. Generally Richardson's advice was taken gladly (according to Richardson), for American Friends eagerly sought to follow the advice of English ministers. Also introduced in 1701 were queries concerning observance of Quaker rules, to be answered by subordinate meetings. By means of these questions, the yearly meeting was able to assert its control of monthly meetings as well as see to uniform behavior among Quakers at large.[13]

Four years after the creation of these select meetings came the organization of another level of meetings. Quarterly meetings, patterned on the English county meetings, met regularly every three months. Minutes of meetings before 1705 sometimes refer to quarterly meetings—as did Rhode Island Monthly Meeting, for example, in 1682—but designation was in name only, as the quarterly meeting did not have a supervisory or representative role either for subordinate monthly meetings or the superior yearly meeting. Before 1700 Rhode Island Friends seem merely to have been copying an English name, since the quarterly meeting functioned essentially like the monthly meeting. By 1705 three quarterly meetings had been formed: in Salem to the north, which had subordinate monthly meetings of Dover, Hampton, and Salem; Sandwich in southeastern Massachusetts, with subordinate monthly meetings of Scituate (later known as Pembroke) and Sandwich; and Rhode Island, comprising Rhode Island, East Greenwich, and Dartmouth monthly meetings. Monthly meetings sent representatives, who were to answer yearly meeting queries on the state of their meetings, to the quarterly meetings. The quarterly meetings in turn sent representatives to the yearly meeting.

The establishment of quarterly meetings served to reduce the autonomy of monthly meetings and to put yearly meeting decision-making at a greater distance. In other words, these meetings served as buffers between the local and superior meetings.[14]

Yet another aspect of organization was the establishment of a collection of rules—the Discipline—to guide subordinate meetings. These rules, which New England Yearly Meeting approved in 1708 and corrected in manuscript in 1709, replaced earlier "advices" (advisories) emanating from George Fox, William Edmundson, and others. Implicit in the adoption of new rules was the assumption that they would be enforced. Hence in them were requirements that practices of honesty, simplicity, marriage within a Quaker meeting, and devotion to the faith be observed. Also included was the stipulation that each monthly meeting appoint visitors to inspect every family once a quarter to check on behavior. Discovery of a violation of the Discipline would result first in an admonition, then a more vigorous effort on the part of a committee, and finally a decision by the monthly meeting on whether the erring Friend's membership would be continued. The practice of checking members' behavior was not new, although it took on a special intensity after adoption of formal rules and the creation of a meeting structure in New England.[15]

The New England Yearly Meeting had set off New York as a separate yearly meeting in 1695. There is no readily apparent reason for the separate establishment; indeed all logic at the time would have argued against it. There was only one monthly meeting in New York whose members resided mainly in Flushing and Hempstead, when New York Yearly Meeting became a separate entity. Not until 1698 did Westbury Monthly Meeting begin its existence. The logical creation for New York Friends would have been a quarterly meeting as established later in New England. Flushing had been a quarterly meeting in name only, at least since 1686, but it did not mediate between a monthly meeting and a superior yearly meeting; as in New England, it was the monthly meeting under a different name. In 1697, seven years before New England, a distinct quarterly meeting emerged when New York Friends set up Westbury Monthly Meeting, presumably recognizing thereby the Westbury Quakers' desire to have their own monthly meeting. So few and so geographically confined were New York Friends at this period that every May the quarterly meeting turned itself into a yearly meeting. In effect New York Friends had yearly meeting status with only quarterly meeting activity possible, a situation they later recognized in 1746 when they added a second quarterly meeting in Purchase.[16]

There had been a half-year's meeting in New York before 1671. Like the general yearly meetings found throughout this region, it may have served as a semiannual revival meeting that occasionally made decisions for Friends. Whatever its role, its existence is to some extent a clue to New York's ultimate independence from the New England Yearly Meeting despite frequent trade, good communications, and family ties. As the Irish Half Yearly National Meeting indicated a meeting partially independent of the London Yearly Meeting, so the Oyster Bay Half Year's Meeting probably demonstrated a deliberate attempt to establish quasi-independence of New England Friends. It was not the only monthly meeting to use that term: Scituate also called a semiannual business meeting a half year's meeting, indicating an attempt to keep Rhode Island at arm's length. That did not work out in Scituate, where Friends were few, numbers declined, and Scituate and other southeastern Massachusetts meetings needed Rhode Island's help in resisting the extension of the Standing Order of Massachusetts. Probably a semiannual meeting did serve to foster New York's separation from New England. Persecution in New York was never as intense as in Massachusetts, and thus the need to unite with Rhode Island's influential Friends was less.[17]

Like their New England brethren, New York Quakers also tightened organizational authority. In 1704, three years after New England, New York Friends set up a select meeting of ministers and elders, perhaps as a result of Samuel Bownas' advice and no doubt because of Rhode Island's recent example. More important (because the meeting of ministers and elders apparently did not function as such for almost half a century) was New York's establishment in 1706 of a select preparative meeting, as distinguished from the representative preparative meetings of New England. This standing committee placed control of New York business meetings quite openly in the hands of a self-perpetuating group of Friends, narrowing control to the hands of a few to an even greater extent than did New England Quakers. Whereas New England's organization remained open by being representative, New York's was closed to easy penetration. Consequently, an oligarchy grew up which even the control of business meetings by weighty and wealthy New England Friends could not match.[18]

Development of Quaker institutions before 1710 had a parallel in a substantial numerical growth of the Society, which in some parts of the northern colonies probably exceeded the growth of the population at large. One of these areas was in the vicinity of Salem and Lynn, where the visiting John Richardson found many convinced in 1702. Another was to the north of Salem in New Hampshire and Maine, until Queen Anne's War forced an exodus of settlers exposed to Indian attack. Towns north of Boston had provided converts for Quaker missionaries from the earliest days of Friends' activity in New England, and the growth rate for the generation or so after 1690 was certainly sufficient to attract comment. Chances are that conditions improved for Quakers in these areas: constant danger of harassment under the old charter was now replaced at most by collection of church tithes.[19]

In southeastern Massachusetts, Rhode Island, and New York the growth in number of Quakers probably matched the growth of the population at large. Certainly there was increase, although precise information is lacking. Determination of who was a Friend in these communities contributes to one's difficulties. Many persons who rarely attended meeting, were not born to Quaker parents, and did not marry in meeting may have been considered by the community at large to be Friends. An example is the case of Jamaica, Long Island. Anglican missionaries in that town again and again complained of Quaker influence: there was widespread opposition to the sacraments of baptism and communion, an intolerable situation to Anglicans. Yet Quaker records indicate there were few Friends in town. Rhode Island's Narragansett country provides another illustration of similar difficulties. Although there were few Quakers among its population, outsiders like Ezra Stiles viewed the area reaching from South Kingston to Westerly as essentially a hotbed of Quakerism.[20]

One is uncertain about Quaker growth elsewhere in New York and New England, but Friends made a clear gain on the island of Nantucket. Several of its first settlers had departed Massachusetts in disagreement with the church there, some for having given shelter to Quaker missionaries. Their departure resembled that of several other Bay Colony residents and future Friends who had gone to Long Island. Quaker missionaries do not appear to have visited Nantucket, and the only hint of Quaker activity was the rumored visit of Jane Stokes, a follower of John Perrot. Whatever the religious complexion thereafter, Friends do not seem to have been present in identifiable numbers before the end of the seventeenth century, although some individuals, at least briefly, may have been Friends.[21]

Several Quakers from England and Pennsylvania who visited Nantucket between 1698 and 1704 are credited with making Nantucket into the Quaker stronghold it was before the War for Independence. Thomas Chalkley, the ship captain from Southwark and soon to be from Philadelphia, convinced several residents in 1698. John Richardson, the English minister, was more successful four years later, as was Thomas Story, from Philadelphia, in 1704. The result of these visits was that leading families, especially the Starbucks, were convinced, and probably within a few years most other residents were too. Shortly afterward, in 1708, Nantucket obtained its own monthly meeting.[22]

For all the persuasive abilities of the traveling Friends, there was no doubt another factor in Nantucket's conversion at just this time. Nantucket residents had good reason to fear the extension of Massachusetts church taxes to the island. Unlike mainland towns, Nantucket, added to Massachusetts by the charter in 1692, had avoided the issue of church taxes, yet it was only a matter of time until Massachusetts authorities attempted to establish the Standing Order on the island. Efforts to enforce an established church on towns in Bristol and Barnstable Counties cannot have gone unnoticed. What better way could there have been to counteract Massachusetts religious expansion than to adopt a congenial faith that opposed church taxes? Whether the efforts of Quaker missionaries would have succeeded to the extent they did without this impetus is far from certain, but the clear intent of Massachusetts vis-à-vis recently acquired areas like former Plymouth Colony and Nantucket no doubt made conversion to Quakerism easier for those who might otherwise have remained clear of a religious affiliation as they had been since the first settlement of the island.[23]

New England and New York, 1710–1754

Many English Friends visited New England and New York in the first half of the eighteenth century. Their ventures were essentially hortatory: to see the meetings in America, to carry their message, and to uplift their coreligionists. When they returned, they made detailed reports. A few such reports appeared as published journals; others went into yearly meeting minutes; still others remained in manuscript. At the beginning of the century ministers like Samuel Bownas and Patrick Henderson frequently met opposition and seemed to expect and enjoy it. By 1730 visiting Quaker ministers were no longer meeting that kind of opposition, although they did debate with persons of other persuasions. There were several reasons for this development: Quaker doctrines were no longer feared, as Cotton Mather's later pamphlets indicate; Friends had obtained release from church taxes; English and, to a lesser extent, American Friends adopted the view that Friends should be thankful to have kind treatment and now must live honest, humble lives so that the great favors recently given them should not be withdrawn.[24]

Visiting Quaker ministers from England and Ireland detailed the growth of their sect. Samuel Bownas recorded after his second trip (1726–28) that Quakers were increasing rapidly as "truth" prospered. The total number had grown as much as fourfold in some meetings in the two decades since his first visit. Of fifty-six new meetinghouses built in

North America, New England Friends had twelve and New York six, and in addition, he noted, old meetinghouses had been rebuilt and enlarged. This happy view of American Quakerism was to be repeated by traveling Friends from Ireland in the 1730's and by virtually every other English visiting minister before 1754. They did observe difficulties and sought to have American Friends correct them, but by and large the impression they had of colonial Friends was very favorable, and this impression was reported home.[25]

Also exemplifying the English view was Mary Weston. On an American journey between 1750 and 1752, she spent most of her first year in New England and New York with leading Friends like Thomas Richardson and Abraham Redwood in New England and John Bowne, Walter Franklin, and Benjamin Ferris in New York, who had shared control of meeting affairs for the past half century. Although ultimately numbered among reforming Friends, she demonstrated little interest in reform while on the American continent. On occasion she gave advice to meetings that seemed to be going astray, as in Smithfield, Rhode Island, where she detected what she thought were traces of Methodist enthusiasm, or in Salem, when she labored with the elders. Her visit to New York and New England had an impact not unlike that of a Great Awakening itinerant preacher on other sects, and she and the older Quaker generation were evidently pleased. Crowds were large, and important people who were not Friends attended—by Mary Weston's estimate 4,000 at Newport with the governor in attendance, 3,000 at Apponagansett in Dartmouth, 2,000 at Salem, and 1,500 at Nantucket. George Whitefield would have been pleased. He would also have liked her comments on election, reprobation, and original sin as she recorded them: a sign that at least one current of the Society was moving in the direction of the later Quaker orthodoxy. A Congregational elder supported her right to preach when a young clergyman opposed her addressing a group in Connecticut, maintaining that women should not preach. She was evidently satisfied when he added that she preached sound doctrine according to Scripture—another sign of her orthodox emphasis. Cotton Mather would have approved.[26]

When visiting English and Irish Friends observed that American Quakerism had grown and prospered, at least numerically, they may have been uneasy, for the opposite development had been taking place in England and Ireland since the second decade of the eighteenth century. But even if they indulged at times in unfavorable comparisons, their attitude demonstrated a satisfaction with American Quakerism before 1754 which was not shared by the next generation of English traveling Friends, and to that extent it must have been shared by Friends in New England and New York, for there is no evidence of widespread dissatisfaction among them nor of any attempt to do something about it. In short, if all was not well in the world, Quakerism was content and prospering under the meeting structure set up before 1710.[27]

The basic structure of New York and New England business meetings had been completed by 1710, and most internal practices had been developed—visiting Friends in their families, answering queries on behavior, and setting up methods of record-keeping—the establishment of a formal leadership had only begun. Although a few individuals, generally the wealthy and literate, might have dominated meeting affairs before 1700, there was no pattern of organization sufficiently well developed to say who spoke for the meetings, even though it is clear that from time to time Friends like Walter Clarke, Walter Newberry, and Thomas Maule did so. Once Friends had created the strata of meetings with lines of responsibility and communication, an established leadership within the organization grew up which belied the essentially democratic implications of the meetings for business.[28]

As already noted, those meetings had been instituted to keep Friends from anarchistic implications of mistaking one's creaturely creations for the leadings of the Light. They had also taken on the tasks of overseeing behavior. The belief was that no one could be certain of being correct, hence one should submit to the group judgment. A meeting's judgment was in theory by consensus—there was to be no minority. There was a loophole: those with a minority view could withdraw from the meeting; but basically the system of church government functioned by consensus much as Michael Zuckerman has demonstrated that New England towns did, no doubt making church government by consensus all the more acceptable—at least in New England.[29]

At first glance it seems unlikely that such an organization could develop an oligarchy; yet that is what happened in New England before 1760. Necessary services had to be performed—minutes recorded, committee meetings attended, representatives sent from subordinate to superior meetings—and the men who performed these duties came to dominate their meetings. Because only a few men performed them, a semipermanent leadership grew up. There was nothing insidious about the development; rather it was due in part to the natural abilities of men chosen to perform functions of church government and to the convenience of leaving affairs of the church in the hands of men with proven ability and with sufficient wealth to take the time—men who enjoyed the respect and confidence of their brethren. Nor is there record of objection to this leadership before 1755, and not even then among New England Friends.

One is less certain about New York at this time. The problem there is that records either do not carry information or are missing for periods too lengthy to permit generalizations—as are Westbury Quarterly Meeting minutes for the colonial period after 1720, New York Yearly Meeting from 1720 to 1746, Purchase Monthly Meeting from 1746 to 1772, and Oblong Monthly Meeting before 1757. One cannot be sure which Friends controlled New York affairs and wrote epistles to other meetings. Despite this deficiency of information, it is likely that the existence of select preparative meetings served to establish control by a few weighty Quakers in New York.

The clerk was the most important of the persons active in meeting affairs. He presided over the meeting and was chosen in New England by representatives from subordinate meetings; before 1754 his tenure was undetermined. He opened the meeting with a period of silence, and then proceeded to business. He presided over discussions and like nineteenth-century clerks may have favored a few important Friends who sat near him. If disputants grew overheated, he called for a period of silence until tempers cooled. Technically, he recognized rather than appointed committee members, but in effect recognition was the same as appointment. He also drew up the minutes reporting the sense of the meeting, which on occasions of controversy could be an extremely difficult task. In those rare instances when the meeting did split and several adjournments could not restore consensus, the faction on the clerk's side enjoyed an immense advantage over opponents, for he could draft a prejudiced record, although on appeal he could be overruled by a superior meeting, and sometimes was. More important was the length of a clerk's tenure, for the longer he served, the more likely it was that he could dominate deliberations.[30]

Clerks had been appointed before 1700, but we know little about them or their activities. Their note-keeping was careless at best, and, as in New York before 1746, it was not unusual for a clerk of many years' standing to lose his copy of the minutes. Since clerks served for long periods in New England and probably New York too, the tendency to have power centralized in the clerk's hands began early. Indeed, that a clerk apparently held his position without annual reappointment in New England and probably New York before the reform of the Society began in 1755 confirms that a small group consisting of clerk and a few weighty Friends could dominate monthly, quarterly, or yearly meeting affairs.

The combined terms of two New England Yearly Meeting clerks, Thomas Rodman and Thomas Richardson, endured for over half a century before 1760. They, their relatives, and their Newport friends controlled yearly meeting actions and the activities of Rhode Island monthly and quarterly meetings during this period. A similar situation may have existed in New York, where Thomas Rodman (not to be confused with his New England namesake) was clerk of Flushing Monthly Meeting and perhaps also New York Yearly Meeting after 1733, stepping down from the former in 1759 and only replaced as yearly meeting clerk in 1763 after his death.[31]

Another important office in New England Yearly Meeting was that of treasurer. Like the clerks, most treasurers before the Revolution came from Newport. That is not surprising, for most Quaker wealth was there, and the income from quitrents in lots in that town provided the Rhode Island Monthly Meeting with substantial funds, which were frequently used for purposes of the yearly meeting. Since Newport provided most of the money for yearly meeting expenses until the Revolution ruined income and property values in that town, it was natural for leading Newport merchants to serve as treasurer. Treasurers, like the clerks in this period, served for long periods. There were, for example, only five Friends in charge of New England Yearly Meeting funds (or stock, as Friends then referred to their treasury) between 1720 and 1760. In New York the first yearly meeting treasurer, Samuel Bowne, was not appointed until 1759. One cannot use the treasurer's position as an instance of oligarchy in that yearly meeting, indeed with the probable exception of yearly meeting clerk, such oligarchic features as there were in New York were essentially local.

The appointment of Friends as representatives is another indication of growth in a small group of leaders, a practice in New England in the eighteenth century. In New England Yearly Meeting this was particularly noticeable; several men served as representatives for long periods of time. Of course, many Friends were appointed only once or twice, but overall there was a tendency to return a man again and again. Representatives were not the only persons present at a business meeting, nor did they necessarily have the greatest influence in discussion. Sometimes their service must have been pro forma, but the multiterm representative was unlikely to be chosen simply to fill space and quietly assent to others' decisions. That most of them served again and again on yearly meeting committees further supports the contention that a few men provided leadership for New England Quakerism. Frequent appointment to committees also illustrates the growth of a fairly small group of leaders. This situation was repeated on all levels of New England meetings. Usually a few persons had the largest proportion of committee assignments in monthly meetings, even meetings with a large membership.[32]

Growth of rules coincided with the development of this leading group of Friends. There had not been substantial additions to the New England Discipline in the two decades following codification in 1708—a declaration ordering that no gravestones be erected over Quaker graves in 1712 (reaffirmed in 1717 and 1730), a statement suggesting the discouragement of the slave trade in 1717, and prohibitions of the marriage of second cousins in 1718 and of the use of periwigs in 1722. Some Friends apparently wanted the 1708 Discipline substantially revised in 1733, but the yearly meeting decided against dropping the particular requirements for it, though "friends [should] keep on a watchful care" so as to avoid the abuses that had given rise to the rules in the first place. The revised Discipline emerging in 1738 from these deliberations consisted of the 1708 Discipline, rules adopted since 1708, and the inclusion of a lengthy section from the Philadelphia Discipline which described the process to be used in settling disputes between Friends. The adoption of the revised Discipline completed the growth of Quaker rules before midcentury. Subsequent additions had to await reform of the Society after 1755. Whatever some Friends might have thought, the leadership of the New England Yearly Meeting was content with institutions and enforcement.[33]

Although there were possibilities of the leadership using the Quaker institutional apparatus to raise standards of behavior for New England Friends if not New York Friends, that did not happen before 1755. An essentially benign leadership presided over a Society that had the apparatus to require enforcement of the letter of the Discipline but did not use it. On occasion there seemed to be drives to raise standards. Visits of families ordered by meetings would be carried out with great enthusiasm for a brief period and then pro forma. There would be heightened periods of concern about offenses against rules, but ordinarily these periods were of short duration, and a change in enforcement did not follow. As a result, enforcement of the Discipline did nothing to reduce numerical growth of the Society in New England and New York in the first half of the eighteenth century as it did in the British Isles at that time and in America afterward. Although there are no statistics on the Society's members, a rough indication, particularly of young adults, is the number of marriages. Taking all meetings in New York and New England, there was a steady increase in marriages throughout the first fifty-five years of the eighteenth century; the increase was fivefold between the five-year periods 1700–04 and 1750–54.[34]

At least one reason for the rapid increase must have been that meetings dealt with few Friends for offenses against the Discipline. It is true that Rhode Island Monthly Meeting in the first two decades of the eighteenth century brought a fairly large number of offenders under dealing (appointed committees to investigate breaches of the Discipline); but very few Friends were disowned, and most were permitted to condemn or acknowledge their offense by submitting a paper acceptable to their monthly meeting, usually to be read, at the end of one or more meetings for worship, by the clerk of the meeting or another Friend. But most monthly meetings, including Rhode Island after the second decade of the century, simply did not bring offenders before them unless there was a great scandal. Evidence comes from the Flushing and Westbury monthly meetings, which noted in 1734 and 1735 respectively that there were many marriages outside the meeting by a hireling priest (a clergyman of another denomination) or a justice of the peace—"disorderly marriages," the minutes call them. But neither meeting took many of the offenders under dealing as they did after 1770.[35]

Casual enforcement of the Discipline reflected a loose definition of membership. It had been agreed since at least the last decade of the seventeenth century that children of Quaker parents were Friends unless they were disowned. If children did not uphold the Discipline and were not disowned, they would still be counted Friends. What of those children with only one Quaker parent? The Discipline did not say. In practice it depended on their dress, outward actions, and attendance at meeting: if regarded as Friends, then they were Friends. Another category consisted of people who had married in a Quaker meeting, apparently even if there had been no formal application for membership. If they did marry in a Quaker meeting, they were Friends, as Flushing Monthly Meeting recognized when it took D.H. under dealing in 1723, not because anyone thought of him as a Friend but because he had been married among Friends. There appears to have been no certain method of recognizing Friends before 1755 and in most meetings not for several years afterward. Although near the end of this period the New York Yearly Meeting attempted to set rules for membership in 1746, as did Westbury Monthly Meeting in 1752, in neither case was a definition forthcoming. Certificates of membership had been issued by Westbury Quarterly Meeting before 1737, probably in response to the New York election act of 1733, which required them of Quaker voters, but no definition of membership had accompanied the decision to grant certificates. Such a definition and stated requirements for admission as a Friend would have to await the Quaker reform movement after 1755.[36]

Not that thoughts of an expanded and tighter organization did not occur. But when they did, they were not followed up. In 1729 an attempt to establish a permanent executive committee of the New England Yearly Meeting (a meeting for sufferings) may have indicated a drive for reform. Whether or not it did, the yearly meeting beat the initiative back. There were complaints about young Friends marrying outside meeting. Committees were appointed in 1734 in Flushing to investigate and to follow up with a general visit to Friends' families three years later. There were some changes, as when Flushing Monthly Meeting adopted a representative preparative meeting rather than a select one in 1753, but reform did not follow immediately.[37]

American Friends had not yet acquired the urge to enforce Discipline which was an established Quaker characteristic in England and Ireland in the first half of the eighteenth century and would be in America particularly after 1770. They still retained something of the outward-looking features of the prophetic era, although admittedly these had declined in America as they did in the British Isles, where increasingly the Society looked inward. Elements of the original general or yearly meetings remained, however, coinciding usually with the bounds of monthly meetings, although in some instances more than one monthly meeting was involved and in others, none at all. It was at these yearly meetings for worship that visiting ministers attracted throngs of Friends and others. The general meetings served as revivalistic meetings and as meetings that might attract converts. In some cases they bothered neighboring clergy, as comments of several SPG missionaries in New York indicate.

As a consequence of the still relatively loose organization compared to English and Irish Friends, expansion in New England and New York continued. Because of this growth and migration to new areas, Friends added new meetings. Monthly meetings set up in 1725 in Purchase and 1744 in Oblong reflected migration in the Hudson River Valley. One result of this expansion was the creation in 1745 of a second quarterly meeting in New York (Purchase) and, as a New York Yearly Meeting minute of 1746 noted, the effective beginning of the yearly meeting as more than a quarterly meeting. In Rhode Island, South Kingston Monthly Meeting was set off from East Greenwich in 1743, Swansea in Massachusetts from Rhode Island Monthly Meeting in 1732, and Falmouth from Dover Monthly Meeting in 1761, reflecting settlement in Maine.[38]

In numbers and general enthusiasm it was a healthy situation, but young reformers in the 1750's were not impressed. They saw in growing numbers a reflection of lax enforcement of rules, a corruption that they felt must be rooted out by that small remnant of truly concerned Friends of whom they counted themselves a part.

Chapter 5
Reform and Worship

Preparation for Reform

FOR NEW ENGLAND and New York Friends a turning point came in 1755 when Samuel Fothergill and other English Quaker ministers, bent on reform, visited those yearly meetings and subordinate meetings.

Fothergill was not the first to urge reform of the Society by tightening the Discipline and raising barriers between Friends and the world. Mary Peisley, an Irish Quaker, had already passed through New England and Pennsylvania the previous year and visited New York with him in 1755, urging Friends to enforce high standards and to end the compromises with worldliness, particularly in politics. She had also complained about the beliefs of more than a few Friends. For all her efforts, however, Fothergill had greater influence in carrying reform forward.[1]

The effect of his arrival was similar to that of a revivalist preacher in the Great Awakening, and apparently he was conscious of parallels between his itinerary and that of George Whitefield. Like Mary Weston five years earlier, he drew large throngs. By the time Fothergill reached New York Yearly Meeting, he was certain that he had changed Pennsylvania Quakerism. There, he and others of the Society had brought about the beginnings of a Quaker withdrawal from politics sufficient to make Quakers a minority in the legislature and had obtained a revision and more strict enforcement of the Discipline. His efforts in New England and New York also may have quickened reform, although the full effects were a decade and a half away. Moreover, he did not secure the initiation of a Quaker withdrawal from Rhode Island politics. But there was not the same need for abandoning Quaker political participation in Rhode Island as in Pennsylvania: in Rhode Island the faith had not been compromised in the eighteenth century by a government dominated by Quakers, nor were Rhode Islanders under attack by French and Indians in the war that had just broken out as Fothergill arrived. Perhaps his lack of success in bringing about greater formal withdrawal from politics in New England and New York was also due to the fact that with the exception of Rhode Island, few Friends held colonial office.[2]

Even if they failed politically, Fothergill and his Pennsylvania companions were able to stir up the northern yearly meetings, and they initiated significant changes in administration of church government despite opposition. A generational conflict is apparent in Fothergill's reaction to many Friends who opposed his program. He wrote Israel Pemberton from Flushing: "the lamentable defection of those who would be thought the head but are the tail—I mean the more advanced in years, profession, and station amongst the people—gives a painful prospect. And as it is hard to lift up a hand against grey hairs, my progress has been more difficult and afflicting than I can express." As a result of his efforts, and probably against the wishes of many elderly Friends, both yearly meetings adopted the requirement that subordinate meetings write specific answers to each query on members' behavior and the state of meetings. Monthly meetings were to receive reports on queries from preparative meetings and summarize and forward them to quarterly meetings, which in turn were to perform the same function for the yearly meetings. This practice made it possible for the yearly meeting to have a fairly accurate picture of the state of the Society. Of greater importance, the authority of the yearly meeting to oversee Friends' behavior was greatly enhanced. Formerly, reports on the state of the Society from subordinate meetings could and probably did gloss over difficulties among their members. But now meetings could not avoid detailed, specific answers to queries. In response to reformers' pleas, New England Yearly Meeting adopted the practice without a show of resistance from any monthly meeting, although there may have been complaints about the expanded work for meeting clerks.[3]

When New York Yearly Meeting adopted the requirement of specific answers to queries, it may have expected the resistance that continued for almost two decades, perhaps foreshadowed in Samuel Fothergill's comments on resistance by elderly Friends. It may have been that some Friends resented influence from outside the yearly meeting, whether from London or Philadelphia (the constituent monthly meetings in 1757 had rejected a proposed union of New York and Philadelphia yearly meetings, although Purchase Quarterly Meeting had used the Pennsylvania Discipline for some time). The chances are, however, that refusals to answer queries specifically came because of resistance to reform and to identifying centers of opposition. Westbury Monthly Meeting led this resistance. From 1761 to 1767 Westbury refused to answer queries specifically and in writing. During 1763–66 Newtown Preparative Meeting of Flushing

Monthly Meeting also refused to answer queries, and no doubt shared the sentiments set out by Westbury Monthly Meeting in 1766. To these Friends, queries should not be answered because they "did not find the use of them accompanied with that Peace, Quietude and Satisfaction of mind, as might have been expected from the discharge of a known or real duty." Furthermore, while they agreed that "there is a declension among Friends, can we expect a recovery from such a declension, by Overseers undertaking a Service which they can't conceive to be their duty . . .?" Westbury Friends added that many of their Friends who visited Friends' families would resign before they would perform the new service. There was also opposition to queries in Oblong Monthly Meeting. It came into the open shortly after the establishment of Nine Partners Monthly Meeting in 1769, hitherto one of its constituent preparative meetings. In 1771, four years after Westbury resistance had collapsed, Oblong refused to give specific answers to the queries. Its refusal was short lived, for in 1773 a committee from the yearly meeting apparently so overawed the meeting that opposition to answering queries disappeared.[4]

In 1756 New England Yearly Meeting received a copy of the English Discipline—presumably because Fothergill and visiting Pennsylvania Friends bade it ask for one—and began to consider codifying New England Yearly Meeting rules along the lines of the English Quakers. Not until 1760, however, did New England Friends adopt a Discipline, modeled on the English book and replacing their earlier 1738 revision. The yearly meeting saw to it that all monthly meetings and most preparative meetings had copies. Now because each meeting had a copy sent it by the yearly meeting (an act apparently not performed in 1738), claims of ignorance of rules by members were less likely to occur and be excused. And for those Friends who wanted greater uniformity in observance of rules, enforcement of Discipline could now be consistently applied, for subordinate meetings had to give written answers to queries based directly on the Discipline. Again the yearly meeting had extended its control.[5]

New York Yearly Meeting had no Discipline of its own before 1755; in fact it is uncertain to what extent constituent meetings observed a Discipline at all. When Purchase Quarterly Meeting in 1760 answered a yearly meeting query as to what Discipline it used, it replied that it used the 1719 Pennsylvania Discipline and claimed to have followed it for several years. That the question had to be asked indicates the lack of interest in a Discipline before 1759, when the yearly meeting asked the question. So little concerned had New York Friends been with the niceties of Quaker testimonies that gravestones had been erected in both Westbury and Flushing monthly meetings. New York Friends finally brought their observance in line with Friends elsewhere. Westbury ordered the stones removed in 1753, and Flushing followed suit in 1762. So intent on having the letter of the Discipline observed were these meetings that they even had stones removed which had sunk into the ground and were covered with vegetation. The observance came thirty-five years after London Yearly Meeting had issued a strong advice in 1718—which most monthly meetings in New England had followed, intent, it would seem, finally to enforce their own rule of 1712. Because of such lax enforcement, adoption of the English Discipline in 1763 must have come as a shock.[6]

Related to the institution of queries and detailed Disciplines of the reform period was the establishment of permanent executive committees of yearly meetings, meetings for sufferings, patterned on the London Meeting for Sufferings. Now, difficulties brought about by the French and Indian War led to the establishment of the New York Meeting for Sufferings in 1758, emulating the Philadelphia Meeting for Sufferings created in 1756. Part of its duties related to wartime problems, but its tasks went beyond working to alleviate wartime distress. Its charge in 1759 was to stem the "Declension" and bring about a revival; hence its establishment was related to reform. The New York Meeting for Sufferings may have continued to meet after peace broke out in 1763, but its minutes are missing for peacetime before 1774 (when a change of clerks and a renewed crisis brought a revival of record-keeping), so we know little of its activities before the War for Independence. New England lagged behind both New York and Pennsylvania in establishing a meeting for sufferings, primarily because it was less directly affected by the ravages of the French and Indian War. Not until 1775 and the outbreak of the War for Independence did New England Yearly Meeting create its meeting for sufferings. As executive committees for parent yearly meetings, the meetings for sufferings did not make or administer rules, but they could and did intervene in meetings subordinate to the yearly meetings. They met as often as conditions warranted, although on occasion, as in New York in 1778, the meetings for sufferings could not meet at all because warring armies prevented it. The importance of both meetings for sufferings grew as a result of the additional tasks assigned them during and after the wartime crisis. In addition to administering assistance to Friends caught by war and ameliorating the lot of all noncombatants, New England and New York meetings for sufferings took over the work of supervising publications, helped eliminate slavery from both the Society of Friends and the states, and oversaw the promotion of Quaker education, a concern that accompanied reform. Because their several tasks necessitated frequent correspondence with similar bodies in the new nation and England itself, New England and New York meetings for sufferings served as unifying forces in American and transatlantic Quakerism after independence.[7]

Even before the creation of meetings for sufferings in New England and New York, Friends were institutionally prepared for the turn toward stricter enforcement of the Discipline. But although New England Yearly Meeting sent out a committee to stir up subordinate meetings in 1762 and New York had urged family visits in 1761, unlike Pennsylvania there was no serious attempt before 1770 to purify the Society by driving out all wayward members (except for Oblong Monthly Meeting, which got an early start). Probably the death of an older generation of Friends, the rise of a new one, and a reluctance to move too quickly despite desire for reform, account for the time it took for New England and New York Quakers to start to weed out the unworthy. Thomas Richardson resigned as clerk of the New England Yearly Meeting in 1760 and died the next year. In New York, similarly, an older group (the grey hairs who upset Samuel Fothergill) passed away. For example, Edward Burling replaced Thomas Rodman as yearly meeting clerk in 1763, and John Bowne, so admired by Mary Weston, died in 1757. Quakers who entertained charitable views toward human frailty similar to those of Richardson and Thomas Rodman presumably continued to exert enough influence to prevent an effort to clear the Society of impurities at one fell swoop for the next decade, although there was a gradual rise in dealings for offenses against the Discipline and in disownments of offenders.[8]

By 1770 in New England the statements on need for reform and the new generation of leaders committed to enforcement of the Discipline had their way. New England Yearly Meeting encouraged its monthly meetings to set up committees to drive out slackers that year. New York made a similar effort in 1772, when it appointed a large committee to see to the enforcement of the Discipline. Monthly meetings began to investigate persons who did not attend worship regularly, who failed to maintain the testimonies, and whose conduct might in any way bring disrepute on the Society. Enforcement of standards also helped New England antislavery Friends bring about the abolition of slavery among Quakers. But the primary emphasis was on Quakers observing Quaker rules, and the overall effect of attempting to have rigid compliance with the Discipline altered both the outlook and membership of the Society. Ultimately this important facet of reform, perhaps the most important, depopulated the Society.[9]

The effort to eliminate weak members forced yearly meetings to identify who could be considered a Quaker. Before 1755 there is little record that Quakers were concerned about specific statements about membership other than the New England definition of 1708 that Friends under dealing were not to be permitted in business meetings. As indicated in the previous chapter, it was generally understood that children of Friends would be Friends, but there was no other specific provision for membership. As for the rest of mankind, there were no provisions for convincements, although on rare occasions a monthly meeting would record an application for membership. There were attenders who were not considered members in some meetings, and there were nonattenders who were considered members in others. There was, in short, considerable variation in determining membership and therefore persons who came under the Discipline. Records of convincements before 1755 are few, yet men and women who were not so recorded in the minutes of meetings joined the Society and took part in meetings for business. For example, John Wanton of Newport, who had apparently left the Society before 1700, had rejoined by 1711 and from 1712 frequently served on committees of the yearly meeting and Rhode Island Monthly Meeting. Presumably a person was recognized as a Quaker if he or she observed the testimonies and otherwise followed Quaker belief.[10]

As the tribalistic concern for purity increased, there was heightened concern to enforce the Discipline and to define membership more precisely. The move to make Quaker membership standards more specific started the year before Fothergill's visit and was later reinforced by the need to certify members because of militia laws. The major source of a strict definition was the need to identify the "faithful remnant" among the Friends in a Society in "declension," as many reformers viewed it. Quakers had to be sure just who members were. In moving this way they may have been following the same path as the English and Irish Quakers in 1737.[11]

In New York, when war broke out in 1754 Friends had to deal with the problem of membership. There had already been efforts in 1733 to identify members, for political reasons; now the concerns of the past decade came home when the New York Assembly passed an act requiring Friends to register with county clerks and verify membership with signed certificates from their monthly meetings. Committees in Flushing and Westbury had given certificates to enable Friends to vote or to give evidence in court. War and reform coincided to force the yearly meeting to a further definition of membership. The yearly meeting decided that Friends were persons who requested and were admitted to membership or whose names were recorded in the book of members (that is, were birthright Quakers). But neither this statement nor the adoption of English rules of settlement of 1737 seemed precise enough to reforming Quakers. What if one parent of a child was a Friend and the other not? In 1772 the yearly meeting decided that if both parents of a child were Friends when she or he was born, then the child was a member. If just one parent was a Friend, that child would not be recognized as a member until she or he applied for membership on reaching adulthood. On rare occasions the Quaker parent could apply for progeny successfully, but that was not looked on with favor: the other parent would always be a source of corrupting ways. Despite attempts to change the rule in 1773 and 1774, it stood.[12]

Several monthly meetings in New England also wrestled with the problem during and after 1755, because reform was in the air and because of war and militia laws. South Kingston set up a committee in 1755 to see what could be done about defining membership. With the institution of written answers to queries as an additional impetus to war-related concerns, South Kingston had to decide which persons in its vicinity were Quakers, so that visitors could read the queries to them. The reason for South Kingston's having a particularly difficult problem was that many people in the extensive area regarded themselves as Friends. The monthly meeting decided, without reference to superior meetings, that membership belonged to those who had married among Friends or were the children of Friends and who also were willing to observe the rules outlined in the queries and to accept the care of Friends. It was not a tight definition, but it did indicate a concern and an insistence on seeing that members observed the queries read to them, a concomitant of the reformation of Quakerism.[13]

In 1755 Sandwich and Nantucket monthly meetings also sought to define membership. Probably both were interested first in the reform of the Society, and second, as in South Kingston, in overseers, who were needed to identify Friends in order to answer queries specifically in writing. Wartime difficulties seconded reform concerns to an even greater extent than in South Kingston, however, especially on the mainland, where the province had begun to draft Friends for military service. Both meetings set forth terms of membership, Nantucket limiting it to persons recognized in 1753 and those convinced afterward, and Sandwich to members as of 1755. Ten years later Smithfield Monthly Meeting, acting on the same impulse, stated that membership belonged only to birthright and convinced Friends.[14]

New England Yearly Meeting itself made no formal pronouncement on membership for almost two decades after the first of the above monthly meetings had ruled. Although it made no decision, the practice of tighter standards for Quaker membership was approved by most Friends. Monthly meetings began to keep names of applications and accurate records of acceptance for the first time after 1755. The yearly meeting finally set a rule of birthright membership in 1774 along the same lines as the monthly meeting decisions of the fifties and the New York decision of 1772. According to this rule, children could be Quakers only if both parents were Quakers, otherwise they would have to apply for membership. New England had at last defined membership much as had Friends in the British Isles thirty-seven years or more earlier.[15]

Enforcement of Rules

English and American Friends copied elements of each others' practice. English Friends for the first time set up meetings of ministers and elders below the national level. Most of the cross-Atlantic transfer went the other way, since queries had been answered in detail for years by many English and Irish meetings for discipline. More important in America was the move toward rigid enforcement of the Discipline, a practice that had existed for years in England and Ireland and had helped to bring a numerical decline in the Society of Friends in both countries abroad. Gone was the tolerant outlook of colonial Friends. Gone too would be the growth that Quakers on both sides of the Atlantic had regarded as a sign of a prosperous church.[16]

Unlike Pennsylvania Friends to the south who, as Jack Marietta has demonstrated, began enforcement in 1755, New England and New York Quakers took a more gradual approach. With the exceptions of Oblong Monthly Meeting, which initiated a strict administration of the Discipline in the early sixties, and, to a lesser extent, Flushing and Westbury monthly meetings at the same time, there was no move toward a tighter enforcement of rules in the sixties. The yearly meetings probably thought exhortations would suffice, and the older and more tolerant generation criticized by Samuel Fothergill had not yet passed on. Until elderly and tolerant Quakers were out of the way, no consensus was possible. In New England in 1770 and New York in 1772, the new generation of leaders finally won. Subordinate meetings received committees carrying advice to ferret out persons slack in attendance or who had in the past escaped dealing for various offenses, and if necessary to expel them.[17]

Responding to solicitations from above, most monthly meetings appointed committees to investigate slackness, and the results were soon apparent. In Rhode Island Monthly Meeting, for example, the number of dealings between 1770 and 1775 more than tripled the number for the preceding five years. Even more significant was the disposition of cases. Before 1770 this meeting had permitted most offenders to acknowledge offenses and publicly condemn their actions before the meeting. The decision for tighter enforcement of the Discipline changed that practice. Starting with the visitations of the special committee in 1770, Rhode

Island Friends disowned the vast majority of offenders. There were occasional cases where it permitted acknowledgments, but they were only a fraction of disownments. The phenomenon was not short-lived, occasioned by a sudden decision to expel unworthy members, or because of the War for Independence, as Sydney James has suggested. The practice continued in this monthly meeting through the Revolutionary War and well into the nineteenth century.[18]

Rigid enforcement of rules hit some monthly meetings harder than others, but the effect was the same in all. After 1770, when meetings were more concerned with literal enforcement of the Discipline than in carrying the spiritual message of Friends to a larger audience, there was a harsh unforgiving spirit about dealings. As a result, Quakers disowned many members for small offenses, thereby reducing their membership especially in older meetings.

The most harmful circumstance was that the majority of disownments were of youthful members. Young Quakers may have found it easier to break rules when the meeting disowned so many members. The pattern of frequent disownment may also have created a fashion among many young Friends. How could there be a sense of shame if virtually half of one's contemporaries had been disowned for "marrying out"? And surely the "faithful remnant" among young Friends must have included more than a usual share of prigs. Whatever the reason for so many "disorderly" marriages, many Friends did not observe the requirement that Quakers marry only other Quakers and only after receiving the formal approval of their monthly meeting. Because of rigid enforcement of marriage regulations after 1770, young Friends could not expect to be forgiven, as they once had. Cases of bastardy and of children born shortly after marriage met with a similarly stern reception from meetings. "Marital" offenses (offenses related to marriage, courting, or sexual misbehavior) were similar in that they were more likely to involve youthful members than were other infractions of the Discipline. As accompanying tables of dealings for "disorderly marriage" and similar offenses indicate, the ratio of disownments to acknowledgments between 1770 and 1790 for older areas in New England and New York ranged from two to one to almost six to one, and during 1790–1814 in older parts of New England it ranged from ten to one to almost twenty-three to one. Recognition that "outrunnings" in marriage was the source of most difficulties served to spur meetings to even greater efforts. By 1780 most monthly meetings had decided that members who married out after being warned not to do so—a virtual certainty in small communities where courting practices could be closely observed—would be disowned without further dealing. The decision served to make disownments even more frequent.[19]

Other offenses were dealt with in similar fashion. Although older Friends were more likely to be involved than in "marital" cases, young Quakers nevertheless comprised a majority of those who breached rules governing drinking, gambling, and attending dances. In all monthly meetings surveyed in older areas with the exception of South Kingston, the ratio of disownments to acknowledgments in dealing with these offenses was high, although not as high as for marital dealings. In the older areas of New England Yearly Meeting—Nantucket, Salem, Dartmouth, Sandwich, Rhode Island, the Narragansett—the average was about two disownments for every acknowledgment between 1770 and 1780, rising to more than three to one between 1780 and 1789.[20]

The precise effect of disownments is difficult to measure, but there are several factors which indicate that the new enforcement at least seriously limited numerical growth. One is that the number of convincements and restorations generally lagged behind the number of Friends disowned. Another and better indicator is in the number of marriages over a period of years, for such statistics indicate, admittedly in a very inexact way, growth in members and especially the Society's progenitive capacity. Increase in the number of marriages was steady to 1770 in all monthly meetings. Thereafter monthly meetings in southeastern Massachusetts, Rhode Island, and Long Island—the older meetings—either grew only minimally or shrank. The main cause was the increasingly tight administration of the Discipline, although there were secondary reasons, such as migration to new lands where numbers of marriages continued to increase. The overall effect, however, was to bring to an end the steady increase in Quaker numbers in the first seven decades of the eighteenth century. Most of the decline came in the older meetings, but considering the substantial immigration, especially to Hudson Valley meetings in New York, there must have been a decline there too, compensated by migration.[21]

Meetings in the Hudson River Valley and areas under settlement in New England did not show the effects of numerical decline. The primary reason for the growth of Hudson River meetings, especially Nine Partners and, after their creation, The Creek, Saratoga, and East Hoosuck monthly meetings, was that hundreds of Friends moved to this area after 1760, especially after the War for Independence broke out. There was also migration to parts of Smithfield, Hampton, Dover, and Falmouth monthly meetings in New England. Although movement was not on the scale of that to the Hudson River, it was sufficient to help maintain growth. There were other reasons for increase in these New England meetings. David Sands, a convinced Friend of Nine Partners Monthly Meeting, visited Falmouth and Dover meetings during the War for Independence, and his preaching caused the convincement of a substantial number of Friends. In both the Hudson River meetings and the newer areas of New England there was continued growth because of another factor: the ratio of disownments to acknowledgments was lower for Friends taken under dealing in newer areas than it was in the older areas. Taken together, both migration and a significantly milder disownment pattern helped to ensure continued growth in those areas to which Friends moved in great numbers during the War for Independence.[22]

Worship

Important though it was to debate with leaders of other churches and to development of Quaker institutions, the central aspect of Quakerism for both Friends and mere attenders at meeting was worship. The worship was, of course, free of formal liturgy, appointed reading from the Bible, and formal sermon. Like some twentieth-century Friends, in the seventeenth and eighteenth centuries when Quakers met to worship, they met in silence, waiting for God's will to be revealed. From time to time someone would break silence by praying or revealing some aspect of God's truth to those gathered. If that person had spoken frequently enough, the meeting would recognize her or him as a minister, a process that varied in the 1650's from apparently spontaneous acceptance, perhaps even self-appointment, to formal examination and decision by the business meeting in the early eighteenth century. Once recognition of ministers by meetings had become accepted practice, ministers and elders began to sit on a raised "facing bench," one that faced the assembled worshipers. By then meetings for worship seemed less threatening to outsiders and had probably become self-consciously more decorous than in the early years of Quaker presence in the northern colonies.

In their worship meetings, Friends would seek to "center down," much as they do today in those meetings that are not programmed. In centering down they attempted to shut out worldly cares and in silence wait for God to speak. Whether all present would or could effectively center down we have no way of knowing. There are indications that young people did not at times—"the youth," especially, requiring adult supervision. There seem to have been outbreaks of going to sleep during the meeting, lapses sufficiently serious for meetings to comment on inattentiveness. Manifestations like snoring drew reprimands. There must have been many cases of day-dreaming that went undetected; unhappily, contemporary evidence is lacking. What remain are accounts of occasional censure for sleeping and descriptions of the ideal centering down, but how well members practiced the ideal we have no way of knowing.[23]

The basic format of meetings for worship remained the same throughout our period, but there were some changes that reflected both institutional reform within Quakerism and Quaker reaction to events external to the Society. Thus in the period when there was singing and ranting, more than a few messages and the thoughts of those in meetings must have turned to controlling unruly Friends on the one hand and challenges posed by clergy and civil authority on the other. In the quiet period of oligarchic domination from the 1720's until the onset of reform in the 1750's, American Quaker ministers probably spoke about the prosperity of Quaker meetings much as visiting English and Irish Friends did. Then with the beginning of reform, at first rhetorical in the 1750's and after 1770 actively disciplinary, the viewpoint and statements of ministers changed as yearly meeting statements turned to the declining state of the Society compared to the mythical standards of the seventeenth-century founders as eighteenth-century reformers viewed them. In that period, messages must have become jeremiads, occasionally laced with comments about Quaker help for the unfortunate.

No doubt the physical characteristics of meetings were influential in determining the nature of worship. Originally, meetings were held in private homes and continued to be in areas of recent settlement or with small Quaker populations. Where Quakers were numerous or affluent enough, they built meeting houses, which varied in size from small buildings capable of holding perhaps thirty people to large structures that could hold upward of a thousand, packed in. Ministerial messages and prayers would thus vary from those uttered in the quiet simplicity of a home, for a gathered few, to the almost theatrical performances of Job Scott, a Providence, Rhode Island, Friend at the end of the eighteenth century.[24] James Moore, one of Scott's auditors, described his preaching:

> Our Esteemed friend Jobe Scott from Rhode Island Government Newengland Visited Sadsbury Meeting Who I think may be in a good Degree Accounted one of the Sons of thunder, for Before the Meeting was Scarcely Settled he arose on his feet pulled of his great Coat and hatt, and Began as truth opened the Way in a very Moving powerfull Manner in the Line of the Gospell, Saying be still for it is in Stillness and Silent of all flesh that god is to be Worshipp'd in Spirritt—Mentioning his own Expearience when god was pleasd first to visset him In his Yong Days by Drawing his mind Inward into an Awfull Silence before God Saying it was in that Silence I Learned to Unlern all I had Learned in My Own Will and Become anew Creature Which must be performed in humble Waiting upon god in Spirrit in the Secret Chambers of our hearts—or words to

that purpose . . . and so proceeded on for perhaps an hour. Except at times would Make a full stop to clear his passage for Delivery Wipe his face and get his Breath.

And Being so powerfully Led even in the Delivery of the testimony that was committed to his Charge he had to stop pull of his other Coat and Neckcloath from about his neck Laid them Aside and Left only a small under Jacoat without Sleeves, unbutend that and so went on in Avery Moving and Encourageing menner in order to Draw the attention of the peoples mind Inward untill he seemed to be allmost Spent. And Sat Down as it were to Refresh himself or to get Breath, for as I sat Beside him I thought he seemed Like a Vessel Ready to Burst for Want of vent for the Sweat Ran of him Like Watter, and after a Short time he Rose Again and Went on in the Same Line of Doctrine for perhaps three quarters or near an hour Longer. Which I believe was to the astonishment of the people in Generall Especially them that are Led to Beleive the Gospell of Christ Cannot be preached to edification of the people unless it Be By those that are Colledge Bread.[25]

Scott's theatrics were unusual for eighteenth-century Quakers and may have reflected a tendency of some Quaker ministers to copy the methods of itinerant preachers in the late eighteenth and early nineteenth centuries. More typical performances were described by the visiting Finnish naturalist Pehr Kalm in Philadelphia in 1750. He set out his observations on one meeting in some detail:

Here we sat and waited very quietly from ten o'clock to a quarter after eleven, during which the people gathered and then waited for inspiration of the Spirit to speak. Finally, one of the two aforementioned old men in the front pew rose, removed his hat, turned hither and yon, and began to speak, but so softly that even in the middle of the church, which was not very large, it was impossible to hear anything except the confused murmur of the words. Later he began to talk a little louder, but so slowly that four or five minutes elapsed between the sentences; finally the words came both louder and faster. In their preaching the Quakers have a peculiar mode of expression, which is half singing, with a strange cadence and accent, and ending each cadence, as it were, with a half or occasionally a full sob. Each cadence consists of two, three or four syllables, but sometimes more, according to the demand of the words and meaning; e.g., *my friends*// put in your mind// we can// do nothing// good of our selves// without God's// help and assistance// etc. In the beginning the sobbing is not heard so plainly, but the deeper and further the speaker gets into his sermon the stronger becomes the sobbing between the cadences. The speaker to-day made no gestures, but turned in various directions; occasionally he placed one hand on his cheek; and during most of the sermon kept buttoning and unbuttoning his vest with his right hand. The gist of his sermon was that we can do nothing good of ourselves without the help and support of our Savior. When he had stood for a while using his sing-song method he changed his manner of delivery and spoke in a more natural way, or as our ministers do when they say a prayer. Shortly afterwards, however, he began again his half-singing mode of expression, and at the end, just as he was speaking at his best, he stopped abruptly, sat down and put on his hat.

After that the group sat quietly for a while looking at each other until one of the old women in the front bench arose and immediately the whole congregation stood up and the men removed their hats. The woman turned from the people to the wall and began to say extemporaneously a few prayers with a loud but fearfully sobbing voice. When she had finished praying she sat down, and the whole congregation with her.

Kalm visited many other meetings and noted their differences.

But now I shall describe how it was often conducted otherwise. Many times after a long silence a man preaches first, and when he gets through a woman rises and preaches; and after her comes another man or woman; occasionally only the women speak; then again a woman might be the first, and so on alternately; sometimes only men rise to talk; now and then either a man or woman gets up, begins to puff and sign, and endeavors to speak, but is unable to squeeze out a word and so sits down again. Then it happens, also, that the whole congregation gathers in the meeting-house and sits there silently for two hours, waiting for someone to preach; but since none has prepared himself or as they say feels moved by the Holy Spirit, the whole audience rises again at the end of the period and goes home without the members having accomplished anything in the church except sit there and look at each other. The women who hope to preach and therefore sit in a special bench generally sit the whole time, keeping their heads bowed, or holding a handkerchief with both hands over their eyes. All the other women on the other hand sit upright and look up, and do not cover their eyes.[26]

There was no uniform experience in the Pennsylvania meetings Kalm visited, and a similar lack of uniformity was typical of New England and New York.

Worship was not restricted to these meetings. As J. William Frost has observed, the basic emphasis for Quakers was a quest for holiness in which all parts of life were as a sacrament. Thus business meetings opened and closed with silent periods. Similarly the life of the family was a constant pursuit of holiness. Each meal began with a period of silent devotion, and the decor of the home pointed toward the peaceful, contemplative nature Friends sought to encourage. The garments of family members were also to be plain, for gaudiness was not a part of Quaker worship. Even one's business dealings were a part of this pursuit, although if Irish Quaker strictures against mixing business and Quaker affairs had any validity for American Friends, worship in this sense was on a lower order. Still, honest transactions unaccompanied by false flattery reflected the simplicity of Quaker ceremony.[27]

The worship remained in essence the same throughout the period considered here, varying little according to time and place. It was important to all aspects of life; but unlike churches where a liturgy, formal or an informal, is part of worship and where the sermons of some preachers are known and heard in detail, for Quakers there is always uncertainty. Sources for the period before the nineteenth century are scanty, however, and conclusions must be speculative.

PART III
Testimonies and Politics

TO MOST SECULAR HISTORIANS, dissent in American colonial churches focuses on the separation of church and state—that is, elimination of state tax support for churches. Thus William McLoughlin's study of dissent in New England focuses primarily on Baptist efforts to eliminate church taxes. Yet for the student of Quaker history such a focus is unfortunately narrow, for it misses many of the significant parts of dissent held by churches that inherited the radical mantle of the Reformation, principally groups which either descended from or owed a substantial debt to the early Anabaptists. Sects like the Mennonites, some Baptists, and Quakers could not be comfortable with merely eliminating church taxes. For them dissent meant abdication from governmental participation, refusal to swear oaths, pacifism, and efforts to assist the needy.[1]

One may or may not be sympathetic to Quaker testimonies, but they developed in the colonial period and were of considerable importance both to Quakers and to those who dealt with Quakers. In addition to their refusal to pay church taxes, Quakers developed testimonies concerning oaths, pacifism, charity to outsiders, and antislavery. These testimonies are examined not in terms of Quakers moving from strength to strength, but to see in what manner northern Quakers refined and developed testimonies in the seventeenth and eighteenth centuries.

Chapter 6
Quaker Politics and Oaths

SOME COLONIAL DISSENTERS, like the Men-
nonites, eschewed office-holding and the responsibilities that went with
it, but Quakers before the onset of reform were eager to participate in
government at all levels. They were limited in how they could participate
outside Rhode Island, however, because of the requirement that office-
holders swear oaths. On the colonial level there was only one recorded
instance when laws requiring oaths were relaxed; in that case New
Hampshire permitted a Quaker to take an affirmation. Because Rhode
Island had no requirement on swearing, Quakers there were able to seek
election to offices at all levels.

Although election to colony office was limited to Rhode Island,
Quakers in Massachusetts and New Hampshire were nevertheless able to
serve in town governments, though sometimes illegally. New York was
most restrictive where Friends were concerned: before 1733 sheriffs indulged Quakers by permitting them to vote. It was only in 1734 that
New York election law let Friends affirm their qualifications to vote. But
never in the colonial period were New York Quakers able to qualify for
office, either provincial or local.

Their political participation may have compromised some of their testimonies, but there was a positive side to it. Quakers in Rhode Island
politics could assist their coreligionists directly by intercession with royal
governors in the colonies or by using their colonial agents in England.
Participation in Massachusetts town politics also had a happy side to it:
Quakers were able to use the principle of town autonomy to resist church
taxes and eventually to obtain both official acceptance of their refusal to
take oaths and the substitution of an affirmation.

Rhode Island

Individual Quakers may have participated in Rhode Island government from the time when the Society first made its appearance in the

colony, but it was not until 1672 that they entered politics as a faction, if not a party. Whether they and their allies remained an identifiable group after King Philip's War—that is, whether they had formed a party fighting elections for predetermined ideological ends in alliance with other factions in the colony—is a question that lies beyond the scope of this volume and awaits a detailed study of seventeenth-century Rhode Island politics. It does appear that even if a party with clear ideological ends did not form, Friends continued a potent force at the polls, strong enough to elect leading members of their group year after year. Being a Friend helped Quakers at the polls, especially if one came from Aquidneck Island in the late seventeenth century. Sometimes they had merely a share of office, as in 1678–82 and in the first three quarters of the eighteenth century. To the extent that they were elected to leading positions in government, one can safely conclude that coreligionists voted for them, joined by a sufficient number of other freemen who supported their secular politics and who probably admired their material and social standing.

Of course Quakers in Rhode Island had little reason to enter political lists as a distinct political group. They had never been persecuted in Rhode Island. Their testimony against swearing did not hobble their entrance to government: Rhode Island required no oaths. Only their peace testimony was a potential issue, and as we have seen, though individual Friends avoided military service in King Philip's War, Quaker officers of government signed commissions, authorized the deployment of troops, and served on committees to direct the war effort to the limited extent that Rhode Island was involved. Thereafter, as noted below (Chapter 8), some Quaker political leaders compromised their peace testimony, an issue that caused division among Friends but did not lead to the formation of a Quaker party. Furthermore, there was no established church to which one had to pay taxes. Friends in Rhode Island did not have sufficient issues around which to organize and contend with other groups: an ideological basis was lacking for Quakers to enter politics waving a party banner. They did participate, but when they did, they were concerned about secular issues on the local and imperial levels in much the same manner as were other members of their communities.

Perhaps the fact that Rhode Island leadership was in the hands of Quakers both before and after the Dominion of New England temporarily interrupted Rhode Island self-government led to the charge that there was a Quaker party around 1700. Royal officials as various as Edward Randolph, Governor Joseph Dudley of Massachusetts, and Jahleel Brenton of Newport complained about Quakers alleging that Friends would not admit men of substance to office and that they dominated government. These complaints should not blind one to the fact that the real issue was not whether Friends were in office. Rather, elected officials in Rhode Island, many of whom happened to be Friends, resisted efforts of crown officials to expand imperial control, as most Rhode Islanders would have done. It is with these factors in mind that one should read Edward Randolph's charge to the Board of Trade in 1698 that "the management of the government (such as it is), is in the hands of Quakers and Anabaptists. Neither Judges Jurys nor Witnesses, are under any obligation [that is, an oath] so that all Things are managed there according to their will and interest." Even given Randolph's exaggeration to make his point, his statement surely demonstrates not that there was a Quaker party, but rather that he disliked Rhode Island independence.[1]

Randolph's letter to the Board of Trade had complained of the leading Friend and onetime governor Walter Clarke. Clarke had served seven terms as deputy governor and (counting the period of the Dominion as only one term) was elected governor for four terms. When faced with the possibility of having to take an oath to uphold the Acts of Trade, Clarke resigned in 1698 and was replaced by his nephew Samuel Cranston, who was not a Friend and who could swear to uphold the acts. Clearly the oath was an issue in the early eighteenth century on which Quakers would not compromise. When no longer able to avoid or ignore the requirement that he swear rather than engage, Clarke gave up his position, although subsequently in 1700 Rhode Islanders elected him deputy governor, a post which did not require an oath and which he filled until his death in 1714. Beyond this resignation, there does not appear to have been any further reaction by Clarke or any other Friend to the struggle with imperial officials other than what one would ordinarily expect of a Rhode Island leader not tied to imperial officials.[2]

Friends continued to be elected to Rhode Island office in the eighteenth century, and, like Walter Clarke, many of them also held leading positions in New England Yearly Meeting. As many were merchants substantially involved in the transatlantic trade, they also possessed effective ties with Friends in England. Richard Partridge was their best link with English Friends in the first half of the eighteenth century. A native New Englander who became a Quaker in England, Partridge was a member of the London Meeting for Sufferings and after 1715 was also the agent for Rhode Island in London. Partridge had business as well as religious associations with Quaker merchants in Rhode Island who served in colony governments, like Thomas Richardson and John Wanton. Again and again these merchants and other Friends were elected to assembly seats, especially from the town of Portsmouth. Their position did help Friends in neighboring colonies in the struggle to eliminate tithes, but that was not an issue in Rhode Island. Friends simply turned out to be leaders because the community regarded them as such. Although they led both Rhode Island and Quakerdom, voters were increasingly likely to divide over secular issues and Friends to be concerned with matters well outside Quaker testimonies.

Typical of this focus was the debate over the Rhode Island land bank. The issue of specie versus bills of credit was not new: it had been argued for almost two decades when in 1731 Governor Joseph Jenkes attempted to veto an act of the Assembly authorizing a land bank. Unwilling to accept easily this defeat of the paper-money faction's plans, Deputy Governor John Wanton, a leading Friend, called the Assembly back into session to memorialize the Board of Trade and to test the legality of Jenkes's veto. Jenkes's supporters, led by Nathaniel Kay, the customs collector, thereupon petitioned the Board of Trade to sustain the veto. One of these petitioners was Abraham Redwood, a wealthy Quaker and member of Rhode Island Monthly Meeting. The assembly party won when the Board upheld the veto, but it is significant that the debate and the party organization focused on issues other than religious, and that Friends could be found on both sides of the issue. Clearly Quakers no longer acted as a party.[3]

Elections the following year brought the Wanton brothers to undisputed power. William, an Anglican, was elected governor. Within two years he had died, and John was elected to succeed him. John, the first Quaker governor since Walter Clarke, apparently did not scruple to take an oath, as had Clarke, nor did other Friends who were subsequently elected governor in this colony: when faced with the choice of having office and power or not having it, John, his nephew Gideon, and later Stephen Hopkins, the Quaker politician of the Great War for Empire and the American Revolution, apparently were sworn in as chief executives. They compromised the testimony on the oath, as they also did their peace testimony, without receiving censure of their meetings for doing so. Many Friends in neighboring provinces and probably Rhode Island as well could not have favored their assumption of office in this manner. Friends in other New England colonies had suffered imprisonment and fines for refusing to swear, and lobbied successfully to have an engagement (affirmation) for town offices.[4]

The reform of the Society which came after 1755 did not bring an immediate change in political participation of Rhode Island Friends. There was no need for Friends to abandon a dominant position, as there was in Pennsylvania, for, as we have seen, they did not hold government as a party. In addition, they did not have war pressing in on Rhode Island as in western Pennsylvania: no outraged multitudes protesting a lack of preparedness descended on Newport as they threatened to in Philadelphia. But the demand for purity was a signal for change, which the American Revolutionary War brought about. Before the War for Independence began, the last Quaker governor of Rhode Island, Stephen Hopkins, had been disowned for refusing to free a slave. It is likely, however, that his activity in government had brought criticism upon him, much as it also reflected on others. A Quaker justice of the peace in South Kingston, for example, came under dealing for having performed a marriage service. The issue had been raised in 1770 by South Kingston Monthly Meeting. Three years later he acknowledged his offense. In a sense he had broken the implied rules of Friends on marriages by performing the ceremony, rules which hitherto had probably not been enforced. More important, his activity in politics demonstrated an irreconcilable difficulty in this era of reform. The period of Quaker participation in Rhode Island government was drawing to a close.[5]

As in other parts of the northern colonies the outbreak of the Revolutionary War brought demands for withdrawal from government. New England Yearly Meeting, like other American yearly meetings, urged Friends to "dwell alone." Friends were to be a people set apart, avoiding compromises with the world. This was a response to wartime threats to the peace testimony, but it was also the logical outcome of the tribalistic drive which the more rigorous enforcement of the Discipline implied. If there had been a slippage of standards when John Wanton became governor, a decline that continued under Gideon Wanton and Stephen Hopkins, after 1770 there had to be an end to compromises at all levels of government: Quaker testimonies could no longer be ignored. Only in voting for and lobbying of government officials could Friends participate as an interest group with definite ends in mind. In Rhode Island that interest was considerable, for Quaker votes were sufficient in towns like Portsmouth to tip elections, and Rhode Island politicians received Quaker lobbying with the favorable hearing it deserved, especially where antislavery and charitable activities were involved. Friends withdrew from the direction of affairs in Rhode Island, only to participate in politics on a higher level.

Massachusetts

Massachusetts in the 1690's was much enlarged and religiously more diverse than it had been before the Dominion of New England. All of former Plymouth colony and Nantucket Island had been added to it by its new charter. As a part of that charter, Massachusetts was to have "liberty of Conscience allowed in the Worshipp of God to all Christians (Except

Papists) Inhabiting or which shall Inhabit . . ." the colony. To that extent, Friends were no longer to be harassed in their worship. But the charter did little to change political disabilities.[6]

One of the major Quaker difficulties, not encountered by most other dissenters in Massachusetts, was, as usual, the oath. Although Friends could now participate in elections in the colony as a whole, much as they could after 1681 in Plymouth Colony, they could not hold electoral office without taking an oath. Some of them do not seem to have avoided the requirement of an oath early in the eighteenth century when elected to town office and jury service. Dartmouth Monthly Meeting referred the matter to New England Yearly Meeting in 1702, and that meeting sent Dartmouth Friends to Walter Clarke for help. Shortly thereafter they unsuccessfully petitioned the General Court for permission to serve on juries and in town offices simply by making an affirmation.[7]

Only indirect evidence suggests that Friends later served in town office for a lengthy period of time without taking an oath. In the Quaker-dominated towns of Dartmouth and Tiverton, assessors and constables were imprisoned for refusing to assess or to collect church rates, which may indicate that those officers served without taking the oath. Friends also served in other offices in these towns, including selectman, as did Friends from Nantucket, where Quakers were a majority after 1708 until land squabbles, migration, and the enforcement of the Discipline seriously depopulated the Society on that island in the second half of the eighteenth century. So many Quakers served in these town governments that serious questions arose as to the legality of actions performed by town officers who had not taken an oath.[8]

Friends petitioned the General Court in 1734 to pass an act "for granting [an] Affirmation or Declaration" in lieu of an oath. But although passed by the Council on June 27, the House of Representatives refused to concur because the petition "contains in it divers inconvenient Expressions." It voted to set up a joint committee with the council to draw up an act permitting an affirmation, and there the matter rested. The problems were not resolved, as a letter to Governor Jonathan Belcher from Dartmouth Monthly Meeting in 1737 indicates. The problem for Dartmouth was "the Difficult circumstance we lie under by reason of our Justices not giving us our engagements according to the Indulgence as in times past." Success would not come during Governor Belcher's term, however. Not until Governor William Shirley took office did Quakers obtain their desired end. Then, in response to a petition from Dartmouth carried by John Tucker in June 1742 again requesting the substitution of an affirmation for the oath, the assembly "Ordered That the Petitioner be allowed to bring in a Bill for the purpose mentioned." Two weeks later

Tucker brought in his bill, but although the House passed it, the Council failed to act. Over a year later, in October 1743, the selectmen of Dartmouth petitioned for an affirmation act "representing sundry Difficulties they labour under occasion'd by the Refusal of several Persons who were chosen Officers in *March* last to take the Oaths required by Law, they being of the People called *Quakers*." A House committee brought in another bill for relief of Friends, which passed the House but again failed to obtain concurrence of the upper chamber. In February 1744 the House passed still another measure, like other Quaker relief acts temporary (of three years duration). It confirmed the right of Friends to take an affirmation to serve in town offices, except for assessing the clergy's rate when one half or more of the assessors or collectors were Friends. It also added a retrospective clause, giving legal force to many acts of Quaker officers who had "neglected or refused to take the oaths to such offices by law annexed, and yet have continued in said offices." The rationale for the assembly's actions was that "should consequent proceedings of such town be called in question as illegal, and so set aside . . . much confusion would arise." Accepted by governor and council in 1744, it was passed again three years later for ten years, renewed periodically until the end of the colonial period, and renewed by the revolutionary government in 1778. The act was not without disabling clauses, however, for the affirmation did not extend to criminal cases, nor could Friends hold office at the provincial level where an oath was also required. They were not, in short, granted equal treatment with other residents whether dissenter or Congregationalist, even though punishment for breach of the affirmation was the same as for perjury under oath.[9]

That the act passed at all was remarkable, given the early experience of Quakers in Massachusetts. But in 1743 Friends were no longer regarded as a threat and had not been for some years. The Great Awakening may have taken some of the resistance out of the Standing Order, again helpful—as similar bills before the Awakening had failed under the decidedly pro-Quaker Governor Jonathan Belcher. Governor William Shirley was not as favorably disposed to Quakers as Belcher had been. The English Quaker lobbying machinery was also of little help in this instance: Friends could not use the dissenting status of Congregationalists in England or of the Society for the Propagation of the Gospel in New England, as they did on the issue of church taxes. Whatever the source, there was a changed attitude toward Friends as the appointment of a joint committee of House and Council to consider what had been done for such "Sufferers, as Quakers, and or on Account of Witchcraft," made clear, even though no compensation was forthcoming.[10]

For the balance of the colonial period Massachusetts Friends seem to have been elected to local office in places where they were numerous, especially in the town of Dartmouth and on the island of Nantucket. With the inception of reform of the Society and the outbreak of the Revolutionary War, however, Friends initiated the withdrawal from government office which became characteristic of them for the remainder of the eighteenth century and the early part of the nineteenth. As in other colonies and states they could and did lobby, particularly where their testimonies were concerned, and vote in town meeting. But temporarily, they excluded themselves from even town offices.

New Hampshire

New Hampshire's requirements for office-holding were similar to those of Massachusetts, yet the rigorous application was never there: New Hampshire did not attempt to impose a provincial system on hostile towns. There was from the outset a milder treatment of dissenters than in the Bay Colony. One sign of New Hampshire's tolerance was its legislation permitting the affirmation.

From 1696, as in other colonies and England, New Hampshire Friends received the privilege of taking an affirmation of fidelity to the crown. Later, in 1718, Friends were able to take the affirmation to serve on all juries, a right they did not receive in Massachusetts, where the suspicion lurked that unless an oath was involved, one could not really be trusted in cases of life and limb, a view shared by many members of the imperial administration, particularly at the beginning of the eighteenth century.[11]

New Hampshire law also provided for oaths for town and provincial officers. A statute of William III (1699) required oaths of justices, and a statute of George I (1718) established oaths for all officers from town through province. Since these remained on statute books printed in 1729 and 1761, it is probable that legally at least they continued in force throughout the colonial period. As a consequence, Friends were in theory legally prevented from serving in office before Independence.[12]

In practice there was Quaker office-holding, particularly in local government, despite the oath-taking requirement. Even the statute books gave tacit recognition to the fact that Friends were elected to local office, such as the undesirable office of constable. An act of 1731 relieved them of the necessity of collecting church taxes when serving in that office. Since participation went beyond the office of constable, one can conclude that the statute requiring oaths was honored as much in the breach as in the observance. In fact, when confronted with the election of a Friend, colony officials proved eager to accommodate, as in January 1742 when Friend

John Canney, an elected representative from Dover, where many Quakers lived, refused to take the oath because he was a Friend. The Assembly conceded that he had a point and accepted him, since "he was willing to make a solemn affirmation which was accepted afterwards." There is no record that Friends served in provincial office subsequently, but the readiness with which the requirement for swearing was waived for Canney indicates an openness in New Hampshire. The colony gave the broadest possible interpretation to the 1718 statute permitting affirmations, although the clear intent was to have that affirmation restricted to jury service and to affirmations of allegiance to the Crown and the Hanoverian succession.[13]

As for withdrawal from governmental office during the Revolutionary War, one can only speculate that most if not all Friends who had served did withdraw. In any event as there had been few if any leading Quaker politicians before the War for Independence in New Hampshire, the change for Friends as a group was minor. They continued, where necessary, to lobby for their testimonies, most of which were recognized by statute by the end of the colonial period anyway. Where they were temporarily unsuccessful, generally it was because of their reluctance to accept the new state government until after peace had been signed with Britain, particularly on the issue of paying taxes to the state during wartime.

New York

New York developed institutions of representative government on the provincial level later than did other colonies. Not until the accession of William and Mary was the existence of an assembly finally confirmed for the colony, although there had been demands earlier which had been frustrated during the Dominion of New England and which in part lay behind a rebellion in New York by Jacob Leisler against the Dominion of New England. When New Yorkers finally elected an assembly in 1691, it was numerically small, was influenced by continuing factional interests, sat for lengthy periods, and frequently was the stage for contention between the governor and his allies and their factional opponents of the moment. The full implications of these struggles are still debated by historians and do not concern us here except as they involved Friends—which they did on several occasions.[14]

While Quakers were not legally able to serve in town and colony offices because an oath was required (and there is no evidence to indicate that communities ignored the requirement), Friends were given liberty in 1691 under "An Act to ease People that are Scrupulous in Swearing" to give evidence and to serve on juries, a considerably greater freedom than they enjoyed in eighteenth-century Massachusetts and one which they gained despite some provincial suspicion of their refusal to take oaths. Like Friends in other northern colonies after 1690, they also apparently had the right to vote and did so during Governor Benjamin Fletcher's administration, until in 1698, after an apparently tumultuous election, the assembly passed a comprehensive election statute setting a 40-pound property requirement for each voter and giving each sheriff the right to determine the qualification of electors by demanding that they swear under oath that they had sufficient property to be qualified as voters.[15]

It is probable that the act itself was not intended to be used against Friends, for they apparently had the freedom to vote under the next governor, Richard Coote, Lord Bellomont. As a Quaker petition to his successor, Edward Hyde, Lord Cornbury, in 1702 indicated, Bellomont permitted them to vote when they requested his intervention. Bellomont was not enthusiastic about Quakers in government, and the caretaker regime after his death under Lieutenant Governor John Nanfan, even less kindly disposed, refused them their franchise because they would not swear. Nanfan and supporters no doubt had a factional motive that originated in part from an election in 1699. The Earl of Bellomont had called for elections in that year primarily to obtain an Assembly more favorable to him, much as he had turned out of the Council such men as William Nichols. Nichols was an ally of Bellomont's predecessor, Benjamin Fletcher. Fletcher had been recalled to England to answer a number of charges, especially failure to enforce the Acts of Trade and Navigation. Nichols, Bellomont alleged, consorted with pirates, smuggled goods, and was a Jacobite, as was his anti-Leislerian party. Because Nichols' faction was particularly strong in Queens County, Bellomont had required an oath of allegiance, theoretically to smoke out Jacobites. It was at this point that he probably indulged Quakers because of their scruples about swearing. As Bellomont reported to the Board of Trade: "A Great many men in that county pretended themselves Quakers to avoid taking the oaths, but soon after at the election, those very men pulled off the mask of Quakerism, and were got very drunk and swore and fought bloodily, their padrone, Mr. Nichols, being a spectator all the while." While Nanfan and his allies saw to it that at the next election there were neither Friends nor pretended Friends voting, the newly arrived Lord Cornbury was happy to pass on the Quaker complaint annexed to a letter alleging misgovernment under Nanfan. Thereafter, until 1733, as there is no evidence that Quakers were denied the vote, it is likely that they were in fact permitted to vote and to that limited extent to participate in government, allied with onetime anti-Leislerians like Nichols and Adolph Philipse.[16]

Their support probably continued with the Philipse group for many years, until in 1733, when one next encounters a denial of Quaker votes, many Friends supported the group led by Lewis Morris. That year Morris' faction was locked in a contest with Governor William Cosby. Cosby had appointed a new sheriff, one Nicholas Cooper, and in an attempt to have his candidate elected Cooper had thrown out the votes of Quakers in Westchester County (Friends had voted for Morris). This time Quakers had their franchise defended by the aggrieved Morris faction. Rip Van Dam, an ally of Morris, complained to the Board of Trade that Morris' opponent was a known Jacobite, a typical and useful charge to make against opponents when addressing imperial authorities for assistance, and probably untrue. Similarly unreliable was his charge that the sheriff "is a stranger and a person of no visible estate, and is supposed to have been by you put into place in order to defeat the late Chief Justice" (Lewis Morris). Cosby's tactic had failed to prevent Morris' election. Despite a favorable opinion from the court, which upheld the Quaker disqualification, Cosby was happy in 1735 to send to the Board of Trade an act passed in 1734 which permitted Friends to vote if they had a certificate from their quarterly meeting. Although New York politics continued on a troubled course, Quakers ceased to be an issue.[17]

Despite the clear evidence that Friends supported Lewis Morris, both before and after this case, they may not have supported him when he moved his political activities to New York in 1710 and actively began to participate in politics. Probably not until he released a legacy given by his uncle, William Morris, to Friends—a legacy he had refused to give them for years—did Friends support him. This suggests not that Quakers sold their votes for the legacy, but that Morris, a difficult character at best, was prepared to withhold the legacy until Quakers proved politically useful to him. He had already headed a faction representing Scots and Quakers in New Jersey, so it is not unlikely that Friends would find him unappealing. Unhappily, there is no evidence to indicate how Friends in Queens County voted, and Morris' Quaker support in 1733 may have been limited to the mainland. It is clear that Friends favored the landed interest represented by such as Morris and Henry Beekman in the Hudson River Valley, but that is the extent of certain knowledge.[18]

Since one had to take an oath to serve in any office in eighteenth-century New York, it is unlikely that Friends served in any but the lowest offices, and not in them either unless there was collusion to permit their taking an affirmation. Quakers in New York seem to have been firm in dealing with any Friend who took the oath. For example, Flushing Monthly Meeting disowned Thomas Betts of Newtown in 1750 for taking an oath and qualifying as a justice of the peace.[19]

New York Friends came to the period of reform of the Society and of the Revolution without having to abandon participation in government: so far as we know, they had not served. The transition must have been easier for them than in New England and in Pennsylvania. But they still continued to vote in elections and apparently to support established politicians like the Beekmans in places where many Friends lived—the Oblong, and towns in Nine Partners and The Creek monthly meetings. And while they were not immune to unrest over land during the troubled decade of the 1760's when squatters fought with landed proprietors, with but few exceptions it seems their support went to those with clear title— that is, to the group that dominated the region socially and economically.[20]

Like most other colonies, New York, after the outbreak of the War for Independence, continued its practice of permitting Friends to vote and to give evidence, although there were difficulties at times. Apparently, authorities permitted Quakers to vote if they were recognized as Friends—a practice confirmed by statute in 1787, based on earlier legislation before 1783 which was unacceptable to the yearly meeting, since Quakers officially refused to recognize the new government until the 1783 peace treaty. Friends could and did participate, but they faced uncertain prospects because they were frequently identified with loyalists.[21]

Chapter 7
Church Taxes

FROM THE LATE SEVENTEENTH through the first three decades of the eighteenth centuries, Quakers in the Northeast, like other dissenters, found the issue of church taxes distressing. Most difficulties were encountered in Massachusetts, enlarged in 1692 by Plymouth. In a losing struggle lasting almost four decades, the Bay Colony sought to impose requirements for tax support of its ecclesiastical system on these dissenters and the recalcitrant towns where they lived—Dartmouth, Tiverton, Little Compton, and Sandwich, to name a few with a substantial Quaker population. Elsewhere in New England there was relatively little struggle. New Hampshire virtually exempted Friends from church taxes after 1692. Even Connecticut caused few problems, for there were not many Friends there until 1727 and in 1729 Connecticut exempted Quakers from paying taxes once they had satisfied certain criteria.

The struggle to escape New York church taxes illustrates both the strength and the weakness of the Quaker position. To wage their battle, New England dissenters found it useful to have Anglicans as allies against the established New England churches. In New York, Quakers could not resort to such an alliance, for church taxes helped support the Anglicans in the four lower counties. It was one thing to struggle against the Congregationalists and quite another to take on the church headed by the Crown. Neither town resistance nor the Quaker transatlantic connections which had served Friends so well in New England could help at all. New York Friends were destined to face church taxes until the Revolution.[1]

Massachusetts and Connecticut to 1708

Friends and other dissenters in Massachusetts may have briefly thought in the late 1680's and early 1690's that they would be free of compulsory church taxation. Before 1680 church taxes had been at least 50 percent

higher for Friends who refused to pay than for other residents, because
of fees charged for forced collection, because the sale of goods distrained
would not equal the amount due and, so far as we know, because Friends
if not other dissenters would not accept a refund of excess charges. But
under Governor Edmund Andros, those taxes had been ordered remitted
in both Massachusetts and towns in the former Plymouth Colony which
had continued to assess Friends and Baptists. After the overthrow of
Andros, there was still hope, even if some English Friends were suspected of alliance with James II, that William and Mary would favor persons who dissented from the Massachusetts way. To be sure, Increase
Mather, the Massachusetts agent in London seeking a new charter, was no
friendlier to Massachusetts dissenters after the Glorious Revolution than
he had been before. But it was not unreasonable to expect the new mon-
archs to continue tolerant efforts begun under Andros.[2]

In many ways, the charter granted by William and Mary fulfilled
Mather's hopes even if it did not free dissenting colonists from church
taxes. It did restore a measure of autonomy to Massachusetts voters, who
either directly in the case of the Assembly or indirectly in the Council,
elected provincial officials. But it also contained a clause providing for
liberty of conscience, surely a comfort for Friends and other dissenters,
which required "liberty of Conscience allowed in the worship of God to
all Christians." The definition included Quakers, but what would the
phrase mean in practical terms? Would it mean, as it ultimately did in
neighboring New Hampshire, that faithful members of other churches
would be freed from the necessity of supporting the established church?
As it turned out, Massachusetts had no such intention. If Friends in
towns like Salem thought their difficulties over church taxes were at an
end, they were soon disabused of that notion, as were Quakers and Baptists in southeastern Massachusetts towns which had had no clergy paid
by public funds.[3]

The General Court began immediately to reestablish public support
for orthodox ministers in old Massachusetts. It also tried to impose it
piecemeal on old Colony towns. It extended the system town by town,
until such towns as Dartmouth and Tiverton in Bristol County (to
mention only major mainland Quaker centers) were locked in combat
with the General Court, resisting efforts to establish the Massachusetts
way.

In November 1692 the General Court passed an act providing for support of ministers and schoolmasters. As it related to dissenters, the section on ministers was the most important part. All towns were to have a
"learned orthodox minister, or ministers." The meaning of that phrase
would give trouble in the future even if the intent was clearly to establish

the Standing Order. Anglicans, Baptists, and Quakers might well ask who was learned and who orthodox. The act also required courts of quarter sessions to make contracts for the support of orthodox clergy, if no contracts existed, to see that no town was without a minister for more than three months, and to appoint a clergyman if the town refused. All taxpayers were to share the obligation to support a minister, and a town majority was to choose him. The act also affirmed congregational autonomy: "That the respective churches in the several towns . . . shall . . . use, exercise and enjoy all their privileges and freedoms respecting divine worship, church order and discipline." The autonomy suggested gave towns a chance to select clergy who were not the "learned, orthodox" men the General Court and ministers like the Mathers had in mind, even though it fitted the Massachusetts practice of recognizing town autonomy.[4]

Because of its ambiguities, the act was amended, in February 1693. This first amendment provided that the traditional Massachusetts practice of "approval" was necessary for a minister's installation. Custom dictated that this approval meant certification by neighboring ministers (a good means of having only Congregationalists settled). It also freed Boston from compulsory taxes but, as McLoughlin has pointed out, Quakers outside Boston could argue, if Boston Friends are free of church taxation, why not all Friends? When Massachusetts Congregational clergy recognized the danger to the Standing Order of giving the town a veto in the choice of a minister, the General Court in 1695 further amended the original act. This second amendment permitted a council to meet at the behest of the church, if church members and town disagreed. The council was to be composed of representatives of between three and five neighboring churches who would arbitrate the dispute. If the council found for the church, the minister was to be appointed; if not, the church would have to choose again, subject to the veto of the town, and get another hearing by a council if the town vetoed the choice. This last amendment struck directly at town autonomy, as indeed did the province's imperial venture to impose the Standing Order. The practice of established Congregational churches ran head on into dissenter resistance and the tradition of town autonomy. Time was past when this kind of system could easily be imposed. The attempt to expand the Standing Order was doomed from the outset, although that was by no means clear in the 1690's. Compulsory cultural assimilation of old Plymouth towns was to be the rule, thought Massachusetts leaders.[5]

For most of the province enforcement was immediate and resistance was minimal. Many towns in southeastern Massachusetts went along with the legislation, but they were the towns that had supported a clergyman before Plymouth colony's demise. In old Massachusetts not all was well. Boston Friends reported sufferings in 1695, as did Salem Monthly Meeting in 1696. In that year Salem town imprisoned Thomas Farrar and John Hood for failing to collect church taxes. Moreover, authorities in predominantly Congregational towns like Salem, Scituate, and Marshfield, where many Quakers lived, probably collected church taxes from Friends by distraint under the law of 1693, much as they had before the time of Governor Andros. Nor did Quaker problems stop there, for one could be elected to the lowly town office of constable and, if permitted to serve without swearing, still have to face the likelihood of imprisonment for refusing to collect taxes. The situation was exacerbated by many Lynn residents who had become convinced of Quakerism in the 1690's. Taken with the proximity of a small enclave of Quaker merchants in Boston who had good transatlantic connections, especially with members of London Meeting for Sufferings, it is hardly surprising that the first efforts of Friends to work for repeal came out of Salem Monthly Meeting, which was the monthly meeting for Friends in Boston, Salem, and Lynn.[6]

Lynn Friends drew up an account of their sufferings and through the New England Yearly Meeting petitioned Lord Bellomont, Governor of Massachusetts. Bellomont (New England Yearly Meeting informed London Yearly Meeting) had responded that he would "Send home the Petition and that we [Friends] would have to answer to them, for this Law for the Priest was Confirmed in England and he Saith he cannot help us without order from thence." Friends now came to the unhappy realization that recent Massachusetts church tax laws had received royal assent, without Quaker protest.[7]

Apparently royal assent had been given because English and American Friends had not yet developed the transatlantic intelligence network or the familiarity with English administrative agencies which proved so useful later. Many English Friends were also unaware of the political-religious realities in New England—another limiting factor. In the London Yearly Meeting epistle of 1700 English Friends were astonished that Bellomont would do nothing for Friends, which thereby demonstrated their ignorance of Massachusetts affairs. The English Friends wondered if the Massachusetts charter permitted nonconformists from the Church of England to impose "forced maintenance" on other dissenters. They had also "enquired and do not understand that your Petitions are remitted hither by the Governour" and so urged New England Friends "to Send a true State of Your case and a petition for the King" to English Friends "to Solicite on your behalf." Presumably they still thought that something could be done. As it turned out, the Crown could not repeal the laws that had received royal assent. Only by a patient and long-term commitment to resist assessment and collection of church taxes could Quakers and Baptists in southeastern Massachusetts beat back these acts. Until then, dissenters who had been forced for years to pay church taxes would continue to suffer distraint.[8]

Though English Friends could not help their Massachusetts coreligionists, they were able to demonstrate that in the future they would be better organized to cope with additional New England church taxes. The demonstration came over publication of a Connecticut anti-Quaker law, even though this law had very little directly to do with Friends in 1702 despite its language, for there were few Friends in Connecticut and those at the turn of the eighteenth century were only along the border with Rhode Island near that colony's town of Westerly. The assistance to Friends in Massachusetts came about in this way:

Anti-Quaker laws passed before 1660 in Connecticut and New Haven had been renewed when those colonies were joined under the 1662 charter. Details and language were essentially the same: fines and whippings were in store for any Quaker coming to proselytize, for anyone entertaining a Quaker or having Quaker books (other than magistrates and church elders), and for any shipmaster bringing in Quakers. The law essentially fell into disuse as the Quaker "threat" diminished in the 1660's, and because of diplomatic efforts by Friends with Indians in 1675 before the outbreak of King Philip's War the General Court suspended "the penalty for absence from o[u]r publique assemblyes, or imprisonment of [Quakers] . . . provided they do not gather into assemblies in this Colony nor make any disturbance." In brief, individual Friends were free to live in the colony but not to have meetings there.[9]

There matters would probably have remained had it not been for a sect of Baptists, known as Rogerenes, led by John Rogers of New London, and a codification of Connecticut law published in 1702, probably at the behest of imperial authorities. The Rogerenes were as strident in their defiance of Congregational authorities in Connecticut as were early Friends, but they were resident in the colony and both wealthy and determined enough to make a stand from the year of Rogers' conversion in 1675. Over the next two decades members of the sect suffered distraints, imprisonments, and other harassments at the hands of authorities (John Rogers was divorced by his wife with alleged official connivance). Although the Rogerenes advocated adult baptism, holy communion, and sabbatarian worship and did not accept the Quaker belief in the Inward Light in all, they were on good terms with Friends. Though John Rogers debated with William Edmundson in 1675 and Samuel Bownas in 1703 (when Bownas was imprisoned in New York) and published an account of his differences with Quakers in 1705, clearly he and Friends did not compete; indeed Connecticut people thought the Rogerenes were Quaker Baptists! The Rogerenes may have been the intended victims of the revival of the anti-Quaker law in the 1702 code, but it is also possible that the law remained by accident on the books in much the same form as it had before 1675. The legislature and various committees appointed by it reviewed the code from 1696 until publication in 1702, which effectively repealed any intervening law, including the relaxation for Friends in 1675.[10]

Publication could not have come at a more opportune time for Friends. The laws were published in Boston, which led the Connecticut agent, Sir Henry Ashurst, to conclude later, probably incorrectly, that Massachusetts Governor Joseph Dudley had a hand in continuance of the act so as to embarrass Connecticut. Connecticut's charter, like Rhode Island's, had been under attack by royal authorities led by the Board of Trade and including, on the American side, Dudley and New York Governor Lord Cornbury, and the attack could again be renewed. The policy of the home government now was to gain the compliance of Rhode Island and Connecticut with the Acts of Trade. Publication of laws was one potential means toward that end. Daniel Zachary, Boston Quaker merchant, sent a copy of the law to his brother in England, Thomas Zachary, who in turn brought it to the attention of the London Meeting for Sufferings, of which he was a member. Now the meeting for sufferings had something it could work on, for the act had not yet received royal assent, and, hopefully, the meeting could influence Queen Anne to repeal it. The meeting decided to have a committee check on the law to see whether it was still with the Board of Trade. The committee was also to apply pressure via the English "Preachers of the Presbyterian and Independents" in the hope of having something done by them to demonstrate to their American brethren the inconsistency of Connecticut's actions against the spirit of its charter, which promised freedom of conscience. The dissenting English clergy also would be able to point out the potential danger to dissenters throughout the empire if some of them outside the Mother Country persecuted persons not of their own faith.[11]

The meeting for sufferings soon discovered that not only the Connecticut code but other laws as well (probably the Massachusetts Act of 1702, discussed below) were before the Queen. It decided that one of its members should speak to Sir Henry Ashurst, incorrectly identified by the clerk in the minutes and perhaps by the meeting itself as agent for Massachusetts (no doubt another example of the basic unfamiliarity of the meeting as late as 1703 with colonies and the imperial administration— an instance of misinformation that was soon to be rectified). The meeting for sufferings also sent copies of these laws to the English dissenting clergy, who, shortly thereafter, sent the meeting a copy of their letter to their New England brethren in Boston concerning recent anti-Quaker laws. In spite of the dissenting ministers' good intentions and good efforts, it appears that their efforts had no substantial impact. On inquiry, Friends Thomas Maule and Richard Estes could not find if any letters had reached Boston, although of the two sent, one eventually arrived. The London Meeting for Sufferings tired of waiting and in 1704 prepared a petition for submission to the Queen. Its choice was to deal with the Connecticut law first, perhaps in the hope of tarring Massachusetts with the same brush. The strategy was successful only to the extent that Governor Dudley wrote William Crouch of the Board of Trade to deny that Massachusetts law even remotely resembled that of Connecticut.[12]

Through 1704 and 1705 the meeting for sufferings pressed the case and Sir Henry Ashurst sought to delay consideration. Ashurst needed time to obtain a memorial from Connecticut, he said; moreover, the law was of no effect against Friends: made thirty-two years before, it was obsolete. The meeting for sufferings replied that indeed the law had been used and had a substantial deterring effect on local residents who might otherwise have been willing to receive Quaker books or permit Quaker meetings to be held in their homes, and Friends had a letter from a resident in Fairfield, Connecticut, to prove it. They cited the persecution of John Rogers to indicate that the law was still used and noted two other instances from George Bishop's *New England Judged*, which gave substance to the suggestion that where Quakers were concerned the law was obsolete, since these cases had occurred decades earlier. But these examples gave the meeting for sufferings a chance to show that Connecticut law and Massachusetts tithes were cut from the same cloth, inasmuch as the original Connecticut and Massachusetts laws were virtually identical.[13]

Eventually the Queen disallowed the law. The likelihood of her doing so probably inspired Connecticut to void provisions of the act relating to Friends even before word of repeal reached the colony. It is even possible that Connecticut may have wanted to remove the odium of having a seventeenth-century anachronism in its recently published code. Whatever the case, the heresy law with the catch-all phrase "whether Quakers, Ranters, Adamites, or such like" was no longer valid.[14]

Friends did not give up. They continued efforts to secure the blessings of toleration, making the rather useful point that English toleration policy did not extend to Connecticut and called for the Queen to repeal or disallow Connecticut acts that authorized taxes to support churches, a useful precedent vis-à-vis Massachusetts. Sir Henry Ashurst disagreed: the Queen had no precedent to confirm or disallow Connecticut laws concerning Quakers. The Quaker presentation, moreover, was filled with misinformation, he thought: "They give some scraps of Laws, without mentioning what went before or followed after what they object against." He added significantly: "There are not above seven Quakers in that Colony." English Friends had high hopes for Connecticut after the successful disallowance of a New Hampshire law in 1706 for the maintenance of clergy, but they had to be satisfied for the moment with a new Connecticut law which promised toleration of dissenters from Connecticut's Standing Order to the extent that they were free to meet for worship. But neither the oath of fidelity required of Connecticut dissenters nor the added clause that dissenters still had to pay religious taxes provided comfort for Quakers or Rogerenes who could neither swear nor pay church taxes. If Friends were to obtain release from church taxes, they would have to obtain it by other means. The Connecticut case had provided useful training and an occasion to restate the case against New England persecution and reinvoke the Quaker view of mistreatment of the first Quakers in New England—the London Meeting for Sufferings gave copies of the 1702 edition of Bishop's *New England Judged* to members of the Privy Council and the Board of Trade.[15]

Massachusetts and Connecticut after 1708

Southeastern Massachusetts was the theater for successful Baptist and Quaker action on church taxes, but the issue was not so much over payment of taxes as assessment and collection of them. When Quaker and Baptist towns resisted the Province's demands, Massachusetts confronted the problems of town autonomy, dissenter refusal to pay taxes, and the well developed network of Quaker lobbying in England. The Massachusetts attempt and failure to impose its way inevitably led to unraveling of the skein of clergy maintenance, where Friends and others were concerned.[16]

In 1702 Massachusetts added new legislation to that of the nineties. Dartmouth and Tiverton refused to call and pay ministers qualified to lead them as Massachusetts understood the act of 1693. To deal with those recalcitrant towns, the General Court stated that as "in some few towns and districts within this province, divers of the inhabitants are Quakers, and other irreligious persons averse to the publick worship of God and to a learned and orthodox ministry, and find out ways to elude the laws provided for the support of such, and pervert the good intentions thereof" it was amending the original clergy maintenance law. Now if a town did not support the clergyman according either to its contract with him or one made for him by the Court of General Sessions, that court was empowered to appoint freeholders to assess for the selectmen and to require town constables to collect the tax. Since Dartmouth and Tiverton continued to refuse to appoint orthodox ministers, the General Court went farther and in 1706 passed another act, this time itself undertaking the burden of providing clergy. If, as had happened, court orders continued "not duely observed, or by contrivances and practices of ill men be eluded," then the courts were to inform the General Court, which would see to the employment and payment of an orthodox minister and add the cost to town taxes due the colony.[17]

All that remained was for the General Court to find clergymen who would agree to appointment. Courts had had little luck before in obtaining preachers, and on several occasions had faced claims that Dartmouth and Tiverton had learned and orthodox (though not Congregational) preachers. In each case, the men named were Quakers. Perhaps Baptists saw the utility of employing English Quaker lobbying. In any event, Baptists' interests were reflected in the nominations, for had Friends alone been responsible for the nominations, they might have offered women recognized by the Society as ministers, thereby baiting authorities even further. As they were working with Baptists, they could no longer employ the confrontation tactics they had used in the seventeenth century. In 1708 the General Court, with the promise of salary virtually assured, found two clergymen willing to go to Dartmouth and Tiverton, the Reverend Samuel Hunt for the former and the Reverend Joseph Marsh for the latter. Salaries of 50 pounds for Hunt and 30 pounds for Marsh were added to the province taxes for both towns. Surely that would take care of payment.[18]

The General Court did not reckon on the degree of resistance. Assessors of both Dartmouth and Tiverton refused to comply: they assessed the province rates but omitted the salaries of Hunt and Marsh. Both towns had officially taken the position that assessors should not assess church taxes, because the majority of inhabitants were dissenters who had not previously paid these taxes, and as a matter of principle refused to do so now. They petitioned Governor Joseph Dudley. Throughout the autumn petitions flowed in from the towns, from Massachusetts Quakers, and from Rhode Island Monthly Meeting. The General Court now found itself facing not just individual or Quaker refusal to pay, but town defiance of provincial authorities in what Tiverton and Dartmouth residents clearly regarded as local matters.[19]

Town autonomy was one thing, lack of orthodox clergy another. The General Court ordered the Bristol County sheriff to assess the estates of the assessors, or to imprison them if their possessions were insufficient. Eventually, failing to obtain sufficient funds from the assessors to pay the delinquent rates, Sheriff Samuel Gallop imprisoned three assessors: Quakers Richard Borden and Deliverance Smith, who were both selectmen and assessors (contrary to the law requiring oaths), and Thomas Taber, a Baptist. Petitions followed to Governor Dudley to secure the release of the prisoners, with the certainty that if they were not released, Friends would petition the Queen.[20]

Just what the precise effect was on Governor Dudley one cannot be sure, but he had already felt the strength of Quaker pressure and no doubt was unwilling to quarrel with Quakers again. Sir Henry Ashurst's charge that Dudley had a hand in the Connecticut Heretic Act did not please. In 1706 Dudley had protested to the Board of Trade that he had nothing to do with that act: he was in England when the code was passed. He had also been embarrassed by John Campbell's article in the *Boston Newsletter* suggesting that English Quakers had misrepresented Massachusetts to the English dissenting clergy. Dudley had Campbell write an explanation to William Popple, Secretary of the Board, because the article had given offense to the Board of Trade. Dudley had also reprimanded Campbell, and he suggested that as governor he had always treated Friends well. In 1708 he informed the Board of Trade of the imprisonment of assessors Borden, Smith, and Taber, because, he thought, the Board would probably hear a complaint. There would be no great difficulty, he noted, as a result of freeing Friends from the tax, except that many people not really Quakers might claim to be Friends to avoid the tax. Either by collusion with the General Court or simply on Dudley's initiative, Friends in Bristol prison were released. Dudley added this information as a postscript to his letter to the Board. For the next few years after 1711, Massachusetts helped pay Hunt's salary (he remained in Dartmouth until his death in 1729), but Tiverton had no minister and only occasional attention from visiting clergymen, as Cotton Mather's diary notes.[21]

There matters rested until 1722, when Congregationalists in Dartmouth requested help that would be on a permanent footing—they had been receiving only occasional grants and were not able to support Mr. Hunt. The General Court responded with a revival of the campaign of 1708–09 under the clergy-support law, which had been renewed in 1715 essentially in the same form as the 1706 enactment. In June the General Court voted to add 100 pounds to Dartmouth's rates and £72 11s. to Tiverton's—the purpose of the increase not disclosed. The issue clearly was joined when both towns petitioned the General Court, and the various meetings of the Society of Friends became involved.[22]

Friends had already protested concerning the 1715 legislation. In that year Dartmouth Quakers petitioned the General Court, opposing re-enactment of earlier legislation, but without success. News of these petitions crossed the Atlantic to the London Meeting for Sufferings in 1718 and 1720, and there were reports of a sharp rise in distraints of Quaker possessions in the vicinity of Salem. Now both Dartmouth and Tiverton refused to comply with the 1722 assessment. Town meetings authorized petitions to the General Court and to England and promised their financial support of imprisoned assessors. Imprisonment of four assessors followed in the next year when the General Court, faced with defiance of its authority, determined on punitive measures despite action by the Council to remit taxes.[23]

In the meantime the Quaker lobby had swung into action. Thomas Richardson, a young Newport merchant and former resident of Boston, was sent to London to join the meeting for sufferings in petitioning for repeal of both current tax legislation and the 1715 law. There he joined Friend Richard Partridge, a London merchant, member of the meeting for sufferings, and Rhode Island agent. Business connections, family ties, and expertise in the meeting for sufferings once again combined to produce a successful lobby. It was a propitious time, for the Quaker lobby, as N. C. Hunt has observed, had in 1722 successfully promoted an amendment to the Affirmation Act and had identified and skillfully used powerful members of Robert Walpole's administration. Quaker lobbyists were well placed to continue that pressure on behalf of Massachusetts Friends.[24]

Richardson, Partridge, and their solicitor, John Sharpe, argued that the several Massachusetts tithing acts had worked against the liberty of conscience promised in the 1692 charter, had nullified majorities in towns by attempting to impose ministers of their own dissenting orthodoxy, and had recently and illegally added amounts to the provincial rates not to support necessary provincial services but to impose unwanted paid ministers on the towns of Dartmouth and Tiverton. In defense of the province, Massachusetts pointed out that all of the laws in question had received royal assent except taxation laws, which were temporary. Ultimately the issue was decided not on narrow points of law but on the moral force of arguments—and, one suspects, the Quaker lobby's influence with the Government. As a consequence, the Crown repealed the Tax Act of 1722 and subsequently the Tax Act of 1723.[25]

Repeal did not obtain immediate release of imprisoned assessors. Four—Joseph Anthony, John Sisson, John Atkin, and Philip Taber—were still in prison, and the Privy Council ordered their release (part of the background for their imprisonment had been the traditional dissenter tactic of appointing one of the Quaker-recognized ministers as minister of Dartmouth in May 1723). But the following December two more of the Dartmouth assessors were imprisoned: Baptist Jacob Taber and Quaker Beriah Goddard. In August the four assessors confined in May 1723 were released, after fifteen months in Bristol County jail. The two imprisoned the previous December were set free in November.[26]

Release of the assessors and repeal of the tax laws of 1722 and 1723 meant more than just a setback for those laws; it signaled an imminent change in church taxes. The Privy Council had reversed its previous policy concerning Massachusetts. The Quaker lobby had succeeded to a degree it had probably not expected. In addition to being infinitely more powerful than it had been in the earlier confrontation in 1706–09, it had two other factors working for it: Anglican interest in reducing Massachusetts orthodoxy and the General Court's stubborn prosecution of the Dartmouth and Tiverton cases despite the fact that the Massachusetts Council attempted to shape a conciliatory policy.[27]

As a consequence, the Massachusetts system as it affected Friends and other dissenters was in shambles, and relief acts followed. The immediate effect is hard to measure, but Cotton Mather's interest in reconciliation with Philadelphia Friends was at least in part recognition of the reality of Quaker political power, despite his recently reiterated position favoring state support of orthodox clergy. First to be aided were the Anglicans, who were benefited in 1727 by a law exempting them from church taxes (lobbying by Church of England bishops was clearly superior to that of Quakers). The following year both Friends and Baptists received a temporary law freeing them from taxation, although the law was not entirely satisfactory to them. The 1728 law had imposed a five-mile rule: Baptists or Quakers were to live within five miles of the meeting they attended. The dissenters were to be identified by certificates granted by business meetings, although there is no evidence that this spurred Friends on to a more precise definition of membership.[28]

Friends were displeased with the five-mile rule and pressed to have a new law, this time with additional help from Jonathan Belcher, the new governor, brother-in-law of Richard Partridge. In England before he returned to his native Massachusetts in 1730, he had been impressed by the strength of the Quaker lobby and intended to serve Quakers as well as he could. In January 1732 he informed Partridge that he had met with Friends after the passage of another act solely intended for the relief of Friends—a slightly more permissive certificate system was included, and there was no five-mile limitation. Quakers had dined with him and assured him of their gratitude, although he observed that Anglicans were unhappy because they had not received a similarly favorable act. In April he continued on that theme and asked Partridge to apply to the Bishop of London to answer his letter. He would do as much for the Anglicans, he asserted, if they would only apply to him. Nor did Friends in either New England or England forget the favors done them: they sent petitions when Belcher needed them to help him retain his governorship, and they and their Baptist neighbors attempted to obtain a permanent salary for him by causing the representatives from Dartmouth and Tiverton to vote for that measure when all other representatives voted against it.[29]

Friends were not again seriously bothered by church taxes in Massachusetts, although they did have to petition colony authorities from time to time for relief from taxes improperly assessed. It is noteworthy, however, that the struggle over Massachusetts' imperial extension never reached Nantucket, where Friends were more numerous than in any other place in Massachusetts and which, after Dartmouth and Tiverton, would probably have been the next point of struggle had the General Court had its way on the mainland. Nor did Friends or other dissenters win relief from the requirement that all residents of new towns were required to contribute to the building of a Congregational meeting house and the settlement of a minister—a requirement that shut them off from the frontier settlements in Massachusetts. Despite efforts of Quaker petitioners in 1738 to obtain a township for their people, Friends never obtained relief. If Quakers were to escape land pressure in southeastern Massachusetts (including Nantucket), they either had to move away from Massachusetts (many Friends from New England migrated to the Hudson River Valley) or compromise their testimony on state support of churches, as several did just before and during the Revolutionary War in the town of East Hoosuck.[30]

Connecticut followed Massachusetts in granting relief from taxation. As in Massachusetts, the Anglican lobby led other dissenting faiths in obtaining relief in 1727. If Massachusetts could not hold out, neither could Connecticut. Two years later New York Friends on behalf of recently convinced Quakers of New Milford petitioned the colony for relief. There had been a revival in the town located near the Quaker settlement in the Oblong, and individuals meeting by themselves had come to a position like that of Friends and had applied for and received recognition as a meeting for worship. New Milford Meeting for Worship was the largest group of Friends in Connecticut in the colonial period, although its members never numbered more than a dozen or two (in 1760 there were only two families, three bachelors, and two spinsters there). The act in 1729 excused them and Friends on the eastern border near the Rhode Island town of Westerly from paying church taxes, whether they attended meeting in or out of the colony. And there matters rested for Friends in Connecticut. Apparently there were too few Quakers for issues of oath, governmental participation, or peace testimony to arise. Instead it is likely that local officials released Quakers from restrictions whenever necessary without legislative enactment.[31]

New Hampshire

Since New Hampshire had never been fully assimilated into the Massachusetts orthodoxy before its separate establishment in 1679, it is hardly surprising that it was much less persistent in enforcing religious taxation than was Massachusetts. Friends had been persecuted before 1690, but persecutions had virtually died out, leaving collection of church taxes, the matter of oaths, and the peace testimony as potential issues. Where church taxes were concerned, Friends may have had some relief before the arrival of Governor Andros, but as McLoughlin surmises, Andros probably interfered to prevent distraints on Quaker dissenters. A test case came in 1687 in Dover when Edward Wanton, patriarch of the Wanton clan, resident of Scituate in old Plymouth, and an apparent property holder in Dover, petitioned the legislature for relief from distraints, and the legislature granted it. He may have been chosen as the best person to test the law, for he lived outside New Hampshire and had no fear of community pressure. At any rate, New Hampshire thereby set a precedent to relieve dissenters from church taxes, a precedent this province sustained when in 1693 it added provisions to the church-support law passed that year favoring Friends and other dissenters.[32]

The law was similar to that of Massachusetts in that the state was to support the church. It left several matters as options, however, which Massachusetts made obligatory. Town control was clearly set forth: the town would call and pay the minister (there would be no clergymen imposed on towns by the colony). Furthermore, the law exempted conscientious Protestant dissenters who regularly attended their churches. By the 1693 law Friends obtained relief from tithes which they would not obtain in Massachusetts and Connecticut for several decades.[33]

Probably Friends did thereafter escape church taxes, but the initial decision to exempt was a local one, and relief from local decisions could only be obtained by petitioning the General Court. If there were distraints for church taxes, they were few if any, for surviving Quaker records do not indicate conclusively that there were such distraints in New Hampshire—the one case mentioned in Hampton Monthly Meeting in 1701 could have referred to distraints of Massachusetts Friends. Nor does intervening legislation in 1716 and 1719 seem to have been enforced with any immediate rigor. The 1716 Act required towns to call a minister (some towns had used the loophole in the 1693 law to avoid the expense of a clergyman). The 1719 Act required church taxes of all inhabitants and contained no exemption for conscientious dissenters. But Quakers continued to enjoy exemption, as the 1731 Act relieving Quaker constables from collecting church taxes indicates (some Quaker constables had apparently suffered distraints because they refused to collect church taxes). If New Hampshire law was not always consistent, at least it does not seem to have placed a burden on the many Friends in the towns of Dover and Durham. In fact Dover was so solicitous of Friends' welfare that in 1733 it granted land to Friends for use as a burial ground, a remarkably early instance of town support for Friends and a case in which Friends by accepting the land came dangerously close to tacit recognition of the validity of church taxes for all but those of faiths that were exempt from taxation.[34]

Other towns were not as generous as Dover, nor were provincial authorities when it came to settling new townships. In these towns proprietors were required to build a meeting house and settle a minister within a short time (three to four years). Where Friends were concerned this requirement may have been quietly overlooked, for Friends did settle in new areas. If they settled only after a meeting house had been built and a minister called, they missed the advantage of low-priced lands available to the first settlers. The only instance of a complaint encountered was that in Nottingham, New Hampshire, where Quaker proprietors sold some of their land to support a minister. As the issue did not arise again, one suspects that the requirement was either not enforced on Friends, or they moved in after initial settlers had built a meeting house.[35]

In balance, New Hampshire demonstrated a remarkable openness in regard to dissenters from the established Congregational churches. Recorded instances of distraints are so few that only on rare occasions, one suspects, did Friends encounter difficulty. Such was the case of Constable Daniel Meader, who petitioned the General Court in 1744 for relief because, contrary to the 1731 law, as he thought, the town insisted on his collecting rates to pay the overdue salary of the Reverend Hugh Adams. Adams had been petitioning for some years for recovery, and the town apparently treated the matter as a bad debt, not a church tax. The case itself drops from view: apparently the next constable made the collection, and, one suspects, not from Friends. But this was the only significant exception in regard to Quaker exemption from clerical taxes. New Hampshire, although not offering Rhode Island's degree of freedom from taxation, nevertheless offered a province free of the rigorous enforcement of law typical of Massachusetts until 1731 in taxes, and, it appears, in most cases in the settlement of towns throughout the eighteenth century.[36]

New York

New York is a useful standard against which to evaluate the activities of Friends in England and New England on the maintenance of clergy. Like eighteenth-century English Friends, New York Quakers could not obtain relief from church taxes, since the Church of England was established in the four lower counties of New York, Westchester, Queens, and Richmond. Nor did New York Friends engage in activities for repeal of these tithe disabilities either in New York or by solicitation of the Quaker lobby in England. Presumably, until tithe repeal could go through in England (the English Quaker attempt to obtain relief in 1736 failed and did not revive again in the American colonial period with the strength it had mustered that year), New York Friends were in a hopeless situation given the polyglot character of church membership in the colony and quasi-Anglican establishment in the four lower counties.[37]

From the time of Dutch rule onward there had been some form of colony support of churches, whether Dutch Reformed, Congregational, Presbyterian, or Anglican. The Duke's Laws had provided for churches to be supported by public funds, and the act of 1693, passed by the New York Assembly and urged along by Governor Benjamin Fletcher, required Protestant ministers in the four lower counties—one each for Richmond and New York counties and two each for Queens and Westchester. Although Friends suffered distraint on their goods as a result and reported them to English Quakers, there is no sign that they mounted the lists to obtain repeal: they simply lacked the effective lobbying of English Friends; they had never possessed the political power of Friends in other colonies; and they probably feared that if they attacked the Anglican church, Governor Fletcher would no longer permit them to vote.[38]

The only certain activity of New York Friends against tithes came in 1702 and accompanied their petition for restoration of the franchise. In that year they complained to Lord Cornbury that they had suffered because of a tax levied to build a nonconformist meeting house. Presbyterians in Queens County had built a church and supported a minister at Jamaica. Quaker protests on this score were occasioned by their recent loss of the franchise. What better way could there have been to curry favor with the Anglican governor? Cornbury had that year thrown out the dissenting Presbyterian minister and appointed an Anglican. The dispute was to continue for the next twenty-five years, until the Jamaica

Presbyterians seized the glebe lands, church, and rectory. By that time Friends had long since dropped out of the argument, their petition having helped to restore their franchise. As in England, New York Friends had to secure their political rights first.[39]

It could be argued that New York Quakers followed an opportunistic policy pursuing the franchise and ignoring the tithe. To advance that argument one would have to ignore the shifting sands of New York politics and the essential powerlessness of Friends there. They had to attach themselves to the faction that could offer protection, and under the circumstances if they failed to obtain release from Anglican taxes, one must note that so did their English brethren, who were more effective politically. In addition many of them in the Flushing, Westbury, the Oblong, and later Nine Partners monthly meetings may have escaped church taxes altogether through informal relief. To that extent New York Friends had been fortunate even if the law was not as kind to them as in New England after 1728: the effect was the most important thing. And perhaps the best measurement of the effect is to be found in Quaker settlements in the Hudson River Valley, for freed of the Connecticut, New Hampshire, and Massachusetts restrictive clauses requiring proprietors to build meeting houses and call clergy, land-hungry New England Friends, particularly from southeastern Massachusetts (including Nantucket), undertook the journey to polyglot New York, where they were able to take advantage of cheap lands in the Oblong or low rents elsewhere in the Hudson River Valley without having to suffer distraints for church taxes. Under the circumstances, their long-standing support of the Beekman-Morris faction was a small price to pay, and a price that did not undermine the essential openness of New York to people with scruples like theirs.

Chapter 8
Peace Testimony

OF ALL THE EARLY Quaker testimonies, that on peace is even better known than that on the affirmation. Throughout the colonial period and since then as well, this testimony proved to be the most difficult not only to have recognized by external authorities but also to define and to require of members. Moreover, it is difficult for the academic community to agree on its place as an element of religious dissent. Implicit in the existence of colonies was a need to defend themselves, and when war came to their borders from New York north, there was no realistic choice other than to maintain an active defense, no matter how well placed Friends were in these colonial governments, or how effective their lobby in England. Still, except for wartime, Friends seem not to have been severely persecuted for their pacifism, and this in part accounts for their failure to achieve recognition of this testimony, which they had achieved for the issues of the affirmation and church taxes. In addition, they faced the problem that some of their coreligionists, usually occupants of major colonial offices, clearly compromised their pacifism. Although these leaders may have helped to modify militia requirements to favor Friends, it was beyond their capabilities to stay in office if they failed to direct war efforts. Still more significant in this regard was the fact that when Friends suffered most for this testimony, the communities in which they lived were in a state of emergency. That a minority group like Friends received the relief granted them testifies to both the good opinion in which they were held and the liberality of their hard-pressed communities. In sum, Friends' pacifist testimony was neither easy to maintain within the Society nor easy for others, often others hurt by war, to tolerate.[1]

Friends in Government

Rhode Island was the only colony in which Friends attained full recognition of the peace testimony, and even there, as we have seen, that recognition was short-lived, extending to no more than 1677. Thereafter, if Friends did exist as a major political entity and function as such, they did not have the political effectiveness to secure complete repeal of compulsory militia service; instead, the best they could obtain was a provision for some form of alternative service, such as serving as watch or caring for noncombatants.[2]

Political participation did not bring with it elimination of required alternative service, but it did require duties and obligations of Quaker members of government which compromised to some extent the peace testimony. Several instances, detailed above in Chapter 2, occurred in King Philip's War, in which leading Friends had an active role, even though their efforts were not sufficiently active for non-Quaker colonists in New England. It appears that after that war there was no similar difficulty for over a decade, since there was no war that affected Rhode Island. After 1690 and the resumption of charter government in wartime, Quaker leaders temporarily abandoned part of their pacifism because their role in government implicated them in wartime measures. At least one Quaker governor in this period, John Easton, appointed military officers, approved the expenditure of funds, and commissioned privateers.[3]

Despite the complicity of some leading Friends in war-making, many Friends did not approve of these activities, and three Quaker members of the Assembly—William Anthony, Jacob Mott, Jr., and Ebenezer Slocum—in 1709 spoke out against war and the support of it, "giving the reason it being contrary to our Principles which was offered to both houses" of the Rhode Island Assembly. Nor were some Friends before 1740 as prepared as those before 1700 had been to accept military participation even to the extent of a governor's signing commissions. It is not possible to trace in any detail the background of the case, but when John Wanton succeeded his Anglican brother, William, as governor in 1734, he signed military commissions, and Rhode Island Monthly Meeting, of which he had up to that date been a leading member, took him under dealing, excluded him from active participation in meeting affairs, and obtained the backing of New England Yearly Meeting for its action. There is no evidence of his formal disownment, but it is clear that Wanton never again was able to make a mark as a leading Friend, as he had for over two decades. With his exclusion from meetings for business, Rhode Island had in effect disowned him, but beyond that conclusion it is hard to penetrate, given the fact that after 1740 many of the same members of the Rhode Island Monthly Meeting that excluded Wanton compromised their pacifism by active participation in wartime military activities. There are at least two possible explanations: one, that the adherence to Friends' testimonies weakened after Wanton's death in 1740 until the onset of reform in 1755, the other, and more likely, that someone within the monthly meeting was evening an old score—Wanton's political activities in 1731, which favored a land bank, had roused the opposition of Quaker Abraham Redwood and presumably many others of the Rhode Island specie party. One should note that even after reform began, monthly meetings did not deal with political leaders who had modified their pacifism. Whatever the reason (evidence does not exist), that as prominent a Friend as John Wanton could be taken under dealing indicates the strength of the peace testimony among some Friends and their probable dissatisfaction with political compromises.[4]

If the peace testimony was alive in 1734, one cannot say the same thing for it after 1740, at least insofar as Rhode Island leadership was concerned. John Wanton's nephew, Gideon Wanton, was treasurer from 1733 to 1743 and then governor in 1745–46 and 1747–48. In one or the other office he was involved in disbursing funds, directing the war effort in King George's War, and signing commissions, and he remained active in Quaker business meetings. So did Richard Partridge in England, a member of the London Meeting for Sufferings, who defended Wanton's and Rhode Island's conduct of the war before the Privy Council in 1746. Thomas Richardson, yearly meeting clerk for over three decades before 1760, was colony treasurer during the Great War for the Empire. Nothing seems to have hindered his handling of funds specifically designated for military use or from continuing as yearly meeting clerk until 1760, five years after Friends had begun to reform the Society. Perhaps most notorious of the Rhode Island politicians who compromised their peace testimony was Stephen Hopkins. Hopkins, it should be noted, was ultimately disowned in 1774, not for having directed the Rhode Island war effort in the Great War for the Empire or for seeking a defensive union of English North American colonies, but for refusing to free a slave woman who had small children. Hopkins insisted on retaining ownership until her children no longer needed her care. The meeting did not agree, but then Hopkins was really no more than an attender who had obtained membership before rules were set out clearly.[5]

So it was that Quaker participation in Rhode Island government did not bring with it freedom for the ordinary Quaker from all aspects of military service. For colony officers it meant sacrificing some aspects of their pacifism. Some Quaker politicians did not get away with doing so, as the case of John Wanton indicates. But lacking evidence, we cannot say whether Quaker assemblymen from Quaker centers like Portsmouth voted for war taxes without scruple. If they once had done so, in 1757 five of them—William Anthony, Jr., Gideon Wanton, Jr., John Shearman, Jr., Giles Slocum, and Isaac Barker—acknowledged their error in so doing, a sign perhaps of the influence of the reform if not conformance to the Philadelphia Pembertons' position. At best one suspects that the influence of Quaker politicians may have helped obtain easy laws and easier enforcement where Rhode Island Friends were concerned until the outbreak of the Revolutionary War.[6]

In other areas where Friends participated in government there does not seem to have been any effect at all on peace testimony. Quakers did not occupy provincial office, and so they could not as in Rhode Island hope to modify militia policy so that Friends could escape service or fines in place of that service.

Quakers, Compulsory Service, and Military Taxes before 1750

Quaker accounts of sufferings before 1732 frequently mentioned church taxes, but instances of conscientious objection to military and alternate service, to fines paid for replacements of those conscripted, and to military taxes (sometimes specific, sometimes mixed with other taxes) were few in peacetime. As a consequence, there were few instances of fining and impressment outside the war years. Even in those times Friends were free of strict military obligations in Rhode Island—a happy consequence of having their leading members in high governmental office—although at best cold comfort in the other colonies where Quakers not only faced financial loss and occasional imprisonment, but also the hatred of fellow colonists who did have to serve and did not care to see others escape risking life and limb.

Rhode Island had never seriously backed away from its liberality concerning Friends and the militia service, set out in statute for the first time in 1673, briefly repealed and reinstituted in 1676, and then finally repealed in 1677 under Governor Benedict Arnold. Despite the law, Friends do not seem to have suffered hardship for the remainder of the century, although Rhode Island Monthly Meeting found it necessary in 1698 to issue "A Testimonie by an Epistle . . . to Cleare Truth and Friends of an Aspersion tht hath beene Cast upone Friends heare as if wee allowed of Training wch Our Testimoney is against [a]ssisting or Learning to war" or to permit children to do so. Two years later the colony apparently accepted the point when it gave militia officers the freedom to excuse those persons with a conscientious scruple against military service. In effect the law probably gave the force of legality to accepted practice. But this law was not clear enough, and when Friends petitioned in 1730, requesting relief for pacifists, the colony granted their request.[7]

Despite their release from military service, Friends still had to contemplate alternative service much as they had in the seventeenth century.

Such service was not without its problems, however. In 1704 during Queen Anne's War, Newport apparently wanted Friends to take the watch under arms. The monthly meeting was firm: Friends could only watch without arms. Two years later the monthly meeting apparently successfully petitioned the General Assembly to permit Friends to watch without arms, for the issue does not appear again. Alternate service remained a requirement, and Rhode Island Friends apparently observed it during the colonial period to the extent that they served when required. They did not raise the question whether specific alternative service, by contributing to the war effort, compromised their pacifism. It was sufficient to avoid carrying weapons.[8]

But what of tax? Surely paying even indirectly for war was as bad as paying indirectly for a hireling ministry. Here Quakers faced the dilemma of how to support civil government if military appropriations were part of a general levy, a currency issue, or a direct military tax. Some Friends in the Rhode Island Assembly did speak out against war in 1709 and again in the Great War for the Empire, as already noted, but Quakers generally seem to have paid those taxes. English Friend John Richardson indicated as much to Rhode Island Quakers when he told them that English "Friends did not see an effectual door opened to avoid" mixed taxes. Like the complicity of Rhode Island Quaker leaders in wartime finance, one is struck by the inconsistency of struggling to avoid church tax on the one hand, yet paying war tax on the other. But the war tax was not continuous, as was a church tax, and there was also support from other religious groups against the tax for the Standing Order in Massachusetts and Connecticut. In short, political realism dictated the course Friends adopted, when most Rhode Island Quakers apparently accepted the compromise and continued to do so until the reform of the Society and the added complication of the American Revolutionary War forced them to face these issues again.[9]

Massachusetts and, before 1692, Plymouth had no tolerance for men who refused military service in wartime. Plymouth had experienced one officer and fifteen men walking away from the campaign in King Philip's War, and we have seen Massachusetts' anti-Quaker legislation of that period directed against a detested Quaker minority whose heterodox views also included refusal to defend themselves. Massachusetts reenacted its previous military law in 1693, requiring males of eighteen and over to train, to watch under arms, and to be impressed for service. There followed additional legislation expanding the watch to include males of sixteen upward. Friends received no relief; they must suffer if understanding officers did not grant them relief; and this remained the law where Friends were concerned until the Great War for the Empire brought changes.[10]

We cannot be sure how extensive the conflict with civil authorities was on this issue, but in many towns it was considerable. For one thing, assertion of town autonomy did Friends little good where military service was at stake: having Quaker selectmen, assessors, and constables was no help; command was centralized directly under the governor. For another, there was Nantucket, where no military preparations went forward. In some cases Friends may have simply escaped with a nod and a wink. But not always in southeastern Massachusetts. Young Friends John Smith and Thomas Maccomber were arrested for refusing to serve and taken to Boston in 1703, where they were imprisoned for four months despite intervention with Governor Joseph Dudley by English Friend Thomas Story and others. We do not know how many other Friends were imprisoned, or when, but one suspects only in wartime and especially in towns like Dartmouth where the relatively numerous Quakers made service particularly onerous for everyone else. Instances of imprisonment recorded in 1740 and in 1750 indicate that Quakers of both Barnstable and Bristol counties had been incarcerated for refusing military service. In 1750, presumably because war was over, the Bristol sheriff released four of them.[11]

As for taxes, again one has little specific and direct evidence as to general behavior in Massachusetts, but as in Rhode Island, one assumes that Friends paid the mixed taxes even if reluctantly, and sought whenever possible to avoid direct military taxes. Perhaps Friends had sufficient trouble with the clergy tax. Before 1730 to combat the clergy tax they needed to maintain their alliance with Baptists. How could they mount an even less promising offensive where war taxes were concerned? One suspects that struggle remained reserved for another day.

Similarly, New Hampshire did not exempt Friends from military service, nor did Friends escape military taxes, or effectively campaign against them before 1750. Several Dover Quakers had been confined in 1705 when the Council and General Assembly ordered their release because they refused to work in Fort William and Mary. Nor was any legislation passed to improve their situation before 1750. A militia act in 1718 granted Friends no relief from training or other military service, although one suspects that as long as there was no war, they encountered only occasional attempts to compel them to train.[12]

It was in this northern part of New England that Friends encountered the greatest challenge to their pacifism. Most of them would carry no arms when Indian warfare was most severe at the beginning of the century. Journals of visiting Friends provide evidence of this struggle that is both impressionistic and didactic. Thomas Story, Samuel Bownas, and Thomas Chalkley all tell of difficulties with Indians and generally suggest that Friends who went unarmed and did not go to blockhouses were not molested by Indians. One doubts that life was as simple or safe for those without arms in the first three decades as visiting Friends thought; indeed, accounts in epistles from New England Yearly Meeting to London Yearly Meeting and the relief sent to Friends in those parts suggest that Quakers suffered just as much from war as did their neighbors, whether armed or not. Like the rest of the population, many Friends were forced to leave northern New England, and many were probably killed. Charles Clark's conclusions on the general depopulation in the region at this time match the New England Yearly Meeting accounts of an end to Quaker expansion during wartime. What one can conclude, however, is that most if not all Friends refused to bear arms, thereby establishing the importance of their pacifism although gaining no more than a grudging acquiescence to it from the community at large.[13]

New York provides some evidence of Friends vigorously maintaining pacifism. Perhaps the fact that Quakers could not seriously press for relief from Anglican church taxes in New York as they did against Congregational establishments to the north released some of their energies to seek a greater acceptance of the peace testimony than in Massachusetts. Perhaps, too, the proximity of Pennsylvania could have been a factor: if there was no required military service in Pennsylvania, why New York? Whatever the reason, Friends are on record as actively resisting military preparations in New York and enduring penalties for it. They did not obtain satisfaction in New York before 1750, for law throughout the English period required them to train. They had protested the building of a fort in 1672, to no avail. In 1675 Friends in Flushing reported sufferings for refusal to train. Whether before 1686 they continued to have difficulty over compulsory military service we do not know, but in that year New York Friends requested the New York Council (which included Friend William Morris) to relieve them from training because the recently passed Charter of Liberties granted religious freedom to law-abiding people, and one of their principle beliefs was in peace. The Council determined that no one could be exempt. Mixed with other distraints that year were nineteen levied on sixteen different individuals for refusal to train, totaling £41/3/1 and ranging from 6 shillings to £15/13/4— the latter, on Albertus Brandt (who may not have been a Friend), being remarkably high. Nor, apparently, were these exceptions for the New York epistles to London Friends during wartime noted sufferings for military service although the epistle for 1693 indicated the magistrates used restraint.[14]

After their seventeenth-century efforts, New York Friends seem quietly to have accepted the London Yearly Meeting advice of 1708 on religious and military sufferings to "be thankfull to and pray for those tht have been Instrumental in affording us our Liberty and for the Continuance of it by the Queen and those in authority." Such submissive sentiments could not promote a Quaker challenge to New York authority. There continued to be occasional instances of authorities distraining Friends for refusing to train, like those reported in the 1720 and 1725 epistles to London, but Long Island Friends do not seem to have encountered great difficulties when they were punished. The apparent restraint of New York authorities may have been due to Friends' participation in military exercises, as several did in Huntington, Long Island. The area of major difficulty for Friends turned out to be the mainland counties to the north. If minutes were extant for Hudson Valley meetings, one could probably say more. As it is, before 1750 there is only the indication in the 1742 New York epistle to London Yearly Meeting that militia sufferings were particularly great in northern meetings, a condition, one might add, that continued through the Revolutionary War in that most expansive part of Quakerdom, the Hudson Valley meetings.[15]

By way of summary one can note that before 1750 Friends had generally maintained their position against serving in strictly military forces. In many instances they performed alternative service when that option was available provided they did not have to carry arms. That they might thereby have contributed to the war effort does not seem to have occurred to them: like the Mennonites to the south in times of invasion, refusal to fight was enough—certainly enough to arouse resentment among neighbors and, consequently, to make it that much more difficult to uphold their pacifism. Another compromise of many Quakers of later generations and some in the colonial period was the apparent willingness to pay military taxes mixed with other rates and, since no evidence remains that would indicate refusal to pay, direct taxes assessed either as poll taxes or as new currency issued to finance war. The apparent compliance with taxation of this sort seems to have suggested a solution to authorities which they had assemblies enact in the Great War for the Empire—a solution that enlarged the issue of the Quaker peace testimony.

Compulsory Militia Service and Military Taxes, 1754–1763

The Great War for the Empire brought to a head many issues that had been simmering for a generation or more. It was, in the North American setting, first and foremost a war for the control of the continent between France and Great Britain and as such directly affected

Friends, particularly in potential theaters of war and in periods during the war when provincial governments sought to raise large numbers of troops. The indirect effects were also considerable, for attendant crises stemming from this war, the financing of it, and the peace treaty that followed were intimately linked to the subsequent imperial crisis. It is hardly surprising that in this greatest of colonial wars Friends faced the most serious challenge to their pacifism. As a consequence of their reaction to the war and of the drive for purity within the Society, Quakers sought to raise standards on the peace testimony. The most serious aspect of the challenge stemmed from new legislation, but it was not limited to that.

New York was the first of the northern provinces to adjust its militia law for Friends. In a comprehensive militia act in 1755 it set out provisions relieving Quakers of carrying arms. If they refused, Friends were not to pay a fine greater than twenty shillings. They were, if required, to stand watch or, if pressed, to send armed replacements or pay a ten-shilling fine. In times of invasion they were to serve as laborers, building field works. Finally, the act required Quakers to register with their county clerk, handing over a certificate and paying a registration fee of one shilling sixpence. While some portions of the act ultimately proved to be unacceptable, Friends in New York City and Dutchess County set about registering, monthly meetings granted certificates, and all seemed well in the province. But not for long. Westbury Friends objected to payment of fines, as they would have probably objected to alternative service provisions that required Quakers to build field fortifications. As a result, New York Friends refused to comply with the act and began to suffer distraints. Data are not precise, but the incomplete records suggest that military sufferings came to over 100 pounds a year for each year between 1756 and 1762, reaching a peak of over 800 pounds in 1759. Figures cited included distraints for church taxes, but the vast majority were for military expenses. Given the probability that church distraints were always less than 100 pounds, a conservative estimate of total distraints for the war is 1400 pounds, and it is likely to have been closer to 2000—no mean sum in those days. As New York was a major theater of the war, Quakers there faced greater penalties than their New England coreligionists, and the legislation was of no help. New York Friends do not seem to have challenged war taxes, however; that was left for New England to do.[16]

Massachusetts also changed its militia law to meet the stress of this war, but as the theater of operations was distant, it could afford to delay. First to receive attention in March 1756 was Nantucket. Although the issue of clergy tax had never spread to that island, that of militia did. In

February the General Court sought to force Quakers to carry their share of the burden of war. Eventually, something would have had to be done about the exposure of Nantucket, over thirty miles away from the mainland. Distance and the fact that many of its residents were mariners made it difficult to contribute troops to the war, and the problem might have been resolved administratively rather than legislatively. The act subsequently passed to deal with Nantucket "and Quakers elsewhere" noted in its preamble the primary reason for the legislation: "the greatest part of the inhabitants being of the people called Quakers."[17]

The legislature rather ingeniously pursued the frequently used tax loophole. As Friends had paid war taxes before, why not add the cost of replacement for each soldier pressed to the Nantucket provincial tax bill? The taxes would still be mixed, and Massachusetts would have its troops. The cost of each soldier was set at £13/6/8. To ensure compliance, captains of militia companies in towns other than Nantucket were to supply a list of Quakers, and no town would have to furnish more troops than its proportion of non-Quakers, making up the difference with the £13/6/8 poll tax for each Friend drafted. Friends were not to collect the tax. Only men recognized as Friends from March 1, 1756, were to count as Quakers. By this means authorities managed to have their army and avoid jailing Quakers by the score. To be sure, there were still problems—some residents resented Friends being excused, and not everyone understood the act—but there was nothing on the order of what might have occurred had the act not passed.[18]

It did not take Nantucket long to protest its ill use. On January 15, 1757, Jonathan Coffin on behalf of Nantucket inhabitants pleaded that recent great losses (one fifth of all ships and one hundred men "or at least the benefit of their service") had weakened Nantucket, and with so many fatherless children and widows to care for, it could not afford the £1506/13/4 assessed. The House of Representatives was sympathetic and reduced the tax to £1000. Most important in the context of this discussion is that many Nantucket residents paid. It must have been clear to Massachusetts authorities that they had a way to avoid confrontation over the peace testimony.[19]

If the Nantucket Act resolved military sufferings for that island, it apparently did not extend effectively to the mainland. Perhaps the law was to be tested first on the island. Whatever the intent, Friends were still being fined 20 pounds for not attending muster, and fines built up in Dartmouth in 1755, 1756, and 1757 to 380 pounds 4 shillings. As a consequence, a number of petitions went to the General Court requesting relief. After a period of legislative manipulation beginning in December 1757, Massachusetts Friends received essentially the same act that had been passed for Nantucket, but with disabilities removed. Some features of the act were not acceptable: as in New York, meetings did not grant certificates, for that would implicate them in war-making. Since earlier there had been a willingness to grant certificates for relief from church taxes, Quakers (unlike the Baptists) thereby reversed their previously co-operative position. Furthermore, the allocation of replacement funds, in essence a direct tax, did not go down well. To get its lists, Massachusetts revised the act in April 1758 to permit colonels of regiment to draw up lists of Friends. As on Nantucket, many Friends probably paid the tax in 1759. Massachusetts Friends who paid objected to the amount, not the principle: sums assessed Quakers exceeded the cost of hiring troops to replace them. Friends wanted the tax reduced, and the General Court relented in part, using provincial funds for relief of towns with large numbers of Quakers.[20]

There had been confiscations and some imprisonment in Barnstable Court before 1758. Quakers Joseph Wing and Melatiah Gifford had refused militia service in May 1757 and had been imprisoned and fined. The relief act that December did not save them, and authorities seized some of their possessions. In February they asked for redress, and a year later got it—on payment of expenses to Moses Swift, the man who had the property. The land was returned. If there were any other successful petitions, no record remains.[21]

Though some Friends paid the tax, many others were uncomfortable. Distracted by a flare-up of the long-standing dispute over Nantucket commons land, the monthly meeting appointed a committee in 1756 to give advice to Friends, but took no further action. So serious was the Nantucket land squabble that Quaker opposition to Massachusetts relief laws had to come from elsewhere. Once the acts had taken effect on the mainland in 1758, Dartmouth and Sandwich monthly meetings appointed committees to decide what to do. Unsuccessful in determining whether Friends should comply with the act, Dartmouth then referred the question to the yearly meeting. There was no solace, for the Rhode Island Quarterly Meeting had already tried unsuccessfully to determine whether Quakers could vote for war measures, raise money for war, or pay men to go to war. The best it could do was to observe that there was "a manifest Differance and it is hoped Friends will generally understand it so." The yearly meeting was no more likely to act than the quarterly meeting had been: Thomas Richardson was clerk of both and as Rhode Island Treasurer was active in the war effort. The yearly meeting referred the issue to London Yearly Meeting (not that London's decision would be binding, for too many Friends disagreed on whether Quakers could pay war taxes). London's reply in 1760 came too late to affect Quakers in this way, but it did serve to set a precedent for many in the War for Independence. To English Quakers, Massachusetts Friends could not pay a tax in lieu of military service, for "such payment is inconsistent with the religious Testimony we have to bear in the world." All Friends, the epistle concluded, should "Suffer the penalty the law inflicts rather than violate their Testimony."[22]

Massachusetts legislation proved to be instructive for New Hampshire. In May 1758 Governor Benning Wentworth recommended passage of "an Act similar to an Act passed lately in the Government of the Massachusetts . . . obliging the people called Quakers, to bear a proportionable part in the present Expedition, either in men or money." Wentworth went on to outline some of the difficulties of raising troops where some men claimed to be Friends. It was not until the next March that the New Hampshire legislature took the matter up again, adding a fine of 10 pounds for Friends refusing to serve. Friends protested the act; some even suffered distraint; but New Hampshire was determined to use the tax in support of the war effort if Friends refused to enlist.[23]

There followed numerous petitions from Friends seeking relief, but while war continued, the New Hampshire legislature would not yield. It dismissed Dover Monthly Meeting petitions in 1761 and 1762. With the exception of a few Friends who served as scouts or soldiers, the full measure of the tax apparently was collected. But New Hampshire Quakers, unlike many Massachusetts Friends, officially do not seem to have acquiesced in the tax. On balance, despite the military service of at least ten Quakers, several of whom were not disowned, New Hampshire Friends seem to have had the desire to uphold the peace testimony without compromise, a position that helped them considerably after the outbreak of the War for Independence.[24]

Compulsory Service and War Taxes during the Revolution
The developing imperial crisis that led to independence coincided with the drastic increase in disownments of Quakers in New England and New York and confirmed developments previously started during the Great War for the Empire. As a consequence the Quaker peace testimony was sharpened and issues previously only touched on indirectly now were at least faced if not settled. Loyalty to civil government, payment of taxes, and even land ownership became issues affecting Quaker pacifism as Friends raised their standards.

The reform movement reinforced the tendency of the Society in the eighteenth century to give thanks to those in authority for their favors, and to refrain from disrupting government. Quakers interpreted "render unto Caesar" as giving quiet acquiescence to all acts of civil government. Because they attached a seemingly disproportionate amount of emphasis to being a peaceable people, they entered the period of heightened imperial crisis with a stance ready made for loyalism. That Friends survived the revolutionary period at all was in part due to the practical genius of Quakers like Moses Brown, a wealthy merchant of Providence who was willing to accommodate revolutionary governments and give aid to noncombatant victims of war. Mixed with a tendency toward loyalism under all circumstances, the peace testimony was to make Friends seem more suspect than they otherwise would have been, and more so than other pacifist groups, like the Pennsylvania Mennonites, who remained aloof from government.[25]

The issue of loyalty caught all Friends in one way or another. Without regard for personal preference, could Quakers recognize the revolutionary government and defy London Yearly Meeting's injunction "to keep out of the Spirit of parties, and to cherish in your hearts the principle of peace and Good will to all"? And how could they dwell in the midst of a colonial war, at times a civil war in the strictly colonial sense, without recognizing revolutionary governments when those governments controlled their state or at least those portions of the states in which they resided? For a people who had protested their loyalty throughout the eighteenth century, how could Friends break with Britain? There were obviously no simple answers to any of these questions—no answer at all, in fact, for many Friends as long as war continued and control of territory remained in dispute.[26]

New York was one of the most difficult areas. There Friends were split by warring armies as from late 1776 to 1783 the British controlled New York City, Long Island, and a part of the mainland opposite Manhattan, while the Americans held the Hudson River Valley. The territory of Purchase Monthly Meeting turned into a no man's land contested by both armies. For Friends under British occupation the question of loyalty at least until the end of the war was relatively simple: there was no change. Anyone in this area who was disaffected by British rule would be well advised not to advertise his dissatisfaction either to the British or to Friends. The consequence of such an indiscretion would be imprisonment by the British or disownment by his monthly meeting. A more serious problem lay within American lines. In 1777 the yearly meeting decided that Friends were not to subscribe to the affirmation of allegiance required by the state of New York of citizens in areas of American control. If any Friends did so and would not acknowledge their error, they would be disowned. The chances are that as a result of refusing the affirmation, individual Quakers found themselves at odds with local authorities and their neighbors. Pacifism aside, could Quakers who refused the affirmation be trusted?[27]

New York Friends had many significant encounters with opposing military forces, varying from arrest for crossing lines to attend meetings to refusal to supply services demanded. Of greatest interest to later generations of Quakers, especially small children (who know it as the story of Fierce Feathers), was the encounter between some of General John Burgoyne's Indians and Quakers attending a meeting for worship near Saratoga. In 1777 as Burgoyne's disastrous campaign neared its conclusion, a scouting party of his Indians interrupted these Friends during silent worship. Accompanied by two Frenchmen and one American prisoner, the Indians eventually went away. But although the record does not indicate Quaker consternation, at that meeting they must have been at least apprehensive, if not frightened out of their wits, for word of the recent scalping of Jane McCrea by Indian allies of the British had circulated widely. In this and other encounters, Quakers survived New York's warfare with difficulty, but with their pacifism nevertheless intact.[28]

Perhaps because Rhode Island had been a seat for Quaker political leadership for a long time, withdrawal from government was particularly difficult for Friends. Withdrawal raised a question of Quaker devotion to either side. Certainly the Rhode Island Monthly Meeting's declaration of loyalty to George III did not help Newport Friends after the British evacuated Newport in 1779 and American forces returned, nor could it have helped Friends in other parts of Rhode Island, although there are no clear indications of retaliatory action. Major emphasis outside Newport was on a positive neutrality, with no allegiance to either side. To this end the activities of Moses Brown and others on the New England Meeting for Sufferings relief committee for noncombatant sufferers must have helped relations with other New Englanders, an effort described in the chapter that follows.[29]

In Massachusetts and New Hampshire, loyalty was not a major issue in most places: American control of both states from early 1776 helped resolve questions for Quakers on the mainland. But for Friends on the island of Nantucket the issue was not so easy. They needed to continue their whale fishery, and because of it needed and obtained from Massachusetts permission to land whale oil. They had received freedom from harassment on the high seas because the British blockade of the continent specifically exempted Nantucket. The island also needed supplies from the mainland, for it was not self-sufficient. The answer had to be, and was for most residents, a declared neutrality. Given some freedom to continue their whale fishery, they still faced privations, for their vessels and crews were subject to seizure and their market was now limited. They also had to face hostility of revolutionary state authorities and consequently the possibility of being charged with treason because of antimilitary activities (Quaker merchant William Rotch destroyed a quantity of bayonets) or for seeking release of Quakers imprisoned by the British (again William Rotch was involved and in this case only barely escaped imprisonment himself in Massachusetts). Nantucket, however, was an exception to the general rule, for the nature of the conflict simplified the question of allegiance for most Friends in this province.[30]

A much more difficult question than loyalty, especially in New England, turned on tax and currency. If Friends accepted and used money of the states or Confederation and paid taxes even indirectly to support the war, might they not be said to participate in wars and tumults and in the overthrow of lawful government? Some Friends like Job Scott, a recent convert, Providence schoolmaster, and recognized minister, thought so and wanted to have a strict, literal enforcement of the peace testimony, with no payment of war taxes in any form. Fortunately for Quakers in general, the Society did not adopt this position, for it would have increased the suspicion of Quaker untrustworthiness among revolutionaries. To be fair, the adoption of Scott's position would have been consistent with Friends' attitude toward clergy rates throughout the century, but consistency would have cost Friends dearly. Encouraged by Moses Brown among others, the yearly meeting advised mutual forbearance. Friends who could in conscience use continental currency and pay war taxes—either mixed or direct—presumably did so. Not everyone was happy with this decision, for the Revolutionary War was nudging Friends into a more rigid position. The attempt to prevent payment of taxes represented a change in recent Quaker policy: although payment of war debts, acceptance of currency, and payment of taxes had not been enthusiastically received by some Friends, most had gone along in earlier wars.[31]

The change in emphasis did not please Timothy Davis, a leading member of Sandwich Monthly Meeting and a supporter of the Revolution. Davis had submitted an unsigned, short manuscript to Moses Brown of the New England Meeting for Sufferings but had not formally applied to the meeting itself requesting permission to publish. Without obtaining approval of that body, he engaged another Friend, Caleb Greene, to publish it for him. Davis, argued, correctly, that there was nothing novel in Friends paying war taxes or in using currency issued to pay for war. Moreover, since a change in government had taken place, Quakers were obliged to recognize the new authorities and to support them. As the "government of Massachusetts Bay is better than none, and [as] the inhabitants receive . . . advantage from it," asserted Davis, "they ought to be willing to bear a proportionable part" of its support. He buttressed his argument by referring to Thomas Story's justification of mixed taxes and to the Biblical injunction: "render unto Caesar . . ."[32]

The New England Meeting for Sufferings was taken aback. This pamphlet would divide Friends, some of whom had reached new and radical conclusions on pacifism, and could demonstrate that Friends were neither neutral nor consistent. Those who refused to pay taxes or to accept new currency would also be exposed to the charge that they were loyalists (which, of course, some of them were). By exposing divided opinion at a very difficult time, Davis compelled some disciplinary action and no doubt fully expected it. He had knowingly breached the Society's rule that publication of members' views having a direct bearing on Quakerism as a whole had to receive the imprimatur of the responsible committee of the yearly meeting. It was a practice established for several decades in New England, and the meeting for sufferings had recently been charged with administering it. For publication without permission and for airing views that were divisive within and embarrassing without, the meeting for sufferings urged that Davis be taken under dealing.[33]

More than Davis' views were now exposed to public scrutiny, for the proceedings that followed demonstrated the weakness of the constitutional structure of the Society. Davis had to be dealt with by his own Sandwich Monthly Meeting. The problem for yearly meeting leaders was that a majority of Sandwich Monthly Meeting supported Davis. The yearly meeting therefore had Davis and his firm supporters disowned by the group, and the affair dragged on for several years before Davis and many of his followers returned to membership. Before they did, a majority of Sandwich Monthly Meeting members, joined by a few Friends in neighboring Dartmouth, had organized a separate monthly meeting which claimed meeting property and the right to use the meeting house with the officially recognized group. Overall, however, relatively few New England Friends left to join the schismatic group, and its effect was limited.[34]

The tax question continued to bother. Some New England Friends wrote a memorial in 1780 against the payment of any taxes, mixed or otherwise, which might support the war effort. It did not become official policy. Nor did a South Kingston concern not to pay either war or mixed taxes. New England Friends were to remain divided on the issue, with some paying taxes and using bills of exchange and others not. Independence relieved some of their problems. But not all. Officially Friends now opposed the paper currency that helped fund the war. In 1787 they petitioned the Rhode Island Assembly, unsuccessfully, "praying for repeal or amendment of the act making the paper currency of the state lawful tender, and of the act limiting the bringing of personal actions to two years." The motives for their opposing the limitation of personal actions and making paper currency legal "tender at par on payment of Just debts" centered on the inherent advantage given to speculators (those who favored the land bank), but surely their attitude was also tied to the (in this case) unstated original use of the currency to fund war debts.[35]

Although New England Friends did not come to a clear decision on war tax and currency, New York Friends did. Since New York had not developed a system of taxation in lieu of military service, as had Massachusetts in the Great War for the Empire, perhaps New York Friends were unwilling to accept a war tax, mixed or direct. In any event they refused to pay the tax and for that action suffered many distraints. And not only did Quakers not pay during wartime, but they refused to pay their share of the war debt after peace had been signed. Their position went well beyond that of Friends in New England Yearly Meeting, where only a few—an important few, to be sure—consistently favored nonpayment.[36]

Trade in prize goods was a simpler matter for Friends to maintain in their testimony. If, as seems possible, earlier in the century Friends had sent out privateers, accepted smuggled goods, and even dealt in prize goods, by midcentury the practice was no longer acceptable, and Friends did not escape dealing if they traded in goods tainted by war. Rejection of trade in prize goods and contraband paralleled rejection of the slave trade, as all were fruits of war. New York City Quakers dealt with several of their number who had ignored both a blockade of New Jersey and the prohibition on prize goods. If the situation varied elsewhere in New York or New England, enforcement did not: if anyone dealt in goods of war, he could expect to be taken under dealing. On Nantucket, where the problem was more ticklish—Nantucket Friends trading with one side would come under suspicion of the other—there was enforcement of the requirement that only neutral goods—that is, goods having no role in the conflict—could be traded or purchased.[37]

Related to the issue of prize goods was that of confiscated estates. In 1761 the New England Yearly Meeting had ordered Friends not to purchase forfeited lands. Reaffirmation of that position came during the Revolutionary War in South Kingston when one member was disowned for renting confiscated property. Similar action followed in New York after the war when confiscated Tory estates were put up for sale. The problem on estates like Philipse Manor was that tenants had lived there for many years holding land on long-term leases. But what of Quaker leaseholders? Would the New York Meeting for Sufferings permit them to purchase the lands they had improved? It would not, and although delays in putting lands up for sale followed, Friends lost both residences and improvements. To make matters worse, the meeting for sufferings was so unfeeling that it refused to permit them to count lost improvements as sufferings. Under the circumstances it was an enormous price to pay for one's faith. One is impressed both by the studied callousness of New York Quaker leadership and by the compliance of dispossessed tenants.[38]

Friends had advanced their testimony in this aspect of pacifism. Much land in North America and Ireland in times past had been acquired by conquest, and much would still be in North America. Quakers had shared in the fruits of those conquests to the extent of eventually taking up land: in southeastern Massachusetts and Rhode Island some lands had been taken from Indians by a combination of force and trickery, and Friends settled on them much as Quakers in central and southern Ireland had taken up land seized from the Irish in the seventeenth century. Now the peace testimony had changed to the point where a conscientious scruple would not permit counting seized property as official suffering if one had not foresight enough to safeguard it years earlier by a lease. A lease was not customary at the time, and especially not a lease to which a landlord might not assent. A further question concerning the bearing of previous land struggles in the Hudson Valley also enters here. Could previous disagreements over property, which had been sharp and serious before the war, have been reflected in the New York stand? It is a difficult question to answer and one which must be left to detailed histories of land speculation in that region. But one suspects that previous land contention in Oblong and Purchase monthly meetings, mixed with the divisiveness of the War for Independence, served to influence the decision of the New York Meeting for Sufferings.[39]

Throughout the war Friends maintained their earlier testimony against participating in military affairs, although the price was substantial. Many young Friends enlisted in the army, and this was the major cause for disownments. Friends who maintained the peace testimony elicited a varied response from authorities. New York Friends were exempt from 1775 until 1777, although in emergencies they were to help (that was not the kind of exemption some Friends wanted). In 1777 New York resorted to the practice of a tax in lieu of service; that remained the practice throughout the war and was a major factor in the total distraints of £8894/9/8 in Purchase Quarterly Meeting. Rhode Island, which had exempted Friends, required them to hire substitutes—in effect as legislation in New York and Massachusetts also required. Under British occupation Quakers generally escaped any requirement for service, although there was one instance in 1780 when the British commander attempted to compel New York Friends to serve watch. Unlike their Newport counterparts at the beginning of the century, New York Friends did not acquiesce.[40]

By the end of the Revolution, Quakers had advanced the consistency of their peace testimony substantially. No one was to serve in any capacity furthering a war-making interest. No one was to purchase confiscated lands. There were still differences on taxes mixed or direct and on currency put into circulation to underwrite military expenditures, but Friends were moving gradually in the direction of nonpayment of taxes and nonacceptance of currency. The testimony was enhanced and advanced by the conflict, despite the fact that Friends had not yet taken a consistent position on it.

Chapter 9
Philanthropy

QUAKER TESTIMONIES AGAINST WARS, oaths, and church taxes pointed toward outsiders, especially outsiders in government. Testimonies concerning assistance to the needy and, after it developed, against slavery, had their origin primarily in the relationship of Friends to Friends: the testimonies here looked inward. They partook of the same concern that led Quakers to attempt to settle disputes, maintain high standards of business ethics, and cultivate ascetic tastes in dress. As a religious group, the Society of Friends sought to maintain many of the same services in modern times that guilds, as economic groups, had performed in the medieval period. To that extent the Quaker practice of aiding their own people looked backward to another era, much as did their language. Insofar as philanthropy was concerned, this inward-looking emphasis served well, for particularly in the seventeenth and reaching well into the eighteenth century, Friends had to practice in-group philanthropy.

This practice of restricting the Society's assistance to its own poor continued after the period of seventeenth-century persecution. No doubt individual Friends helped non-Friends in need before 1700, but not until Quakers began to remove themselves from the political arena did they begin to look outward, to help others. In so doing, reforming Friends took advantage of a long-standing implied commitment of the Society to remain uncontaminated by slavery, first by eliminating both slaveholding and participation in the slave trade by Friends, and then by eliminating slavery from society at large. Paralleling the attack on slavery was the practice of aiding outsiders in distress, especially in wartime. In the northern colonies the first signs of this assistance came in the French and Indian War. The War for Independence gave Friends the opportunity to increase their aid to noncombatants who suffered privation in wartime, although in New England and New York most relief funds had to go to Friends, for several Quaker centers were particularly exposed to the ravages of war. For the colonial and revolutionary periods at least, the major philanthropic achievement of these northern Friends related to their efforts to eliminate slavery from North America. Aid to the Indians, an active concern in Pennsylvania, for these northern yearly meetings lay in the future.

Help to the Needy

Early American Friends had to help one another in periods of oppression. Probably first in their minds was the necessity of maintaining their faith in the eyes of the world, which promoted the inward-looking emphasis on charity. Rhode Island Monthly Meeting's seventeenth-century book of rules contains the advice George Fox gave fellow Quakers in the Barbadoes and which New England Friends collected and sometimes used as a Discipline before 1708. Though many of the suggestions—on slavery, for example—were disregarded, care for Quaker poor was an early practice of the Society in England, and Fox's advice on the indigent must have found a receptive audience in both New England and New York as well. He argued that since Friends had put off the old Adam, they should care for all their poor, so as to keep the faith spotless before the world. He also urged children to care for their parents, so that they would not have to rely on towns for support.[1]

In the seventeenth century there were few occasions when New England and New York meetings looked after their poor. At least little evidence survives among the fragmentary meeting records for this century to indicate that care for poor Friends occupied the attention of the yearly meetings or their subordinate groups very often, although it is possible that such assistance was given and not recorded. Monthly meetings at this stage did not appoint permanent committees for poor relief. Perhaps poverty, as defined in the seventeenth century, was so infrequent that monthly meetings had little reason to help.[2]

Usually a monthly meeting solicited its members for funds for the aged or ill and appointed a committee for each case to oversee the distribution of assistance. Sandwich Monthly Meeting cared for Thomas Johnson and his wife in this manner for several years after they applied for aid in 1673. Rhode Island Monthly Meeting cared for John Crossland after 1687 and for Mary Harper's children when she passed away two years later. Flushing Monthly Meeting in 1684, in a remarkable gesture considering the Society's later antislavery position, helped purchase a Negro slave for John Adams, a onetime ranter who had rejoined the monthly meeting in 1676. There were similar instances of assistance in all monthly meetings, and this form of poor relief administered by special committees appointed for individual cases continued to be the pattern of Quaker charity in these colonies until after 1750, much as it remained the characteristic way of caring for the poor in rural and sparsely populated meetings after that date. Farmers in rural meetings were probably self-sufficient and did not need the poorhouses or the permanent committees for the poor which grew up in more populous areas with specialized economies, although it is also possible that having less wealth, they were less able to offer help to the needy.[3]

Friends in urban meetings faced a much different situation. Rhode Island Monthly Meeting included the city of Newport and was the first New England monthly meeting to have the problem of numerous urban poor. It established a committee to care for all the meeting's needy in 1752. Subsequently, committees to care for the poor became a feature of all populous New England monthly meetings there were centered on towns or populous farming communities. Before the Revolution, Salem, Smithfield (which included a growing Providence), Nantucket, and Dartmouth monthly meetings also established such committees. Of the New York meetings only Flushing had a poor committee, set up first in 1756. Newport Friends had set up poorhouses before 1760, the only monthly meeting to do so, although these were short-lived expedients. Usually there was an attempt to find employment for the indigent when they were able to work. All meetings sought to place dependent children in apprenticeships so as to relieve poor families—and, presumably, the meetings—of the necessity of caring for them. In particularly difficult situations, committees would be specially appointed to investigate and give assistance if necessary.[4]

The usual place for assistance to the poor was within the monthly meeting, although neighboring monthly meetings and superior quarterly and yearly meetings sometimes aided monthly meetings. Several cases came as early as the seventeenth century. When Indian wars in New Hampshire and Maine wrought havoc among the Quakers living in those parts in 1697, the yearly meeting sent them 10 pounds. New England Quakers also asked New York and Philadelphia yearly meetings for financial assistance, and those meetings, in an unusual display of financial generosity at this early date, responded with funds.[5]

As already noted, Friends also extended assistance to members imprisoned for refusing to assess taxes to support the Standing Order or to join the militia. Their actions went beyond the simple lobbying that eventually obtained relief for them from these requirements. For example, Dartmouth Monthly Meeting undertook to run a member's business when he was incarcerated for refusing to assess church taxes in his capacity as a selectman and assessor. As instances like this also involved towns as a whole, towns may have also given assistance.[6]

There were also occasions when small meetings with insufficient resources received assistance from larger and wealthier meetings. An example was Pembroke Monthly Meeting. In the seventeenth century it had been a leading meeting, but by the mid-eighteenth century it was poor and faltering. (In fact, Pembroke was so weak that shortly after the Revolution the New England Yearly Meeting briefly considered dissolving it and attaching it to the larger and stronger Sandwich Monthly Meeting, itself somewhat depleted in numbers by the temporary departure of Timothy Davis and his followers.) In 1751 Pembroke had to ask for yearly meeting assistance in providing for one of its elderly women, Alice Howard. Many New England monthly meetings responded, but, as was usual in these years, Rhode Island Monthly Meeting contributed most of the money. This monthly meeting also furnished the largest share of funds when Friends outside Salem Monthly Meeting helped rebuild the Boston meeting house, destroyed in the fire of 1760. Most other meetings helped, too, but Dartmouth Monthly Meeting went farther when it took up a collection and gave it to the Boston selectmen to assist anyone in need as a result of the fire.[7]

Dartmouth's action was one of the few instances of relief given to outsiders before the Revolution. If Dartmouth Quaker Peleg Smith's comments on the Act of 1758 are accurate, the relief given was in part to compensate for the militia law exempting Friends, passed that year. Records of other instances of assistance given outsiders late in the seventeenth century are so few that even if they were designed to help outsiders in distress, the level of concern for innocent victims of war and disaster was not on the same order as in the Dartmouth case above or in the American Revolution. In 1697 the New England Yearly Meeting gave Robert Deeringe funds to rebuild his house after its destruction in Indian wars. Apparently Pembroke Monthly Meeting sent funds to the victims of Indian attacks in Wells, Maine, in 1691, but those unnamed people could have been Friends. In 1697 Rhode Island Monthly Meeting helped a Newport woman purchase her son's freedom from the Turks, but compared to charity within the meeting, these few instances to outsiders were rare indeed before Dartmouth made its contribution.[8]

The American Revolution brought new dimensions to Quaker poor relief. After the outbreak of fighting around Boston in 1775, New England Friends at first assisted only Friends. A change soon came about as Quakers followed (probably unknowingly) the precedent of Dartmouth Friends at the time of the Boston fire, but on a much larger scale. Impetus to expand relief came from Moses Brown and Philadelphia Quakers. Relief funds were not just from one monthly meeting, as earlier; they came from Philadelphia, New York, and the British Isles. The decision to help came in 1775, and it could not have hurt Friends incorrectly suspected of sympathy with the British, or even those who drafted and signed messages of loyalty and opposition to the rebellion of their fellow Americans. The considerable relief funds expended to noncombatant needy stressed Quaker beneficent pacifism in the face of suspicion from both sides. It also helped to establish Quaker neutrality when Friends were suspected of disloyalty by both sides and embarrassed by schisms like that led by Timothy Davis.[9]

As Henry Cadbury indicates, Quaker relief to New England in 1775 and 1776 totaled the staggering amount of £3910/2/1 1/2 from Philadelphia alone. As of April 1776, £1968/5/2 1/2 had been given to a total of 5220 needy people. Sixteen months later the total was £3910/2/1 1/2, in addition to the New England Yearly Meeting contribution. Most of the money spent the first year went to non-Quakers, but after that, of necessity, relief had to go mainly to Friends, although there were instances when non-Quakers benefited. As for the geographical pattern of relief, funds expended away from the vicinity of Boston—in Rhode Island, for example—tended to be used for the support of Quakers, although many non-Friends were helped. Emphasis changed from aid to outsiders to assistance to Quakers after the British evacuated Boston and after refugees from Newport and Aquidneck Island had been absorbed on the Rhode Island mainland. Thereafter, Quaker aid in New England went to Friends almost exclusively, especially to Nantucket, where many inhabitants had been in dire straits even before the war. With disruption by both sides of their trade and with short supplies and raids, a difficult situation became impossible, and hundreds of Nantucket Friends moved, primarily to Quaker areas in the Hudson River Valley. Nantucket Quakers received money to help them move. Administered by William Rotch, a member of the New England Meeting for Sufferings and wealthy whaling merchant, these funds also supported Nantucket Friends unable to leave the island until peace in 1783.[10]

War moved south in 1776, and when it did, Quakers transferred their relief efforts to help outsiders, particularly to the Hudson Valley, as there was less need in places like Long Island and New York, which were under British occupation. In no-man's-land and American territory Friends gave liberally from relief funds derived from internal and external sources. The latter included gifts from English and Irish Friends, whose assistance was especially noticeable after British occupation of Philadelphia temporarily dried up that source. Friends were careful to give aid only to noncombatants. All aid went to the needy, Quaker and otherwise, in the Hudson Valley. Assistance to outsiders lasted longer than in New England, primarily because the war remained longer but also because the Quaker poor, even refugees from Nantucket, seem to have been less in need of help than non-Friends. There must have been assistance to Nantucket immigrants, but as no records survive it was probably personal and direct rather than the occasional financial handout of the Society.[11]

As a result of the Revolutionary War, coming when it did, charitable concerns changed both in degree and direction. Innocent victims of war were to be helped in the future whatever their faith. A useful beginning had been launched in a practice which from this time won Friends well-deserved renown. No longer would their pacifism serve merely to keep them from war. Now there was commitment of relief to all war victims without regard to battle lines. Relief to non-Friends served to balance the rising standards set for observing the peace testimony. Withdrawal and dwelling alone, as Sydney James has observed, brought with it a new sense of responsibility for others.[12]

Antislavery Activity in New England and New York

If, as limited evidence indicates, charity to outsiders became official Quaker policy only after the reform of the Society began in the 1750's and especially after the outbreak of the War for Independence, Quaker concern about Negro slavery was of much longer duration and had its origin within the Society rather than outside it. Slavery had troubled American Quakers from the late seventeenth century. One aspect of the problem was that Friends in all but a few isolated country meetings owned slaves. Unhappily, we lack evidence as to numbers of slaves and the extent of Quaker ownership; but for Friends in such urban trading centers as Newport and New York, slavery was an onerous problem. Newport, the heart of New England Quakerdom in pre-Revolutionary years, had several merchants (some of them Quakers) who participated in the slave trade. Many Quaker residents owned slaves on Aquidneck Island itself and on their Narragansett and West Indian plantations. Even those who did not trade or own slaves were caught up with slavery to the extent that they traded extensively with the West Indies. In New York several Long Island Friends owned slaves, and others occasionally brought in slaves by twos or threes after loading their usual cargo. Though it is impossible to be precise, one suspects that New York Quaker involvement with the slave trade was less than that among New England Friends, especially in the vicinity of Rhode Island.[13]

Early Friends had not approved of slavery. Quite the contrary, for at the same time that the English colonies adopted slave codes and long before the major slave migration took place, George Fox preached against the separation of the races in the Barbadoes. In a rare case of a Foxian retreat, however, authorities there forced him into an equivocal stand on slavery itself. There is no record that this early Quaker leader urged the immediate elimination of slavery or wrote New England and New York Friends concerning their slaves. He did, however, hold egalitarian views insofar as former Africans were concerned. In the book of letters from early Quaker ministers which served as a rule book in New England, he is recorded as favoring intermarriage of slaves and whites. He also advocated joint meetings for worship of blacks and whites. His advice to New England Friends on these matters went unheeded.[14]

Although Fox did not speak out against the institution, at least one of his close associates, the Irish Quaker minister William Edmundson, did. During a visit to New England in 1676, Edmundson wrote Newport Friends about slaveholding. His words were as strong as any of the period. He argued that Quakers were to restrain their slaves "from their former Courses of their accustomed filthy, unclean practices, in defileing one another." He implied that all Friends should consider slaves the children of God and as such to be taken to Meeting "tht they may learn to know God that made them, & Christ Jesus that died for them & all Men." Moreover, Edmundson made clear his position against slavery, a position that antislavery Quaker writers used in the eighteenth century until John Woolman, the New Jersey Quaker saint, raised the appeal to a higher level. Edmundson argued that

> it would be acceptable with God, & answer the Witness in all, if you did consider their Condition of perpetual Slavery, & make their Conditions your own, & soe fullfill the Law of Christ, for perpetuall Slavery is an Agrivation, & an Oppression upon the Mind and hath a ground, & Truth is tht which works the Remedy, & breaks the Yoke, & removes the ground; soe it would be well to consider, that they may feel, see, & partake of your Liberty in the Gospel of Christ, & they may see & know a difference between you & other people, & your selfdeniall may be known to all, & those things (layd upon me to write,) & leave them to your Consideration, who am your unfeigned Friend in everlasting truth.

Edmundson took advantage of New England Quaker opposition to enslavement of Indians captured in King Philip's War to point out the evil of all slavery: "And many of you count it unlawfull to make Slaves of the Indians, & if so, then why the Negroes?" Another decade and a half passed before George Keith and Germantown Quakers opposed slavery on similar grounds: as a moral evil in itself and as a violation of the Quaker testimony against war. Men enslaved as a result of war could not be purchased by Friends, according to this argument; to purchase such slaves was the same violation of Quaker pacifism as purchasing prize goods and was made worse by the sin of owning another human.[15]

Edmundson's advice was not followed at the time, but if his exhortation did not serve as a guide for Quakers then, it remained one of many injunctions gathered in the New England Yearly Meeting's book of rules. Taken with statements from other antislavery Quakers, his counsel must have served as a reminder of the evil of slaveholding even when leading New England Quakers held slaves.

It is impossible to determine precisely how many leading Quakers in New York and New England held slaves, but a few Newport records survive which indicate several prominent Friends of that town owned both Indians and Negroes. Among these Friends was Thomas Richardson. In 1712, the year he moved to Newport from Boston, Richardson requested a correspondent in the Carolinas to purchase two Indian slaves for him. He had heard that they could be bought at little expense, especially when acquired "young and trainable." He asked for "a Verry Likely Boy & Girl Between 12 & 16 years Old or Thereabouts." He made a similar request three years later, in a letter basically devoted to the purchase of horses "to lay Out Some of my Efect in a likely Negro boy or two at a Moderate Price . . . but pray let them be likely and not those tht are half Dead." He was a considerate owner, willing to let his slave Cojo have his way and be sold to Long Island in 1716. But love intervened. Cojo, for whom Richardson had high regard, decided to marry Walter Newberry's slave Sarah, and Richardson and his wife gave their reluctant consent. Thereafter he probably continued to hold slaves until his death in 1761; at least his correspondence indicates no opposition to the institution. In 1739 he was checking the Newport slave market for his Boston Quaker cousin, Benjamin Borden. Eleven years later he asked London Friend Richard Partridge to use his good offices to have a runaway slave returned to a poor Newport neighbor, Isaac Anthony. (That Partridge was willing to do so indicates something of the level of antislavery concern among at least one element of the London Meeting for Sufferings and is yet another aspect of transatlantic resistance to antislavery). It was unlikely that a man engaged in these pursuits would take a stand against slavery or dispose of his own slaves.[16]

Richardson was not the largest Quaker slaveholder in Rhode Island. A fellow Quaker merchant, Abraham Redwood, probably had that dubious distinction. Redwood owned a great estate on the northern part of Aquidneck Island and a plantation on Antigua. The number of his slaves in

Rhode Island cannot be determined, but after 1730 slaves on his plantation in the West Indies totaled from 75 to 230. Nor were Redwood
and Richardson alone among Quaker grandees active in meeting affairs
around Newport. Because there were so many like them, rural Quakers
were restrained from abolishing the slave trade and even slaveholding itself among Friends.[17]

It is also difficult to determine which New England Friends participated in the slave trade. Those who did were probably confined to Rhode
Island, but most offical records which Elizabeth Donnan transcribed usually carry insufficient personal identification to determine the names of
the masters (the name Thurston recorded as shipmaster does not mean
that Thurston was a Friend, let alone to which Wanton Newport Cus-
tom-House entries referred). But although we are uncertain which Quakers were involved in the trade, one stands out. Friend Thomas Robinson
took out insurance against a slave insurrection on the sloop *Dolphin* when
it went on a voyage to Sierra Leone and the West Indies in May 1755. En
route, several of the *Dolphin's* crew were pressed, and the voyage may not
have been profitable. Slave trading, especially in wartime, as with this
venture, was always a risky business, and Robinson, like the Brown
brothers in Providence, may have lost heavily in it.[18]

As for New York, there is insufficient information relating to the early
eighteenth century for one to say whether slave trading and slave ownership had extensive Quaker participation. One suspects that only rarely
did Quaker merchants import slaves and then only in small numbers. Edward and James Burling were owners of ships that brought in slaves sin-
gly—apparently as extra freight. Edward Burling was the New York
Yearly Meeting clerk, but unlike evidence on leading Newport Friends,
there is nothing to indicate that he ordered slaves, shared in major slave
voyages, or traded with the West Indies or Africa. Other than the Bur-
lings, the lists that Elizabeth Donnan provides do not indicate readily
identifiable New York Quaker names. One is similarly hindered in estimates on New York Quaker ownership of slaves. Friends, particularly on
Long Island, did purchase slaves, but it is impossible to say to what extent. In any event, before 1750, since they did not have either the vast
estates or the transatlantic trade of their Newport brethren, New York
Quakers' ties to slavery must have been limited to a few slaves for each
farm—slaves, furthermore, who worked beside the family in the fields
and probably ate at the same table in the home.[19]

Country Quakers in New England and New York, as in Pennsylvania,
were consistently more sympathetic to antislavery activities than were
their urban brethren. These Friends may have disliked the unfair compet-
itive advantage that slaveholding gave to wealthy farmers resident on

Long Island and in Newport, and to Newport merchants. Perhaps publications by antislavery English and Pennsylvania Quakers inspired
them. Whatever the source, there seems to have been a large and vocal
body of opinion in rural areas of New England Quakerdom promot-
ing the abolition of both the trade and the institution, a body that
may have had a parallel in New York, although because of fragmentary
records in the first half of the eighteenth century, one cannot say. Before
they could bring about reform, these Friends had to challenge successfully the control of the yearly meetings by slaveholding Friends in Newport and probably Long Island, and induce other yearly meetings to agree
to antislavery rules.[20]

The first recorded instance of slavery arising as an issue in these northern meetings came when a woman member of the rural Dartmouth
Monthly Meeting had a slave whipped so hard that he died. For this offense she was expelled from the Society in 1711, but such was the leniency
of the Discipline at the time that within three years she was reinstated.
Such brutality would not again be part of recorded Quaker business, although there could have been similar cases that went unreported in these
years of at best sketchy record-keeping in monthly meetings. The case of
brutality in Dartmouth may have contributed to a brief spate of activity
between 1716 and 1720 by some antislavery Quakers.[21]

Whether antislavery activity was spontaneous or inspired from outside—the records do not indicate—New England Quaker concern about
slavery became a matter of record in 1715. Rhode Island Monthly Meeting decided, without reference to the yearly meeting, that Friends should
cease the barbaric practice of branding slaves. In the same year, Dartmouth Monthly Meeting, the scene of the recent whipping, pressed the
Rhode Island Quarterly Meeting to decide whether Friends should own
slaves or participate in the trade. Monthly meetings queried on the subject gave differing answers, but it is significant that the replies of rural
meetings indicated an opposition to slavery. Dartmouth and Nantucket
monthly meetings (and perhaps neighboring Sandwich as well, but its
records for these years are lost), urged that slaveholding be terminated
among Friends. East Greenwich, which had some members who owned
slaves, urged that the trade in slaves be ended. But influential Quakers in
Rhode Island managed to bury the issue temporarily in the quarterly
meeting, which decided to see what Friends elsewhere would do.[22]

New York felt the effects of antislavery sentiment in February 1716
when Horsman Mullenix raised the matter first at the quarterly meeting
and then at the yearly meeting. Mullenix was soon joined in his antislavery protest by visiting English Friend John Farmer. When Farmer presented an antislavery paper at the ensuing yearly meeting, New York

Yearly Meeting deferred action for a year. Delay, one suspects, was the best tactic for slaveholding Quakers to defeat their antislavery brethren.[23]

Farmer the previous month had read his "Epistle Concerning Negroes" to the "satisfaction" of Nantucket Monthly Meeting. Following New York's decision to delay, he went to New England Yearly Meeting not content to abide by delaying tactics already used to stop the antislavery campaign by Rhode Island Quarterly Meeting. He read his paper, apparently proposed to publish it, and refused to accept the yearly meeting's instructions not to do so. As a consequence, the yearly meeting took him under dealing. The result was his disownment, for he refused to turn over his antislavery papers to the New England Yearly Meeting for Ministers and Elders and submit to its authority. He had attempted to move too fast, and Friends were not yet sufficiently unified to undertake such a crusade. They contented themselves with referring the matter to all quarterly and monthly meetings and made a minute suggesting concern. The yearly meeting, following the pattern already established in Pennsylvania, New York, and Rhode Island, stated that Friends must wait for unity before acting. Slaveholding Quakers had frustrated antislavery efforts. They were to succeed in preventing renewed debate in the yearly meeting for over two decades.[24]

Farmer's defeat at the New England Yearly Meeting was apparently a setback for antislavery there, but not in New York, where the cause stayed alive and respectable. In 1718 William Burling wrote a paper against slaveholding, not published until Benjamin Lay included it in his *All Slavekeepers* in 1737. Burling argued that slavery was evil, that Friends should consider the hardships of the slave, and that by owning slaves Friends abused their testimony against war. His position was not significantly different from William Edmundson's, and, like Edmundson's (at least until Benjamin Lay had it published), it stayed in its manuscript form.[25]

Perhaps as Burling did not press the issue and did not smother his concern about slavery with a challenge to meeting authority, he enabled the still feeble efforts to challenge the institution to continue. In 1718 after several Friends, Burling among them no doubt, spoke out against slavery, New York Yearly Meeting decided to query London Yearly Meeting. Its epistle indicated that the debate had been hot: the "Question Whether Friends might Buy, Sell, or keep Negroes Slaves for Term of Life, according to the manner Custom and Practice of these Country's . . . greatly Toucheth Peoples Interst and manor of living in this part of the world." Both sides promised to abide by the London Yearly Meeting decision—one of several instances in which New York and New England Yearly

Meetings tacitly accepted the superiority of London Yearly Meeting. That meeting's 1719 epistle essentially maintained Quaker practice up to this time. It did not urge renunciation of slavery; rather, English Friends hoped, "The Lord Grant you may be there Guided and Directed to Act in a true Wisdom that may be most agreeable to his Divine mind and will and the Honour of our holy Profession, not doubting but you will bear in mind that Just Rule left us Recorded in the Scriptures of Truth. All things whatsoever ye would that men Should doe to you, do ye even so to them." This Delphic advice was sufficiently enigmatic to preserve the status quo. The slave owner could presumably justify his conduct by arguing that he was helping his slaves by feeding them and giving them work, just the sort of thing he would want for himself; the antislavery Friend would regard slavery as an abuse of this commandment, basing his stand on the presumption that no free person would choose slavery as a condition of permanent relationship to others. No decision meant no further action. In any event, the epistle was not received by New York Friends until 1720, and by then, it appears, the movement had temporarily spent itself.[26]

But antislavery ideas did stay alive, especially in rural meetings. Dartmouth, East Greenwich, Smithfield, and Nantucket monthly meetings had members who opposed slavery, and perhaps even rural members of Rhode Island Monthly Meeting and members of Purchase Monthly Meeting (whose records are missing for these years) held a similar position. It is unlikely that antislavery attitudes were ever quiet during the succeeding decades. No doubt there was also an awareness of antislavery opinion in Pennsylvania. Views of Quaker antislavery zealots, like Ralph Sandiford and Benjamin Lay, were bound to be reported by traveling ministers and their published works read by a few members of the Society.[27]

Whether inspired from without or not—the historian of Quaker antislavery, Thomas Drake, thinks these views were home grown—antislavery sentiment was much alive on Nantucket, where a Quaker elder and carpenter, Elihu Coleman, wrote a paper against slavery in 1729. It was published four years later with yearly meeting approval as *A Testimony Against the Unchristian Practice of Making Slaves of Men*. It demonstrated the usefulness of antislavery Friends patiently waiting for the appropriate time so that even slaveholding Friends would assent to publication of their views. Coleman referred to George Fox's admonition not to keep men in perpetual slavery and added to this argument his own that enslavement was a violation of the Quaker peace testimony and an affront to God. His pamphlet apparently did not change the position of the system's defenders in Newport, for there was no move toward reform on the yearly meeting level, and it is doubtful if its impact could have extended to New York or beyond. However, it did represent another instance of "rural" Quakers' ambition to rid the Society of the practice.[28]

The remote and rural monthly meeting of Dover, New Hampshire, had also raised the slaveholding issue in 1731 when it questioned whether Friends should be involved in the buying and selling of slaves. The conclusion of Salem Quarterly Meeting, to which Dover referred this case, was a remarkable case of independence from rule-making by the yearly meeting. It urged that Friends "Refrain from buying or trading in Negroes or Slaves for the futer." Whether disciplinary action was taken against those who purchased slaves is not clear from the records, perhaps in part because records for the meetings of the area north of Boston are fragmentary before 1750. But it marks another instance of rural concern over slavery (and a unique one of quarterly meeting decision-making) in the years when Newport Friends blocked action on the issue. That advice paralleled the position of English Friends, but it is significant that no other group in either New England or New York took this position, and furthermore that at least some Friends had been active in slavetrading in both yearly meetings.[29]

Newport again managed to frustrate antislavery designs of rural Friends in the next decade. In 1742 the New England Yearly Meeting received an antislavery broadside from John Bell of London. It stimulated the rural Smithfield Monthly Meeting to raise the issues of Quaker participation in the slave trade and slavery. Rhode Island Quarterly Meeting passed the matter to the yearly meeting. That meeting made no changes in its earlier position and merely referred Friends to the minute of 1717 and John Bell's pamphlet. It urged Friends not to buy slaves, but this minute was a matter of advice and not of discipline.[30]

Although there was no decision to abolish either slavery or the slave trade, antislavery Friends throughout the northern colonies had created a favorable climate which would give future efforts a good chance of success. Later reformers also had the advantage of developing humanitarianism outside the Society, which stressed rights for all men and which informed and supported reformers within Quakerdom. Both Quaker and secular antislavery, it should be added, occurred at the moment when the Atlantic slave trade reached a high point. Slaveholders who continued to insist that the trade and the institution should be permitted flew in the face of antislavery developments, particularly within the Society and to a lesser extent outside it. The time was coming when Newport slaveowners would no longer be able to delay and obstruct reform.[31]

In the mid-1750's came those changes which ultimately led Quakers throughout the British North American colonies to attack slavery. A first stage was the visit of Quaker reformers who inspired American Friends to raise standards within the Society. The struggle for purity within the Society accompanied growth in the movement to rid Quakers of the blemish of slavery and to raise antislavery to the level of testimony much as reformers wanted other Quaker testimonies to be consistently upheld. One of the leaders both of reform and of antislavery was New Jersey Friend John Woolman. He sought to make antislavery an expression of the sect's concern for the world at the same time that Pennsylvania Quakers were withdrawing from involvement in government and purifying their sect.[32]

Woolman's role in subsequent New England and New York Quaker antislavery successes is difficult to measure. His presence at the New England Yearly Meeting of 1760 certainly did much to help the already considerable antislavery sentiment gain a measure of success as well as to support the position of reformers in general. Decisions by the yearly meeting in 1760 marked a notable change from the hesitant and hitherto unsuccessful steps of rural Friends, for the Quaker slaveholders were still untouched, and some Quakers were still involved in the slave trade. Perhaps Woolman's writings had already excited some members of the Society to contemplate manumission. The reverence subsequently paid to his campaign by New England Friends indicated the effectiveness of his support.[33]

On his arrival in 1760 at the yearly meeting in Newport, Woolman began an effective if quiet campaign against slavery. No doubt he managed some lobbying with other antislavery Friends before the meeting began. He even contemplated having a bill submitted to the Rhode Island Assembly, which was meeting at the same time as the yearly meeting, but it adjourned before he could act. He did speak to the yearly meeting, and he did help to overcome the resistance of numerous slaveowning Friends to the manumission of their slaves. So effective were Woolman's efforts that the yearly meeting adopted a new query, which required Quakers to abandon the slave trade. It also forbade "Buying them when Imported" and required Friends to use slaves "Well where they are Possessed by Inheritence or otherwise, Endeavoring to Train them up in the Principles of Religion." Although slavery itself had not been abolished, an important first step had been taken, and Woolman had a large role in persuading the meeting to adopt it.[34]

Like their Quaker contemporaries to the south, New England antislavery Quakers also managed to overcome the resistance of slaveowning Friends. Most Quaker slaveowners were apparently elderly and were unwilling either to see an end to the trade or an abolition of their property. They had successfully withstood earlier efforts to abolish slavery and the trade among Friends, but now they were losing their dominant position in meeting affairs. Although another decade passed before most of them gave up their position in the New England meetings, it became far easier for the critics of slavery to gain adherents. Once the yearly meeting ruled against buying and selling slaves, it was only a matter of time until Friends would stop slaveholding entirely and expel from the Society obstreperous members who refused to manumit their blacks.[35]

The minute of 1760 which forbade importation or purchase of slaves resulted in only sporadic dealing with offenders. (Probably by this time the number of Negroes sold within New England was minimal anyway.) South Kingston Monthly Meeting was among the first to act. The town of South Kingston had the second highest number of slaves in colonial Rhode Island, but the monthly meeting comprised much more than this town, and available evidence makes it appear unlikely that the slaveholding men of substance were Quakers. South Kingston disowned Samuel Rodman when he purchased a Negro slave in September 1760, and the yearly meeting upheld that decision the following June.[36]

Similar actions were taken by meetings where there were few slaveholding members. In 1760 Dartmouth refused to accept the contribution of Jedediah Wood because he had not made satisfaction with the meeting after his sale of two Indian children. In 1762 Nantucket went farther than other meetings when it managed to persuade Timothy Folger to make provision for "his Negro Girl" to obtain her freedom "at twenty-five years of Age" before he went on a trading voyage. Even Rhode Island Monthly Meeting entered the campaign against the trade in 1760 by taking one of its members under dealing for selling and importing slaves, and extracting an apology from him; but in view of dealings with some errant members after 1772, it may be assumed that several Newport Quakers were still engaged in the trade.[37]

The minute of 1760 had little effect on slavery in Newport. At least one prominent Quaker, Abraham Redwood, continued to have his overseer purchase slaves for his plantation on Antigua, although other members of the meeting were probably unaware of these acquisitions. That he and other Newport Friends continued to maintain slaves in fairly large numbers, however, and may even have continued slave purchases within Rhode Island itself, remained a standing insult to the antislavery trend within Quakerdom. In time the Society would have to move against the institution and against individuals like Redwood who kept slaves.[38]

The first proposal for abolition in New England came not surprisingly from a rural meeting. South Kingston raised the issue in 1769. It charged that slavery was brutal, and it took the matter through the Rhode Island Quarterly Meeting to the yearly meeting. The yearly meeting appointed a committee on slavery to visit all meetings. In 1770 the committee recommended to the yearly meeting that Friends free all slaves except the very old and the very young, and the yearly meeting adopted this suggestion as a part of the Discipline that year.[39]

Friends moved immediately to deal with slaveholding members, much as in the same year they began vigorously to enforce the Discipline in other respects. Rhode Island Monthly Meeting acted decisively this time and set up a committee to talk to slaveholders. Family ties had little to do with the position members held on this issue. William Redwood, the eldest son of Abraham, was on the committee to deal with slaveholders, and for the first time this monthly meeting expelled a member who engaged in slavetrading. Other meetings acted in similar fashion, and by 1772 many older Quakers were under dealing. They either freed their slaves or were disowned. Disownments continued for several years and picked up somewhat in 1773 after the yearly meeting, on the suggestion of Smithfield Monthly Meeting, revised the tenth query to require Friends to free all their slaves.[40]

Smithfield's proposal may well have been occasioned by the long-lived dealing with the last Quaker Governor of Rhode Island, Stephen Hopkins of Providence. When Smithfield took him under dealing in 1772, the underlying purpose may have been to humble him for his continuing participation in politics, but the meeting actually dealt with him for his refusal to free his slave. Apparently the meeting was most unwilling to be free of him, for it had him under dealing for seven months before deciding to disown him. Two months afterward, Smithfield proposed that the yearly meeting forbid slaveholding to any member.[41]

By the time of the Revolutionary War, slavery had virtually ceased to exist among Friends in New England, which suggests that their antislavery decisions owed more to their own than to external forces. An exception, Dover Monthly Meeting, was so far from the seat of major activity that it had not taken any slaveholders under dealing before the outbreak of war. Not until 1777—when Moses Brown passed through, distributing aid—did Friends there, at Brown's behest, set about freeing their slaves. The certificates of manumission tell a lot about the complex sources of Brown's antislavery views once war had broken out and independence declared. Probably composed by Brown, they reflect a rationalism that went beyond usual Quaker emphases, a phrasing that indicates Brown favored the American position set out in the Declaration of Independence, even if he had to assume a neutral position on the war itself. If all people were to be free, there could be no justification of slavery, these certificates argued. There were a few other exceptions which escaped notice during wartime turmoil; but shortly after the war, New England Quakers had no more members who possessed slaves. By this time Quaker antislavery attentions had turned to state legislatures, in the hope of abolishing the trade and in fact the institution.[42]

New York Friends moved against the peculiar institution later than their New England brethren. As in earlier periods, they seem to have hung back, awaiting the actions of other yearly meetings. Perhaps New York delayed because it numbered fewer Friends than its neighbors to the north and south before the war. The New York epistle of 1759 indicates some effort that year to eliminate "the practice of dealing in Negroes and other Slaves." A minute was entered in the New York 1762 Discipline, but Friends there do not seem to have acted decisively against either slaveholding or trading, even though Flushing Monthly Meeting forced an acknowledgment out of Samuel Underhill in 1765 for importing Africans. Indeed, the situation in Philadelphia as described by Gary Nash for this period may have applied to New York as well. Not that antislavery Quakers were quiet, for the country Friends of Oblong Monthly Meeting pressed for the elimination of slaveholding in 1767. Slavery was inconsistent with Christianity, they said. New York Yearly Meeting sought delay: it was inconvenient to press the issue, it stated, because it would divide the Society, but the yearly meeting inserted a hortatory admonition designed to convince confirmed slaveholders to give up their human property, arguing that Negroes are rational creatures. Delay was only of short duration this time: perhaps the admonition and continued appeals worked, although there may have been a parallel to Philadelphia if the need for slave labor declined. In 1771 the yearly meeting prohibited sale of Negroes by all except guardians, executors, and administrators of estates who were, in any event, to seek the counsel of their monthly meetings before acting. Three years later, on the solicitation of Purchase Quarterly Meeting acting on a request for advice from Purchase Monthly Meeting, the yearly meeting required that all slaves be freed on attaining their majority (eighteen for women and twenty-one for men). There followed action by all monthly meetings until by 1782 New York Friends had freed almost all of their slaves—two slaves were still being held in a remote region two years later.[43]

Once they had acted to rid the Society of slavery, both New England and New York Friends turned to the legislatures of their respective states to enlarge the area of freedom. Sometimes alone, sometimes in partnership with other antislavery groups, they worked the political arena in one of the few areas still open to them. New York acted first to ease laws covering manumission of slaves. In addition to having the most severe of northern slave codes, New York also provided almost insurmountable obstacles to manumission. The slave code of 1717 had required two bonds of 200 pounds given by the master for each slave freed. A 1730 act retained the two 200-pound bonds, and there matters rested until after the War for Independence had broken out. In 1777, responding in part to Quaker solicitations, the state legislature eased requirements: if a master could prove the slave was under fifty, he could free the slave after obtaining a certificate from the overseers of the poor. The bill also represented partial success for opponents of the slave trade: the act forbade both the import and export of slaves. But this was as much as New York Friends and other antislavery proponents were able to get in the period before 1789.[44]

New England Friends were more successful in their efforts. They faced less opposition and less restrictive laws on manumission than did New Yorkers. Most of their antislavery lobbying was carried on by the New England Meeting for Sufferings, although in the year before its creation in 1775 the yearly meeting had petitioned the Rhode Island legislature to abolish slavery and slave trade. But the events of wartime prevented further action until after 1783, and by that time the meeting for sufferings had assumed all lobbying activities with state governments.[45]

After the Revolutionary War the meeting for sufferings followed the proddings and example of individuals like Moses Brown, who in 1783 sought to have the Rhode Island legislature prohibit the slave trade and abolish slavery in the state. On Brown's initiative the meeting for sufferings carried a petition to the Assembly in February 1784. It and non-Quaker abolition groups (some of which Friends joined) continued to press the legislature for abolition. Quakers and their antislavery allies succeeded in getting the Rhode Island Assembly to pass a law in 1784 which provided for gradual abolition. Three years later, responding to continuing pressure, the Assembly abolished the slave trade in Rhode Island. Quakers and other antislavery advocates managed to persuade the Massachusetts legislature to enact a law forbidding the trade in 1788. Quaker action there with regard to abolishing slavery itself had been obviated by a court decision in 1783 which declared that slavery had no basis in Massachusetts law. Quakers also lobbied in another New England state. Several antislavery groups, among them the meetings for sufferings of New England and New York, pressed Connecticut to abolish the peculiar institution, and Connecticut passed a law providing for the gradual abolition of slavery in 1784. But one must conclude that it did so largely because of antislavery activities within its borders not connected with Quakers.[46]

By 1789 Quakers in New England and New York had obtained substantial successes in ridding themselves and their states of the blemish of slavery. Only New York had not passed an abolition law. Lobbying had also been relatively successful in getting state laws which prohibited slave-trading voyages from northern ports. And Friends themselves maintained a creditable record in caring for their slaves after they were freed. But there was still much to be done: obtaining a national prohibition on the trade, freeing slaves elsewhere, and overcoming latent opposition within the Society to cooperation with outsiders in antislavery endeavors.

Part IV
Quakers in the World

Chapter 10
Economic and Social Conditions

THERE PROBABLY NEVER WAS a time when northern Friends bore a strong resemblance to one another in terms of wealth and social standing. In the 1650's the great divergence in wealth, among Friends and others, which characterized port cities in the eighteenth century had not developed, and the gap in social and economic standing between town and country Friends may not have existed to the degree it did in the ensuing century. Still, there was a substantial gap between wealthy and well-placed Quakers like William Coddington in Newport and Friends in Salem, most of whom lived in the marginal economy of Salem Woods. The separation then as later in terms of worldly status depended as much on location as on one's faith, with the heavy balance of wealth and talent lying with Rhode Islanders. Quakers in Plymouth Colony and on Long Island were the next notch down, and those in Salem were both the poorest and the ones who most clearly deviated from the customs of the community around them. These distinctions remained and widened in the next century and a half as colonial economies became more complex and specialized and as migration to new areas occurred. So great were the differences that despite the social and economic dissimilarity of Quakers of the original period, they, like other people in their communities, more closely resembled one another at the outset than at any other time. To speak of northern colonial Quakers is to refer not to a broad class of people who were of the same social rank, but to a narrow group that accepted and shared characteristic beliefs and practices—the unpaid ministry, silent worship, and testimonies against oaths, war, and, eventually, slavery. Thus to evaluate the social and economic standing of Quakers one must know something of their communities.[1]

Modern town studies of the communities in which Quakers lived in substantial numbers are still to come, but much can be inferred about Friends in the world from evidence of merchant Quakers—a group that left records but unfortunately was atypical of the non-Quakers around them—and from secondary sources relating to communities in which Friends lived. The method is fraught with problems, and future studies of localities where northern Friends lived—based on tax, estate, and similar records—may ultimately disprove assertions made here. All conclusions, then, are essentially tentative, but nonetheless necessary to fill out the account of Friends before 1790.

Throughout the colonial period, Newport Friends dominated the leadership of New England Yearly Meeting and comprised the largest group of wealthy merchants among northern Friends. In the seventeenth century men of wealth and influence like William Coddington, Nicholas Easton, Henry Bull, and Walter Clarke led their meeting and were governors of the colony. Ann Bull, who survived two husbands (Easton and Bull), sold land to Rhode Island Monthly Meeting which was subsequently divided into lots that provided quitrents to support assorted meeting activities both within the monthly meeting itself and the yearly meeting at large. In the eighteenth century Newporters continued to dominate monthly, quarterly, and yearly meetings. Thomas Richardson and the Quaker Wantons, John and Gideon, provided yearly meeting and colonial leadership. Their wealth and standing in the community derived from their international and intercolonial trading activities. Others with mercantile wealth, like Joseph Jacobs, though active in meeting affairs were less involved in political activities. Some Quaker merchants like Abraham Redwood were prominent in neither meeting nor political matters; Redwood was a faithful Friend until disowned for refusal to free his slaves.[2]

Tied closely to Newport wealth and on occasion resident there were the Hazards and Robinsons of the Narragansett country and Joseph Wanton, brother of Quaker John and Anglican William, a resident of Tiverton, who built ships, farmed, and traded, at least locally. Probably less well to do than the mercantile grandees of Newport, they were nevertheless among the wealthiest of their communities.[3]

Comprising the largest number of Friends in Newport and related communities on Aquidneck Island were a middling group. Quakers like Preserved Fish served actively on many committees, especially those of the monthly meeting. Less well connected in the intercolonial trade and uninvolved in transatlantic efforts, they were farmers in the country and artisans in town. If they lived in Portsmouth or Newport, it was to their homes that Friends from off the island came for hospitality at yearly meeting time, and frequently these Friends also helped guide visiting ministers to and from the island and occasionally provided shelter for them as well.

Few Quakers in the area were indigent, although in the colonial period there were always some. Efforts to help Quakers in straitened circumstances were made in the seventeenth century, but only from 1752, as noted, do Rhode Island Monthly Meeting records indicate a number of poor large enough to require a permanent committee. Consequently, it appears that Quakers on Aquidneck were predominantly of a middling group or higher, the latter group sapped by defections to the fashionable tastes of Newport's Anglican Trinity Church. Such as remained within Quakerism were probably better off than their neighbors. Indeed this general situation seems to have continued after the War for Independence, by which time Newport had lost its position of economic domination in Rhode Island to Providence, and Newport Friends their dominant position within the yearly meeting to Providence, Dartmouth, and Nantucket Quakers. It was in that period that residents of monthly meeting lots in Newport, originally part of Ann Bull's sale to the monthly meeting, refused to pay quitrents, a situation that helped reduce the capabilities of Newporters to dominate yearly meeting affairs. Significantly, few Friends were numbered among those resident on the lots: despite the relative decline of Newport, Quakers there remained somewhat better off than their neighbors.[4]

The town of New York had few Quakers in the seventeenth century, when most Friends lived in the vicinity of Flushing. Indeed, not until the middle of the eighteenth century did Quakers move to New York in sufficient numbers and with sufficient wealth for New York to become the dominant preparative meeting of Flushing Monthly Meeting. By that time the Murrays, for whom Murray Hill was named, had established themselves as substantial merchants, as had Edward Burling. But these men were never as powerful in New York mercantile affairs as were Newport Quaker merchants in the business of that town. Probably a majority of New York Friends, given the absence of extensive efforts for the Quaker poor there, were of the middling sort. Artisans and shopkeepers, they were thankful for the business received from non-Quaker political allies and business contacts. An example is the case of Joshua Delaplaine, a shopkeeper, artisan, and active member of the monthly, quarterly, and yearly meeting committees. In 1752 he was commissioned by Lewis Morris, Jr., to make a coffin for the mortal remains of Lewis' mother, Isabella, and he was happy to be of service, as he had in the past.[5]

Nantucket verged on an urban environment. The island could not produce sufficient food for itself on its marginal land and had to import foodstuffs and wood (both firewood and lumber). The principal economic activity was the whale fishery, cultivated in the eighteenth century, in which the Rotch family developed a major role. Although the Rotches gained wealth, apparently most Quaker Nantucketers did not. With the exception of Cumberland County (one of three counties then comprising Maine), Nantucket had more families per house (1.46) than any other Massachusetts county (the average was 1.20). This cramped situation for individual families had a parallel in land shortage, and in 1754 a conflict erupted between proprietors of the commons and residents who wanted a share. A long struggle followed, which Samuel Fothergill, the London Meeting for Sufferings, the New England Yearly Meeting, and the Massachusetts General Court proved unable to resolve.[6]

The resolution of Nantucket's economic difficulty came from two developments: migration and war. Migration was the solution for some seven families and six individuals who went to New Garden, North Carolina, in 1771 and 1772. An even larger number left the island after the War for Independence broke out. Most went to the Hudson River Valley in 1775 and 1776, until British occupation of New York City in July and August of the latter year eliminated ready access to the Hudson. Even wealthy Friends like the Rotches felt the straitened economic circumstances of Nantucket. During the Great War for the Empire, Joseph Rotch, the initial developer of that family's whaling fortune, moved to Dartmouth to provide a more secure environment for his whale fishery as well as, no doubt, a hinterland readily accessible for supplies. Driven from the town of New Bedford when the British burned it in 1778, the firm of Joseph Rotch and Sons was nonetheless a substantial enterprise, rivaling the Boston Hancock wealth according to tax reports of 1771, which cover only the Rotch Dartmouth interests, not those remaining on Nantucket. Even after the devastation of the War for Independence, Rotch wealth continued to be substantial in the young nation, especially when the Rotches returned to New Bedford. And their wealth in turn provided the means to exercise yearly meeting leadership much as the wealth of the Browns enabled Moses Brown of Providence to move into a leading position in New England Quaker affairs.[7]

Providence itself had relatively few Friends in the colonial period. Most Quakers were rural members of Smithfield Monthly Meeting. Probably most had small farms, but the convincement of Moses Brown in 1774 provided a member of both great wealth and talent and one who used both in helping to direct his new faith. With such as the Rotches he provided leadership at all levels of New England Quakerism for almost a half century thereafter. New England Quakerism would as a consequence be under a leadership with a substantially different location than the comfortable days under Newport domination, but a leadership with wealth and connections like its colonial counterpart.[8]

Salem Monthly Meeting had a longer history as part of an urban environment than Providence. Including Boston, Lynn, and Salem, it had mercantile Friends from the seventeenth century. Though not the wealthiest man in Salem in the late seventeenth and early eighteenth centuries, Thomas Maule was close to the top. On tax returns in 1689 and 1699, he was rated among the upper 2 percent in the former year and the upper 3 percent in the latter of all residents in the town. Daniel Zachary, Thomas Richardson, and Walter Newberry, residents of Boston, were also among the wealthiest merchants, but after 1715 there does not appear to have been a wealthy Quaker merchant in these towns. Well-to-do mercantile Friends probably found Dartmouth, Nantucket, and Newport more congenial in the colonial period, because there were more Friends there. In the territory of Salem Monthly Meeting, Friends in towns were apparently shopkeepers and artisans; others were farmers. None qualified for long-standing yearly meeting leadership, which inevitably centered on those whose means and business connections fitted them for larger responsibilities.

Country Friends were both more numerous and less influential than wealthy urban Quakers. An exception in the colonial period were those on Long Island. If they did not possess the wealth and social connections of Newport merchants, residents of Long Island like the Bownes and the Hickses were of sufficient means to serve actively on yearly meeting committees. Numerous in communities like Flushing, Oyster Bay, and Westbury during the colonial period, their numbers seem to have remained stable. Migration, especially to the Hudson River Valley and New York, seems to have been the way they avoided severe overpopulation of the available land. As for Quakers who did farm in Queens County, most were apparently well to do, with few interests beyond cultivating their lands.

Most Friends of South Kingston, East Greenwich, and Smithfield monthly meetings farmed. If fortunate enough to live on fertile Narragansett land like some of the Robinsons and Hazards, they tended to be wealthy; those in Westerly, Rhode Island, Uxbridge, Massachusetts, and similar agricultural areas were less well off if the conclusions of Jackson Turner Main about those areas for all residents also apply to Quakers, as they seem to do.[9]

In the southeastern Massachusetts monthly meetings of Dartmouth, Sandwich, Scituate, and Swansea, most Friends probably farmed, at least until the Rotch interests built up their whale fishery in Dartmouth. Some may have possessed substantial wealth, but the vast majority were probably like Micajah Ruggles in the next century, whose marriage to Lydia Rodman set Newport and Philadelphia Quaker grandees and their wives gossiping because as the wife of a mere farmer she could not have servants and would have to do her own manual labor. So difficult was it for young

Friends in the land-short villages in this area that they migrated to the Hudson River Valley in numbers only slightly inferior to those who left Nantucket.[10]

Few Quakers from Salem north had significant wealth. Before 1789 the share of yearly meeting collections from these Friends was always low compared to meetings to the south—a fairly accurate indication of relative wealth among Quakers for, much as Newport dominated collections before 1775, Dartmouth, New Bedford, and Providence did after that date. Friends of Hampton and Dover were farmers, probably a good deal like the folk John Greenleaf Whittier later remembered and quite unlike wealthy merchants of urban centers. But this was an area of population growth to which Friends from Nantucket north moved from late in the colonial period. Ultimately, some of them would prosper, although they would not rival their coreligionists to the south in wealth.[11]

The area of greatest growth in the late colonial period and the recipient of most Quaker migrants was the Hudson River Valley. Friends had started moving up the Hudson in the second quarter of the eighteenth century. One attraction was the good land in the Oblong, by chance available in fee simple to those who went there, unlike nearby communities in New York which were open to settlement only on the basis of a lease from the owner of one of the large tracts there. Quakers who moved from Rhode Island, Long Island, and Massachusetts prospered on Quaker Hill and nearby communities. By 1750 they were being joined by Friends from land-short areas, especially southeastern Massachusetts and Nantucket, who were unable to found new towns on the Massachusetts frontier because they would have had to build a Congregational meeting house and call a Congregational minister. In the land-short New England communities, possession of land was a social ideal, but the possibility of realizing that ideal in home communities, at least for junior lines of families, was increasingly remote. A steady migration of people after 1750 quickened in the 1770's and became a flood in 1775, especially to Nine Partners Monthly Meeting.[12]

As with any area to which there has been recent migration, especially under distressed conditions, the circumstances of these people varied considerably. Some in Oblong Monthly Meeting were well-to-do farmers and tradesmen. Like Daniel Merritt, for some years clerk of that meeting and a successful shopkeeper, they had not experienced privation, at least in peacetime. Some had trading connections with New York City Friends and with them, or on their own, speculated in Vermont lands. A breakdown of occupations according to the incomplete registration of Friends in Dutchess County in 1755 indicates that farmers predominated—twenty-seven of the forty-nine listed. Other occupations numbered nine laborers, five blacksmiths, two shoemakers, one carpenter, one weaver, and one tailor. As two laborers were clearly sons of farmers listed and five others may have been farmers' or craftsmen's sons, the likelihood of a large laboring class among Friends in Dutchess County, like the older towns in southeastern Massachusetts, is remote (farmers' sons were likely to inherit farms, and craftsmen's sons probably would acquire their fathers' trade). Friends of the more recently settled lands of Nine Partners Monthly Meeting and, after their creation, the monthly meetings to the north had less wealth, depending on how recent were their migration and the conditions under which they made the move. Like Zebulon Hoxie and others of fame in "Fierce Feathers" (see above, page 141), their circumstances on the frontier cannot have been luxurious. They probably did not, however, know privation. By comparison, those who left Nantucket and other parts of southeastern Massachusetts in 1775 and 1776 must have suffered extreme hardship, at least for their first years in the vicinity of meetings from Nine Partners north. Having left from an area where at best they could have had a marginal economic existence, they moved into a country new to them without the advantage of substantial prior planning, and a country isolated by British forces at the mouth of the Hudson. It could not have been easy to start new lives. The shock of their move and the bitterness of their experience in their old homes at least partially accounts for the difference in disownment patterns between Nine Partners and Oblong monthly meetings.[13]

By the 1780's Friends were settled over wide areas. Whereas just two generations earlier they had been confined essentially to coastal areas from Maine to New York with only modest penetration into the Oblong, they had now moved into the back country under the twin pressures of war and economic privation in older areas. Accompanying this geographic expansion was a shift in centers of wealth and worldly influence. Newport declined as a center, to be replaced by newer areas of New England Quaker wealth. New York City was also to be a center of growing Quaker wealth, although, as should be obvious, Friends hardly dominated there as they would for almost half a century in New Bedford. If the Quaker wealthy were to be found in the cities, so were the poor. In the country Friends ranged from moderately well-to-do farmers like Elias Hicks of Jericho to those who had recently had to move from poverty-stricken areas to frontier settlements. For all that they had recently experienced in common during both their own reform and the American Revolution, Quakers in the northern yearly meetings, like other residents of those states, had by this time probably less in common with one another than at any time since the first Quaker missionaries came to the northern colonies in the seventeenth century.

Chapter 11
Retrospect and Prospect

BY THE TIME OF THE ADOPTION of the Constitution and the institution of Congress and the President, Quakerism from New York north had undergone substantial changes. Some of them one might have expected as the militant movement of the seventeenth century ossified. The chance of Friends behaving in the abusive manner of Humphrey Norton in New Haven and Plymouth had passed by the end of the third decade of the eighteenth century, when Friends had secured both relief from church taxes in New England and a measure of respect from such old adversaries as the Mathers and the SPG. The dissenters from the established ways had turned out to be respectable. Attainment of respectability found a counterpart in continued growth, which almost matched expansion of the population at large in the first half of the eighteenth century. No apparent widespread concern for abandonment of participation in the affairs of the world mark this period. Nor can one detect a drive for reform among these northern Friends. Reform when it came was imported, though it was sometimes popular locally, especially among the younger, influential Friends. But it served to jolt the northern yearly meetings from continued accommodation to the world. In the long run it also helped to stimulate doctrinal apprehensions.

It is paradoxical that reform did so. In the period of accommodation in the 1720's and 1730's, Friends seem to have been eager to point up their doctrinal respectability much as outsiders like Cotton Mather were able to accept their belief in the seed of God within all. The concern to exhibit a doctrinal orthodoxy seems to have survived the period of reform, at least among the most influential Friends at the time. It may have been stimulated by conflicts in other churches brought about by the Great Awakening in the 1740's and the later decline in religious fervor among the older churches which accompanied the era of the American Revolution. No doubt the debate about unitarian beliefs like Joseph Priestley's in England at the beginning of the French Revolution and the attempt to shore up orthodoxy by proponents of the New Divinity in New England made an impact. So did convincement of people from other churches, like David Sands of Nine Partners Monthly Meeting, who probably helped maintain an already developed concern for doctrinal orthodoxy. It is impossible to measure precisely the influence of each of these factors, but it is likely that each was present to some extent in the thrust toward orthodoxy.[1]

If there was such a thrust, toward the end of the period under consideration here there also developed a drive to reaffirm traditional Quakerism. Whether consciously developed or not, the effect was ultimately the same: a debate over doctrine within the Society of Friends, which began at the end of the period under study. The debate ultimately pointed to the schisms within American Quakerism in the third decade of the nineteenth century, although, as Robert Doherty and others have pointed out, there was more to these schisms than just a struggle over doctrine. Representative of the reassertion of traditional Quaker views was the onetime schoolmaster and recognized minister of Providence, Job Scott.[2]

Scott was a convinced Friend. Smithfield Monthly Meeting accepted his application for membership in 1773. He became a recognized minister the next year and thereafter appeared in his own and neighboring meetings and traveled in the ministry from Maine to the Carolinas in North America and to the British Isles in 1792 and 1793.[3]

Scott early betrayed signs of the enthusiastic convert. We have already noted his uncompromising pacifism; he also refused to accept continental currency. When Isaac Backus, the Baptist minister in Middleborough, Massachusetts, published in 1777 the first volume of his *History of New England with Particular Reference to the Denomination of Baptists*, Scott wanted to publish a reply defending early Friends wronged, he thought, by Backus' version of events. Cooler heads prevailed in the meeting for sufferings, and after extended negotiations Backus published a retraction of some of his statements and recommended the Quaker version of events for those who wanted it. Like earlier disagreements with the Rogerenes, Baptists and Quakers differed, but not to the extent of an open and bitter confrontation. The exchange could not have been satisfactory to Scott, however, and his views on this and on pacifism presaged a man who could and would carry traditional Quaker beliefs to extremes.[4]

During his trips in the ministry outside New England, especially on his second trip to the South in 1789, Scott first set forth his novel interpretation of traditional Quaker beliefs. He had always stressed the mystical side of Quakerism—namely, the necessity of following the leadings of the Inward Light. In 1786 he began to branch off in new directions, stressing the universality of Christ and the emptiness of religion unless

one could encourage Christ to grow within. This effort must be man's; as
Scott put it, "he that will *reign with Christ, must suffer with him;* must drink
the cup he drank of, *be baptized* with the baptism *he was baptized with . . .*"
For Scott, Christ must be born again in man, and each man must suffer a
death of natural beliefs. Scott went even farther by attacking the doctrine
of imputation, which implied that salvation should be given to natural
men simply because Jesus had been crucified.[5]

Although Scott's statements had ties with older Quaker beliefs, by the
1790's his sentiments were making some Friends nervous. But they were
not the only reasons for future Orthodox Friends to be concerned. Sometime, either during or shortly after his second southern visit, Scott
launched into some variations on the old Quaker theme of the Inward
Light, or seed of God, leading to spiritual rebirth. He carried the doctrine further by arguing that eternal Christ had to be born in all men and
the natural man crucified. To be saved, one had to put off the old Adam
and have Christ born again in oneself. For, Scott put it, when Christ was
born in converted men, "the souls in whom he is begotten and brought
forth, are all in the relation of parent to him, as well as brethren and sis-
ters." He continued: "In the production of this conception, generation,
and birth there is both Father and mother. He that begets, is the only
possible *Father* of the only *begotten.* The soul in whom this conception and
birth is effected, is the mother." More than that, to Scott the body of
historic Jesus was no more than a temple that had received the eternal
Christ, much as people in earlier and later ages had been saved. Scott
never, strictly speaking, denied the divinity of the historic Christ, but by
stressing continual crucifixion, salvation, and baptism, he challenged in
explicit terms what traditional Christian churches upheld as accepted
doctrine. He carried to extremes the beliefs which critics had always
maintained were basic to Quakers and which Friends had in some fashion
or other denied publicly for a century.[6]

By the late 1780's Scott had arrived at a position within the mystical
tradition of eighteenth-century Quaker preachers, but it was a position
that was becoming increasingly unpopular. In the same period he attacked the doctrine of the Trinity, much as had many of the prophetic
seventeenth-century Friends, though perhaps more explicitly. The Trinity, to him had no basis—Scriptural or otherwise. To suggest there were
separate persons, part of the godhead, was to him an absurdity. Belief in
the Trinity was absurd for it was of worldly wisdom, not inspired by God.
To Scott "this wisdom reads 'there are three that bear record in heaven,'
and will have it, these are *three distinct persons in one God*; and rivers of
human blood have been shed in consequence of the contentions that have
been about this mystery! As they handle it, they advance natural flesh and

blood to divinity; they deify a person of shape and dimensions, and look for his coming, as such, to judgement. They make in short *three Gods*; and yet say there is one God!" Yet Scott was no deist; he emphasized experiential Christianity, the Christianity of divine inspiration, not of reason. He objected to the Trinity because it was not grounded in the mystical form of Christianity he preached. To Scott, salvation could come only when the eternal Christ was born in man, and that occurred only in persons who nurtured the seed of God within them. Christ was not a distinct person with historical significance, enjoying an existence separate from God, and to speak of Him and the Trinity in such a manner, wrote Scott, "is as dark as Egyptian darkness, to talk of three eternal persons in the only one God. He is one forever. . . . There is no twain in him. . . . Thus [Christ] and the Father are one." [7]

About the same time that Scott arrived at these beliefs, some Friends began to oppose his statements openly. Whether the opposition formed as a result of his new positions, the influence of evangelical Christianity, the fear of beliefs similar to deists, or all of these factors is uncertain. It is clear, however, that some Friends felt uneasy about letting him leave New England for a religious visit to the British Isles and Ireland. For a time two of them in Smithfield Monthly Meeting opposed his application for a certificate. Eventually, however, they relented, and he received his certificate to go to England. Once there he apparently set forth his views on the Trinity and atonement and, of course, encountered considerable criticism. Crossing to Ireland in the summer of 1793, he met with a much friendlier reception and continued to preach in the same vein as he had since 1789. [8]

Probably only a few Friends in Providence and elsewhere in the New England Yearly Meeting had objected to Scott's position at first. Their objections paralleled a similar uneasiness expressed by New York Quakers and indicated growth of the long-standing doctrinal tension within Quakerism. For by 1790 Quakerism was taking on a more evangelical cast.

An indication of objection to Scott's doctrinal writings came when he submitted a manuscript on baptism to his meeting for sufferings in May 1792. Although he said little that went beyond what many Friends had been saying throughout the century, he did talk of Christ's birth in man instead of merely upholding the Quaker position against water baptism. Scott's talk of Christ's growing in man bothered many of the members of the meeting for sufferings. An alarmed Moses Brown wrote Edmund Prior of the New York Meeting for Sufferings: "Our friend Job Scott has Written a piece on the Subject of Baptism began when he was to the Southward" and requested Prior's opinion of the manuscript. Brown thought that "the part more Imediately on the Subject of Baptism will doubtless be approved[,] the other which respects more particular the Doctrine of the Seed being the same in all as in Christ . . . will Require great Delicacy to be press [published] so as not to wound some Tender people."[9]

The problem of printing difficult doctrinal sections did not arise at this time, for Scott agreed to changes in his manuscript and elimination of objectionable parts before sailing for Ireland, and in February 1793 the New England Meeting for Sufferings ordered 2,000 copies of *The Baptism of Christ a Gospel Ordinance*. Happily, Scott made the revision, for two months later the New York Meeting for Sufferings objected to sections Moses Brown had referred to and asked to have a hand in checking the manuscript. Apparently New York was satisfied with the result, for there is no correspondence extant indicating the meeting's displeasure over the published version.[10]

The problems created by Scott's views were forerunners of later difficulties in both New England and New York. The censorious spirit to be found in many dealings to keep the Society pure in outward behavior must have had its counterpart in a drive for spiritual uniformity. Both decline in numbers and doctrinal divisions were well established by 1790; that a schism would ultimately arise in an American environment where other churches had split and would continue to do so was a certainty unless tendencies already established could be reversed.[11]

A happier development was the growth of women's participation in Quaker activities. Quakers had always been well ahead of the community at large in encouraging women in church affairs. Jeanette Gadt has argued that the preaching of Quaker women ministers was an essential ingredient in the initial hysteria with which New England Puritan leaders greeted Friends. Hostility on that basis was still to be found when Mary Weston visited Connecticut in 1750, much as the issue of women ministers still encounters opposition in some churches today. In that regard, early Friends advanced the feminist cause before it was organized. But Quakers had a long way to go before equality could be achieved.[12]

It was not as ministers that Quaker women eventually saw to the extension of their importance within Quakerism, but in meetings for business. Women's meetings for business had apparently existed from the time when Fox and Burnyeat helped to establish the structure of the business meeting, but not until the eighteenth century did women begin to take an active role. In the era of the American Revolution they generally participated on an equal footing with men, but not until 1771 did Smithfield Monthly Meeting permit women to make the initial decision on accepting or disowning women members. In New York, the extension of rights came even later: women elders were not appointed in that yearly meeting until 1749. Frequently men's meetings came to the assistance of the women, and while women in Flushing did sign the disownment of one of their number in 1772, a man read it at the end of a worship meeting. It was 1781 before this yearly meeting required men's and women's meetings to concur in disownments. Women had obtained equality in most matters by the nineteenth century in all but having their names commemorated in schisms—perhaps a sign of continued male domination despite an otherwise much more open church government than was to be found in other denominations. By then, any acts of a meeting for business had to have the concurrence of both the men's and women's meetings.[13]

Another harbinger of nineteenth-century Quakerism was the effort to establish schools. The attempt was a part of the effort to reform the Society by erecting walls against the rest of the world. After the Revolutionary War, Friends placed special emphasis on having their children educated only by Quakers. They could see the effects of youthful exuberance in the many defections and disownments during and after the Revolution. In addition to rigorous dealing with offenders, they saw a solution to declension in a guarded education of Quaker children to keep the "blessed youth" from the corrupting temptations and snares of the world.[14]

The idea of separate schools was not new to Quakers. New England Friends had sought without success to have all meetings maintain schools since institution of the 1708 queries. Some meetings had from time to time established schools, and occasionally individual Friends kept school and provided what the yearly meeting considered desirable tuition. Rhode Island was the first monthly meeting to support a school. It founded a monthly meeting school in 1703—it had permitted Christian Lodowick to use the Newport meeting house as a schoolhouse until his disownment in 1691. But even this meeting had been unable to keep a school continuously in operation in the colonial period. Occasionally it imported teachers from England, and it even built a schoolhouse in Newport in 1703. By 1771, however, the monthly meeting had given up educational efforts and used the schoolhouse as a home for poor Friends.[15]

Other monthly meetings were not as successful in establishing schools. Most of them made no effort at all. Dartmouth and Nantucket monthly meetings may have established schools, but it is unlikely. That one Nantucket Friend, Joseph Rotch, paid Timothy White, the Congregational minister, to teach his children in the 1740's indicates there was no meeting school there. Elsewhere records show no attempts to have meeting schools, and if Quaker children received any formal training in a school, they obtained it either from a Quaker who taught in a nonsectarian school or from a person of another faith. They were forbidden to attend other sectarian schools, but this rule was probably honored as much in the breach as in the observance.[16]

Most training in elementary subjects must have been either carried on in the home or offered by a master as part of an apprenticeship. Such an informally organized education was sufficient in the colonial period. Most Friends farmed, and few of them needed formal education. For that reason the little training in writing for most Quaker children probably was based on George Fox's *Primers* and similar Quaker books.[17]

Reform of the Society, increasing demand for a formal education, and the effect of the Revolution changed the educational efforts and outlook of Friends. With urban growth, the little knowledge acquired in dame schools and in a master's home was unlikely to be sufficient to train young men for business. More important, however, was the Quaker commitment to erect a hedge against the corrupting influences of the world's people. Thus meeting schools became essential for Quakers. As the yearly meeting observed, a guarded education was necessary to maintain the sect in the times of decline occasioned by the Revolution.[18]

Accordingly, Quakers sought to provide educational facilities at every level of meeting. At the urging of Smithfield Monthly Meeting, which Moses Brown had inspired to promote the subject, the yearly meeting decided in 1779 that Quakers should be more concerned with the long-neglected subject of raising and educating children. As a result of a hortatory yearly meeting epistle that year, East Greenwich and Sandwich monthly meetings established committees to check possibilities of founding schools, and Nantucket Monthly Meeting set up a committee to check on the schooling Quaker children received on the island. Unfortunately, little could be accomplished in 1779: funds were short; some monthly meetings such as East Greenwich were too small and members too scattered to maintain schools; and many Friends who might have taught school had recently been disowned.[19]

Accordingly, to meet the shortage of teachers the yearly meeting in 1780 yielded to Moses Brown's exhortations and decided to establish a yearly meeting school. Financial difficulties prevented its opening until 1784 when Rhode Island Monthly Meeting pledged quitrent income from its lots in Newport in return for which the yearly meeting located the school in Portsmouth, Rhode Island. But collection of quitrents proved to be virtually impossible, and since other sources of financial support were lacking—distant meetings were not inclined to give liberally to the school's support—the yearly meeting decided to close the school in

1788 until more favorable economic conditions permitted its reopening.[20]

New York Friends also made only limited efforts for Quaker education in the colonial period. Flushing Monthly Meeting took several uncertain steps early in the eighteenth century. In 1703 the meeting sought a lot on which to build a schoolhouse. Six years later Thomas Making kept a school, but it is doubtful if there were any other efforts before 1775— extant records contain no indication of the continuation of this concern. Finally the effect of reform caught up with New York Friends. Philadelphia Quakers seem to have been the source of the idea of setting up a school in 1779. The next year New York Yearly Meeting urged establishment of Quaker schools on its subordinate meetings.[21]

Considering that the recommendation came during the war years, the response of subordinate meetings was heartening, even though some of them were not able to begin operating their own schools before 1790. Flushing Monthly Meeting wrote England and Ireland for a schoolmaster, but with little success. By 1787, however, the meeting had a school in New York. Westbury had greater success. In 1781 that meeting planned to build a schoolhouse of modest size (18 by 24 feet), but had to defer action because there were no workmen available. In 1782 one school was in operation when potential disaster struck. Appalling at any time, in this period of rigid Quaker observance of propriety, the misbehavior of a leading Friend was doubly embarrassing. The Westbury Quaker schoolmaster, a recognized minister and onetime yearly meeting clerk, had himself disowned and the cause of a guarded education set back because of his indecent handling of some little girls in his charge. But Quaker schooling survived in this monthly meeting off and on: in 1784 there were two schools; in 1786 there were none when Bethpage Friends decided to build one; in 1789 Jericho Friends decided to hold school sessions in their meeting house. Quaker meetings in the Hudson Valley were less successful, no doubt, at least in part, for want of funds. Though some Friends taught school, there was no school for Quaker children run by a meeting. A guarded education for the Hudson Valley Quakers had to await the establishment of a yearly meeting school.[22]

These humanitarian activities of the Society also provided happy relief to an otherwise bleak outlook for northern Friends in 1789, but there was much left undone. True, Quakers had eliminated slavery from their ranks and had effectively lobbied to eliminate slavery in New England. They had fought the good fight, although success eluded them on the national level and in New York. But it was not in freeing slaves and ending the slave trade that they had to make progress. It remained for them to overcome their long-standing prejudices against both blacks and Indians, prejudices that had delayed helpful actions for Indians in their states.

Quakers had exhibited sympathy for Indians during King Philip's War, but that sympathy did not endure. In King William's and Queen Anne's Wars, Quakers north of Salem probably suffered just as much as did other members of their communities, despite occasional rhetoric to the contrary. The 1706 New England Yearly Meeting epistle to London Yearly Meeting showed little affection for "The Barbarous Indians— assaulting Killing and Captivating" English colonists thereby ending growth of Quaker numbers north of Salem for the time being. Also instructive was the case of Elizabeth Hanson, taken captive by Indians in August 1725. The Indians killed two of her children before her eyes and some of the men treated her brutally before she was finally released to the French. After his second visit to America, Samuel Bownas repeated her tale, with the evident approval of Friends on both sides of the Atlantic. Indians were thought by Quakers in the northern yearly meetings to be less than civilized. Nor had that view changed appreciably when in 1768 South Kingston Monthly Meeting petitioned the Rhode Island Assembly for a law to prohibit disturbances at the annual Quaker general meeting near South Kingston by "Disorderly People Black Tawnies & others." The tawnies were almost certainly Narragansett Indians, the blacks either slaves or freedmen. That South Kingston was a prime mover in the New England Quaker antislavery movement did not prevent Friends there from seeking help to control obstreperous unequals, free or not. The Rhode Island Assembly complied. The following year there was no disturbance. Where South Kingston was concerned, it was one thing to seek freedom for blacks, quite another to treat blacks and Indians as equals. It would be another twenty-five years (1793) before New York Friends began actively to assist Indians and thirty (1798) before New England would adopt the same concern.[23]

This is not to suggest that Quaker efforts for Indians and people of African descent were false and hypocritical. Far from it. Quakers as a group were well in advance of other churches in their assistance of slave and freed peoples, except in membership and proselytizing, where they were notably deficient. Even in 1815, forty-five years after the New England Quaker decision to free slaves, Newport Friend Stephen Wanton Gould reported both the novelty and for some Friends the feelings of apprehension of dining with someone not of European extraction. "Brother Paul Cuffee [a Westport Massachusetts Quaker shipmaster whose parents were Negro and Indian].—it appeared to be a new experience to most of the company to sit down to a table & eat with a man of colour, but however I am glad to insert that none were displeased & with some it was rather gratifying to have it to say that they had had the opportunity to be with him." For all that they had done for Indians and blacks, only rarely, in cases like that of Paul Cuffe, would Friends mix with either group on an equal footing.[24]

Friends had, in short, come a long way in the approximately 130 years they had been in these northern states. From persecuted and detested zealots, they had developed an important place for themselves in most communities, until they withdrew from the responsibility for political office. But even if they had instituted a reform that had already begun to depopulate the Society, even if they would soon divide over doctrine, they still continued efforts to reform the world in 1790 as they had in 1656, a world which by 1790 had changed the context in which they would have to operate—a new nation and a republic—much as they themselves had altered, from a militant group to one that would seek, without violence, to change the world for the better.

Appendices

Appendix A

Rhode Island Quarterly Meeting Representatives to the Yearly Meeting, 1710–1775

Number of years served	Number of representatives	Representatives first appointed before 1740
1	43	18
2	26	5
3	19	9
4	17	11
5	7	3
6	8	2
7	4	4
8	2	1
9	5	3
10	3	2
13	1	1
18	2	2
21	1	1
25	1	1
29	1	1
32	1	1

Appendix B

New England Yearly Meeting Committee Members in Charge of Writing Epistles to London, New York, and Philadelphia Yearly Meetings, 1710–1775

Number of years on the committee	Number of committee members
1	38
2	15
3	11
4	2
5	6
6	3
7	1
8	1
9	1
10	1
11	
12	4
13	2
14	1
15	
16	2
28	1

Members serving ten or more years	Number of years
Thomas Rodman	12
Thomas Richardson	28
John Wanton	13
William Anthony	10
John Casey	12
Clark Rodman	13
Joseph Jacob	16
Christopher Townshend	12
William Lake	12
Abraham Barker	14

Appendix C

Marriages, New England and New York

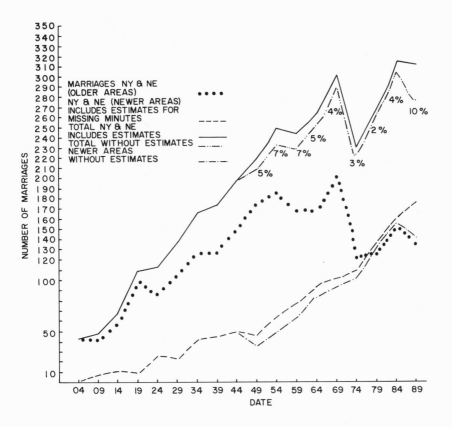

Appendix D

Dealings, Acknowledgments, and Disownments,
Rhode Island Monthly Meeting

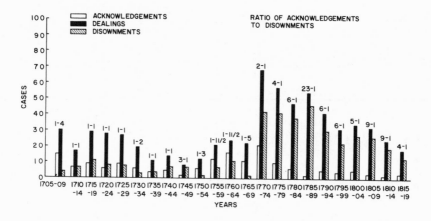

Appendix E

Marital Cases in Older and Newer Areas

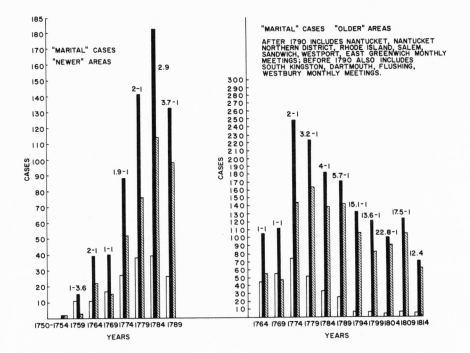

Appendix F

Total Dealings, New England and New York

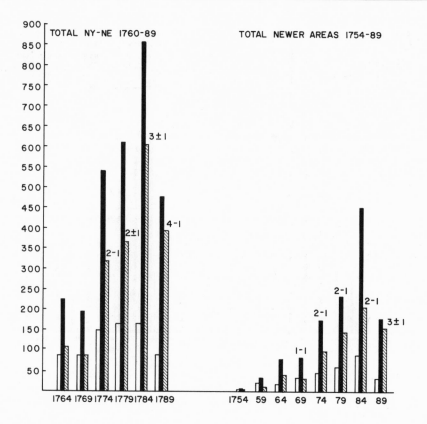

Appendix G

Total Dealings, New England Older Areas

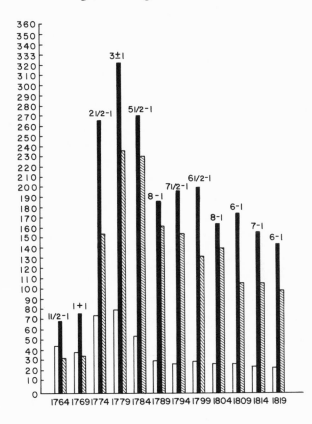

Appendix H

Dealings, Oblong and Nine Partners Monthly Meetings

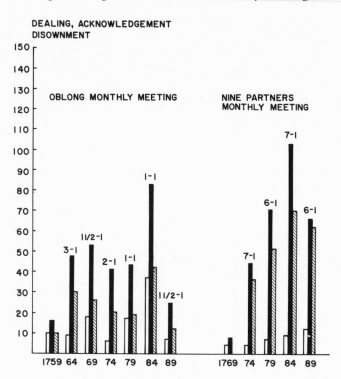

Appendix I

Dealings, New York

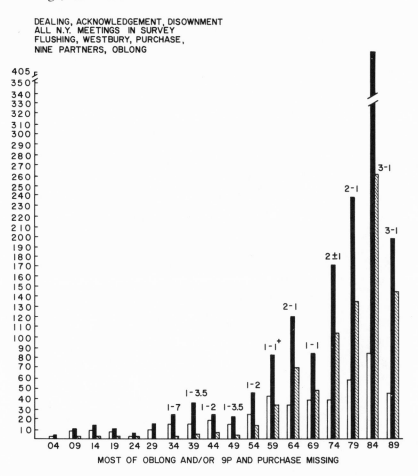

DEALING, ACKNOWLEDGEMENT, DISOWNMENT
ALL N.Y. MEETINGS IN SURVEY
FLUSHING, WESTBURY, PURCHASE,
NINE PARTNERS, OBLONG

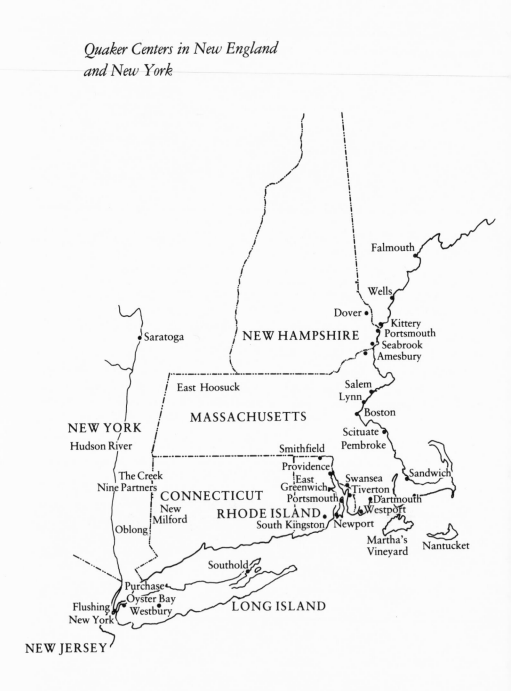

*Quaker Centers in New England
and New York*

Falmouth

Wells

Dover

Saratoga   NEW HAMPSHIRE   Kittery
                                        Portsmouth
                                        Seabrook
                                        Amesbury

                                        Salem
East Hoosuck   Lynn

            MASSACHUSETTS   Boston

NEW YORK   Scituate
Hudson River   Pembroke

                        Smithfield
                        Providence   Sandwich
The Creek   East   Swansea
Nine Partners   Greenwich   Tiverton
                        Portsmouth   Dartmouth
CONNECTICUT   RHODE ISLAND   Westport
        New   Newport
        Milford   South Kingston
Oblong
                                    Martha's   Nantucket
                                    Vineyard

                        Southold
Purchase
Flushing   Oyster Bay
New York   Westbury   LONG ISLAND

NEW JERSEY

Bibliographical Essay

THE BEST SOURCES FOR Quaker history from the last quarter of the seventeenth century are the records of business meetings. They detail most basic decisions affecting the members, as well as how the decisions were implemented. Although there are gaps, the historian nevertheless has a remarkably complete record.

Most New England Quaker records are in the custody of the Rhode Island Historical Society, in Providence. The most useful are the minutes of the yearly meeting; they show how decisions were reached, and the attempts to make subordinate meetings comply with yearly meeting dicta. Quarterly meeting minutes are less useful but provide essential information on how Friends relayed decisions and sometimes made them at this level. Monthly meeting minutes are the best source for how members treated one another.

Most of the extant monthly meeting records are housed with the yearly meeting collection. Exceptions are the minutes of Rhode Island Monthly Meeting, in the keeping of the Newport Historical Society; the Nantucket Monthly Meeting, with the Nantucket Historical Society; and the minutes of Falmouth and Dover Monthly Meetings, with the Maine Historical Society—all of which I read on microfilm at the Rhode Island Historical Society. Dartmouth Monthly Meeting minutes are in a bank vault in New Bedford, but I was able to read a transcript through 1790 in the yearly meeting archives. Minutes of the meeting for sufferings are also with the yearly meeting collection, as are assorted papers dating for the most part after 1750.

New York Yearly Meeting records are in the Haviland Records Room of the New York Yearly Meeting headquarters in New York City. These records before 1750 are much less valuable than New England's. There was little difference between yearly meeting and subordinate monthly and quarterly meetings before 1720, and from that date until 1746 the minutes are lost. After 1750 the minutes of the New York Yearly Meeting are the equal of New England's. Also incomplete for New York are quarterly meeting minutes. Westbury Quarterly Meeting minutes are missing from 1720, important years for a key quarterly meeting, although the ones from Purchase (from 1745) and Nine Partners (from 1783) are extant. Monthly meeting records also have major gaps—Purchase

from 1746 to 1772 and Oblong before 1757. Despite these omissions, the minutes serve well to demonstrate that the New York Quaker organization differed
from New England before the era of reform and in some cases resisted reform in
ways not detected for New England. Also useful are the minutes of the meeting
for sufferings for the years 1758 to 1761 and from 1774. Holdings of mis-
cellaneous manuscripts and correspondence are not as extensive for this yearly
meeting as for New England.

Holdings in other Quaker archives proved useful. Friends House Library in
London contains manuscript collections vital to the study of early Quakers, especially the Swarthmore manuscripts. Also to be found there are correspondence
of English Friends, and correspondence and minutes of the London Meeting for
Sufferings and the London Yearly Meeting. The Friends Historical Library of
Swarthmore College and the Quaker Collection of Haverford College also have
important material, especially the manuscripts of Job Scott at Swarthmore.

Correspondence and other personal papers of northern Friends is scattered in
several collections, most of it pertaining to New England Friends. The Old
Dartmouth Historical Society in New Bedford, Massachusetts, contains the
Rotch papers, as does the Massillon Public Library in Massillon, Ohio. Although most of these records pertain to the period following this study, many
are useful for an understanding of what Friends thought was important in the
late eighteenth century. Also useful for the Rotches and their relatives and
friends are the papers held by Henry Wood, II, of Boston and Newport and
S. A. G. Smith of Philadelphia and Newport. Papers of Moses Brown are in the
Rhode Island Historical Society and are essential for late eighteenth-century
antislavery and the onset of doctrinal differences. The few papers of Joshua Delaplaine and the account book of Daniel Merritt in the New York Historical
Society provide a limited view of day-to-day activities of two prominent eighteenth-century Friends.

Pamphlet literature on early Friends is immense. Among the most useful are
George Bishop, *New England Judged* . . . (London, 1661 and 1667), the basic
Quaker source from the seventeenth century as Joseph Besse, *A Collection of the
Sufferings of the People Called Quakers* . . . (2 vols., London, 1753) is for an eigh-
teenth-century view of Quaker beginnings. John Norton's *The Heart of New En-
gland Rent* . . . (Cambridge, Mass., 1659) provides the initial New England
Puritan response. For other works recording early Quaker debates, notes for the
first three chapters should be consulted.

There are many useful official records. The *Calendar of State Papers, Colonial
Series* (London, 1860–   ), contains ample information from 1698 through
1730 on the struggle against church taxes in Massachusetts. The series is reliable, although for this study I checked relevant sections against the documents in
the Public Record Office in London. Less reliable is John Russell Bartlett's edition of the *Records of the Colony of Rhode Island and Providence Plantations in New
England* (10 vols., Providence, 1856–65). For Massachusetts in the seventeenth
century there is Nathaniel B. Shurtleff, ed., *Records of the Governor and Company
of Massachusetts* (5 vols., Boston, 1853–54), a source not replicated for the eigh-

teenth century. For that century there are a variety of printed sources mentioned in the notes, such as the journals of the General Court and the formal correspondence of colonial governors. David Pulsifer, ed., *Records of the Colony of Plymouth in New England* (12 vols., Boston, 1855–61) serves admirably for that colony, as does Nathaniel Bouton, ed., *Provincial Documents and Records Relating to the Province of New Hampshire . . .* (12 vols., Concord, 1867–83). Charles Hoadly edited both the *Public Records of Connecticut* (15 vols., Hartford, 1850–90) and *Records of the Colony of New Haven from May 1653, to the Union* (Hartford, 1858). *The Documentary History of the State of New York* (3 vols., Albany, 1847–50) and *Documents Relative to the Colonial History of the State of New York* (15 vols., New York, 1856–87), both edited by E. B. O'Callaghan, and *Ecclesiastical Records of the State of New York* (7 vols., Albany, 1901–16), edited by Hugh Hastings, are essential for the early years of New York Quakers.

For the most part I did not consult manuscript sources of local and provincial governments, but these sources are available and would be particularly useful for town studies involving dissenters, an effort in which I have become engaged since completing research for the present volume. Researchers unable to use these records in the East will find, as I have, the microfilm collections of the Church of Jesus Christ of Latter Day Saints in Salt Lake City very helpful. For a modest charge these collections can be borrowed for use in L. D. S. branch libraries.

Of the many monographs on Quaker history, Sydney V. James, *A People among Peoples: Quaker Benevolence in Eighteenth-Century America* (Cambridge, Mass., 1963) is an invaluable introduction to Quakers and a resource for names and locations of primary sources. Though we differ on several points, primarily because James wrote before the era of quantification and I have been modestly affected by it, his book is essential reading for anyone interested in the colonial Quakers. Equally important in helping me place colonial Friends in context was J. William Frost's *The Quaker Family in Colonial America: A Portrait of the Society of Friends* (New York, 1973). Rufus Jones, et al., *The Quakers in the American Colonies*, first published in 1911 (I used the 1966 New York reprint) is a study written mostly by Jones, a leading Friend at the beginning of this century, with assistance from Isaac Sharpless and Amelia Gummere. The work is now dated, and the present volume replaces Jones's sections dealing with New England and New York.

For Quaker origins Hugh Barbour, *The Quakers in Puritan England* (New Haven, 1964) is the place to start. Christopher Hill, *The World Turned Upside Down: Radical Ideas during the English Revolution* (New York, 1972) and Michael R. Watts, *The Dissenters: From the Reformation to the French Revolution* (Oxford, 1978) provide context for Quaker events. William C. Braithwaite's *The Beginnings of Quakerism* (Cambridge, England, 1955, 1st ed. 1912) is a detailed, older work of the first Friends by a Friend. It has stood up over the years—well enough for publication of this second edition, which brings the original edition up to date.

For the Quaker invasion of the northern colonies, James F. Maclear, "The

Heart of New England 'Rent': The Mystical Element in Early Puritan History,"
Mississippi Valley Historical Review, 42 (1956), 621–52; Emory Battis, *Saints and
Sectaries: Anne Hutchinson and the Antinomian Controversy in the Massachusetts Bay
Colony* (New Haven, 1962); and George L. Smith, *Religion and Trade in New
Netherland: Dutch Origins and American Development* (Ithaca, 1973), are useful
starting points among many secondary sources.

Among the many other volumes that provided support for this study are those
which pointed to the context in which Quakers found themselves. Broad treat-
ments of individual colonies are Sydney V. James, *Colonial Rhode Island: A His-
tory* (New York, 1975); Michael Kammen, *Colonial New York: A History* (New
York, 1975); and Patricia U. Bonomi, *A Factious People: Politics and Society in
Colonial New York* (New York, 1971). Suggestive of towns in Massachusetts are
Kenneth A. Lockridge, *A New England Town the First Hundred Years: Dedham,
Massachusetts 1636–1736* (New York, 1970); Michael Zuckerman, *Peaceable
Kingdoms: New England Towns in the Eighteenth Century* (New York, 1972); and
Richard P. Gildrie, *Salem, Massachusetts 1626–1683: A Covenant Community*
(Charlottesville, 1975). Unhappily, there is no town study of dissenting com-
munities, although William G. McLoughlin, *New England Dissent 1630–1833:
The Baptists and the Separation of Church and State* (2 vols., Cambridge, Mass.,
1971), helps untangle some of the dissenters' struggle with Massachusetts, as
does Susan M. Reed, *Church and State in Massachusetts 1691–1740* (Urbana, Ill.,
1914).

Of the Quaker testimonies of antislavery and pacifism, the former has had
ample treatment, the latter little. Most useful for antislavery are James, *A People
among Peoples*, cited above; Arthur Zilversmit, *The First Emancipation: The Abolition of Slavery in the North* (Chicago, 1967); and Thomas E. Drake, *Quakers and
Slavery in America* (New Haven, 1950). On pacifism, Peter Brock, *Pacifism in the
United States: From the Colonial Era to the First World War* (Princeton, 1968), is a
first-rate general treatment that needs to be supplemented by more detailed
studies than Brock was able to make.

Notes

Abbreviations

Dtmth	Dartmouth
EG	East Greenwich
eps	epistles
Fl	Flushing
Hampt	Hampton
Lond	London
mfs	meeting for sufferings
MM	monthly meeting
Nant	Nantucket
NE	New England
NY	New York
Obl	Oblong
PrepM	preparative meeting
P.R.O.	Public Record Office
Purch	Purchase
QM	quarterly meeting
rec	received
RI	Rhode Island
Sandw	Sandwich
SK	South Kingston
Wy	Westbury
YM	yearly meeting
28/VIII/1760	August 28, 1760 (New Style)
28/VIII/1740	October 28, 1740 (Old Style)

Note: The citation of manuscript volumes is in roman numerals. Volumes of printed works are cited in arabic numerals.

Part I. From Heretics to Dissenters

Chapter 1. Quaker Invasion

1. George Fox, *Journal of George Fox* (2 vols., London, 1852), 1:260.
2. Hugh Barbour, *The Quakers in Puritan England* (New Haven, Conn., 1964), pp. 67–68. Kenneth L. Carroll, *John Perrot: Early Quaker Schismatic* (London, 1971), pp. 14–33.
3. For background see Barbour, chapter 1. Reflecting on older origins of Quakerism than those to be found in the Puritan Revolution are Christopher Hill, *The World Turned Upside Down: Radical Ideas during the English Revolution* (New York, 1972), pp. 22–30, 60–68; Donald F. Durnbaugh, "Baptists and Quakers—Left Wing Puritans?" *Quaker History*, 62 (1973), 67–82; Melvin B. Endy, Jr., *William Penn and Early Quakerism* (Princeton, 1973), chapter 1; and Michael R. Watts, *The Dissenters: From the Reformation to the French Revolution* (Oxford, 1978), pp. 187–193. See also William C. Braithwaite, *The Beginnings of Quakerism* (Cambridge, England, 1961), chapter 4.
4. The balance of this section is based on Barbour, chapters 2–6. Hill, chapter 10, also has useful comments on Quaker origins.
5. Richard T. Vann, *The Social Development of English Quakerism 1655–1755* (Cambridge, Mass., 1969), pp. 49–81. Robert W. Doherty, *The Hicksite Separation: A Sociological Analysis of Religious Schism* (New Brunswick, N.J., 1967), pp. 68–73, suggests that Orthodox Friends in the nineteenth century became concerned about the legitimacy of their beliefs, in part because of the vulnerability of wealthy people to social and economic change; see also Emory Battis, *Saints and Sectaries: Anne Hutchinson and the Antinomian Controversy in the Massachusetts Bay Colony* (Chapel Hill, 1962).
6. J. William Frost, *The Quaker Family in Colonial America: A Portrait of the Society of Friends* (New York, 1973), chapter 2, offers a useful comparison of Quaker and Puritan theology.
7. Hill, *World Upside Down*, chapters 9 and 10, shows the close relationship of Ranters and Friends, as does Watts, *Dissenters*, chapter 2, sections 14 and 15.
8. Perry Miller, *Errand into the Wilderness* (Cambridge, Mass., 1956), pp. 4–6, chapter 2. T. H. Breen and Stephen Foster, "Moving to the New World: The Character of Early Massachusetts Immigration," *William and Mary Quarterly*, 3d. ser., 30 (1973), 207–208.
9. One useful discussion among many of the expulsion of Williams is Perry Miller's in *Roger Williams: His Contribution to the American Tradition* (New York, 1953), p. 19.
10. Battis, *Saints and Sectaries*, pp. 247–248, chapters 9, 10.
11. Suggestive of the seriousness of other antinomian crises as well as the personalities of those involved is Nathan Adler, "Ritual, Release, and Orientation: Maintenance of the Self in the Antinomian Personality," in Irving I. Zaretsky and Mark P. Leone, eds., *Religious Movements in Contemporary Amer-*

ica (Princeton, 1974), pp. 283–297. James F. Maclear, "'The Heart of New England Rent': The Mystical Element in Early Puritan History," *Mississippi Valley Historical Review*, 42 (1956), 643–644.

12. Maclear, pp. 650–651. Richard P. Gildrie, *Salem, Massachusetts 1626–1683: A Covenant Community* (Charlottesville, Va., 1975), pp. 150, 165.

13. For early settlement and religious discontent on Long Island, see George L. Smith, *Religion and Trade in New Netherland: Dutch Origins and American Development* (Ithaca, 1973), part IV; Henry Onderdonck, *Queens County in Olden Times: Being a Supplement to the Several Histories Thereof* (Jamaica, N.Y., 1865), p. 4; Nathaniel S. Prime, *A History of Long Island, from Its First Settlement by Europeans, to the Year 1845, with Special Reference to Its Ecclesiastical Concerns* (New York, 1845), pp. 126, 131, 264–266, 269, 297, 334.

14. George Bishop, *New England Judged . . .* (London, 1661), pp. 4–8. Joseph Besse, *A Collection of the Sufferings of the People Called Quakers* (2 vols., London, 1753), 2:177–178. Nathaniel B. Shurtleff, ed., *Records of the Governor and Company of Massachusetts* (5 vols., Boston, 1853–54), 3:415–416.

15. Rufus M. Jones, et al., *Quakers in the American Colonies* (New York, 1966), p. 66, notes that the Salem group was sympathetic to Friends, about whom Quaker missionaries may have had information. Bishop, *New England Judged*, p. 9.

16. Bishop, *New England Judged*, pp. 10–11, 27–29. Besse, *Sufferings*, 2:178–179.

17. Bishop, *New England Judged*, pp. 40–42.

18. Ibid., pp. 42–45. Shurtleff, *Massachusetts Records*, 4:308–309.

19. Bishop, *New England Judged*, pp. 47–48, 58. Besse, *Sufferings*, 2:184–191. See also John Russell Bartlett, ed., *Records of the Colony of Rhode Island and Providence Plantations in New England* (10 vols., Providence, 1856–65), 2:99–103.

20. Shurtleff, *Massachusetts Records*, 4:i, 345–349, 366–367. Besse, *Sufferings*, 2:190. Bishop, *New England Judged*, 77–80. T. H. Breen, *The Character of a Good Ruler: Puritan Political Ideas in New England 1630–1730* (New Haven, 1970), pp. 70–86, details early struggles between the assembly and the magistrates, although he does not refer to this instance.

21. Bishop, *New England Judged*, pp. 83–86, 92–109, 118–119. Shurtleff, *Massachusetts Records*, 4:i, 366–367, 383–384, 419. The Southwicks may have essentially withdrawn from the Salem Church long before Friends arrived, since only one of their children, Mary, was baptized; Richard D. Pierce, ed., *The Records of the First Church in Salem Massachusetts 1629–1736* (Salem, 1974), pp. 8, 17. For a discussion of jails in Massachusetts, see Edwin Powers, *Crime and Punishment in Early Massachusetts 1620–1692: A Documentary History* (Boston, 1966), chapter 8.

22. John Norton, *The Heart of New England Rent at the Blasphemies of the Present Generation . . .* (Cambridge, Mass., 1659), pp. 2–5, 58. *A True Relation of the Proceedings Against Certain Quakers, at the generall Court of the Massachusetts holden at Boston in New-England October 18 1659* (London, 1660). Shurtleff, *Massachusetts Records*, 4:i, 386–390.

23. Francis Howgill, *The Heart of New England Hardened* . . . (London, 1659), pp. 7–9.
24. Joseph Nicholson to Margaret Fell, Boston, 3/II/1660, Swarthmore MSS, IV, 107, Friends House Library, London. Shurtleff, *Massachusetts Records*, 4:i, 433. Watts, *Dissenters*, p. 187 and passim, and Jeanette Carter Gadt, "Women and Protestant Culture: The Quaker dissent from Puritanism," dissertation (University of California, Los Angeles, 1974), p. 109, point to possibilities of contemporary celibate tendencies in George Fox and Margaret Fell.
25. E[dward] B[urrough], *Some Considerations Presented unto the King of England* . . . (London, 1660), p. 31. Shurtleff, *Massachusetts Records*, 4:ii, 19–21.
26. George Bishop, *New England Judged. The Second Part* (London, 1667), pp. 38–40.
27. Shurtleff, *Massachusetts Records*, 4:ii, 2–4. Jones, *American Colonies*, p. 94, indicates the likelihood of a warning that Massachusetts would have to alter its policy.
28. George D. Langdon, Jr., *Pilgrim Colony: A History of New Plymouth 1620–1691* (New Haven, 1966), pp. 58–68. For the consensual nature of Massachusetts towns, see Kenneth A. Lockridge, *A New England Town the First Hundred Years: Dedham, Massachusetts, 1636–1736* (New York, 1970) and Michael Zuckerman, *Peaceable Kingdoms: New England Towns in the Eighteenth Century* (New York, 1972).
29. Langdon, *Plymouth Colony*, pp. 69–72.
30. David Pulsifer, ed., *Records of the Colony of Plymouth in New England* (12 vols., Boston, 1855–61), 3:111, 113.
31. Ibid., 11:68, 100-101.
32. Ibid., 3:124–127.
33. Ibid., 3:138; 11:138.
34. Ibid., 3:140–141; Zuckerman, *Peaceable Kingdoms*, pp. 85–88.
35. Pulsifer, *Plymouth Records*, 3:130, 167; 10:121–122, 125–127.
36. Joannes Megapolensis and Samuel Drisius to the Classis of Amsterdam, New Amsterdam, August 14, 1657, in Hugh Hastings, ed., *Ecclesiastical Records of the State of New York* (7 vols., Albany, 1901–16), 1:400. Bartlett, *Rhode Island Records* 1:374–376.
37. Ibid., pp. 376–380.
38. Smith, *Religion and Trade*, chapter 12, demonstrates how the company's interest in a prosperous colony conflicted with Stuyvesant's interest in a religiously uniform one in the case of the Lutherans who had difficulties with Governor Stuyvesant at the same time as the first Friends.
39. Bishop, *New England Judged*, pp. 159–164. Joannes Megapolensis and Samuel Drisius to the Classis of Amsterdam, New Amsterdam, August 5, 1657, in Hastings, 1:397.
40. E. B. O'Callaghan, ed., *Documents Relative to the Colonial History of the State of New York* (15 vols., New York, 1856–87), 14:402–409. Smith, *Religion and Trade*, pp. 226–227.
41. O'Callaghan, *Docs. Rel. N.Y.*, 14:515. Herbert F. Ricard, ed., *Journal of*

John Bowne (New Orleans, 1975), pp. 19–25, 32–34, 69–71, contains details of Bowne's case.

42. Charles J. Hoadly, ed., *Records of the Colony of New Haven from May 1653, to the Union* (Hartford, 1858), pp. 242, 291, 364.

43. Franklin Bowditch Dexter, ed., *Ancient Town Records*, Vol. 1 of New Haven Town Records 1649–1662 (New Haven, 1917), pp. 339–343.

44. New Haven had passed a law to keep Friends out in 1657; the new law provided for punishment given Norton: Hoadly, *New Haven Colony Records*, pp. 217, 238–241.

45. Ibid., pp. 242–247.

46. Ibid., pp. 291–292.

47. Ibid., pp. 363, 364, 380, 412.

48. Connecticut MSS, Code of 1656 *et seq.*, " 'The Towns's Law Book' of Windsor": October 2, 1656, at Hartford, no. 179; October 7, 1658, no. 195; October 3, 1661, no. 195, microfilm, British Museum. Michael Kammen, *Colonial New York: A History* (New York, 1975), pp. 79–81.

49. For comments on the Lamb's War, see Barbour, *Quakers in Puritan England*, pp. 69, 217–219.

Chapter 2. Schism, Persecution, and Politics

1. Shurtleff, *Massachusetts Records*, 4:i, 442, 451.

2. Ibid., 4:ii, 2–4, 19–21, 34–35, 59, 165–166.

3. Bishop, *New England Judged*, 2:56–59 and passim.

4. Kai Erikson, *Wayward Puritans: A Study in the Sociology of Deviance* (New York, 1966), pp. 114–133.

5. Besse, *Sufferings*, 2:231–233.

6. Ibid., pp. 233–237. Bishop, *New England Judged*, 2:103 and passim.

7. Gildrie, *Salem*, p. 137, suggests relaxation of anti-Quaker efforts as early as 1663 and substantially so from 1667.

8. Carroll, *John Perrot* (above, Chapter 1, note 2), chapters 3, 6.

9. Ibid., p. 75.

10. Ibid., p. 105. Ann Richardson to George Fox, Newport, 1/I/1665, Swarthmore MSS, III, 101, indicates that Nicholas Easton, later governor of Rhode Island, was not sympathetic to Ann's papers against the Perrotonians. There is, however, nothing to be found indicating his sympathy for Perrot or his followers.

11. Ibid. Ann Richardson and Jane Nicholson to [Josiah Southwick], [Salem], I, 1664, Swarthmore MSS, III, 104. Lydia Hynchman, *Early Settlers of Nantucket: Their Associates and Descendants* (Philadelphia, 1901), pp. 130–137. John Barclay, ed., *Journals of the Lives and Gospel Labours of William Caton and John Burnyeat* (2nd ed., London, 1839), p. 207.

12. See Samuel H. Brockunier, *The Irrepressible Democrat: Roger Williams* (New York, 1940), pp. 134–138, 254–255 and passim, for efforts of Connecticut and Massachusetts to dismember Rhode Island.

13. *Rhode Island Records*, 2:373, 381–382, 412–413.

14. Brockunier, *Williams*, chapter 19 passim. *Rhode Island Records*, 2:411–412.

15. J. William Frost, "Quaker versus Baptist: A Religious and Political Squabble in Rhode Island Three Hundred Years Ago," *Quaker History*, 63 (1974), 40. *Rhode Island Records*, 2:429–430.

16. Frost, "Quaker," 41, argues that Whipple and Olney continued to support Harris, although the 1673 rejoinder by Olney to one of George Fox's sermons edited by Frost indicates that Olney had by 1673 gone over to the opposition, as does his and John Whipple's election as assistants as part of an anti-Quaker landslide in 1677 indicate that this opposition continued. *Rhode Island Records*, 2:435–443, 565. Roger Williams was an assistant in the April 2, 1672, General Assembly.

17. *Rhode Island Records*, 2:450–451, 455–460. Carl Bridenbaugh, *Fat Mutton and Liberty of Conscience: Society in Rhode Island, 1636–1690* (Providence, 1974), pp. 19, 55, makes reference to Brenton's landholdings. Brockunier, *Williams*, p. 252, refers to the speculative efforts of Brenton and Friend William Coddington. Rhode Islanders long remembered the muzzling act. Francis Brinley, writing the Earl of Bellomont on December 26, 1699, noted that the act was "so ill resented by the people in general that they turned out of place those that were the cause of that Act, choosing a Quaker to be their Governor." *Calendar of State Papers, Colonial Series*, 1700, no. 14, p. ix.

18. *Rhode Island Records*, 2:466, 472–473, 477–479.

19. Brockunier, *Williams*, p. 272, suggests the antidemocratic nature of Harris and his allies and generally plays down Williams' role in the repressive legislation. He also errs in stating that the repeal acts were passed in October.

20. For Fox's concern to establish business meetings, see Chapter 3 below. John Burnyeat's efforts to found meetings are in *Journals of Caton and Burnyeat*, p. 197. On Williams' claim to have attempted to debate Burnyeat, see Roger Williams, *George Fox Digg'd out of his Burrowes*, ed. J. Lewis Dinman, Vol. 5 of *The Complete Writings of Roger Williams*, ed. Perry Miller (New York, 1963), pp. 2–3; also ibid., pp. xxi–xxii, in which Dinman claims one of the Friends present was John Burnyeat.

21. Ibid., pp. xxi–xxiii, offers a summary of the origins of the debate. George Fox and John Burnyeat, *A New-England Firebrand Quenched* (London, 1678), p. 2, refer to the fact that Fox was in Rhode Island for several weeks and also in Providence briefly without receiving a challenge from Williams.

22. Williams, *Fox*, p. 1.

23. Ibid., pp. 72–83, 305–307, 311–312.

24. Ibid., pp. 56–58, 67.

25. Fox and Burnyeat, *New-England Firebrand*, pp. 12–13, 26–29, 48–49, 56–57.

26. *Rhode Island Records*, 2:465; both Harris and Throckmorton may have become convinced Friends in 1672, and both certainly sided with Quakers in the August debates, although there is no clear evidence on the point. Throckmorton's correspondence quoted by Williams indicates that Throckmorton had adopted Quaker usage. Not even Williams pressed the charge

that Harris had become a Friend. Williams, *Fox*, pp. 8–9, 14–17, 316.

27. *Rhode Island Records*, 2:484, 488–499.

28. Ibid., pp. 495–499.

29. Nathaniel Morton, *New England's Memorial* . . . (Cambridge, Mass., 1669), pp. 157–158. Increase Mather, *Illustrious Providences* . . . (Boston, 1684), pp. 341–356. Cotton Mather, *Memorable Providences* . . . (Boston, 1689), appendix, pp. 6–7.

30. For a Rhode Island Quaker account suggesting the imminence of God's wrath, written before the outbreak of hostilities by the governor elected in 1674, see William Coddington, *A Demonstration of True Love* . . . (London?, 1674). See also George Fox, *Cain Against Abel* . . . (London?, 1675) and Samuel Groom, *A Glass for the People of New-England* . . . (London?, 1676).

31. Douglas E. Leach, *Flintlock and Tomahawk: New England in King Philip's War* (New York, 1966), chapters 2, 8, esp. pp. 245–246. Alden T. Vaughan, *New England Frontier: Puritans and Indians 1620–1675* (New York, 1965), chapter 12. John Easton, *A Narrative of the Causes which led to Philip's Indian War of 1675 and 1676*, ed. Franklin B. Hough (Albany, 1858), pp. 7–15. Brockunier, *Williams*, p. 274.

32. Shurtleff, *Massachusetts Records*, 5:60; on other aspects of Puritan reform see Leach, *Flintlock*, pp. 189-195. The General Court acted on a committee report largely inspired by ministers like Increase Mather; cf. Increase Mather, *A Brief History of the War with the Indians in New-England* (Boston, 1676), pp. 17, 20. In fairness one should note that not all clergy shared this view, as William Hubbard made clear in *Happiness of a People in the Wisdome of Their Rulers Directing and in the Obedience of Their Brethren Attending* (Boston, 1676), pp. 3–4, and in his *A Narrative of the Troubles with the Indians in New England* (Boston, 1677), in which he did not single out Quakers as a cause for the war, as Increase Mather had done. On Hubbard see also Breen, *Good Ruler*, pp. 110–117.

33. E[dward] W[anton] or W[harton], *New England's Present Sufferings, under Their Cruel Neighbouring Indians* (London, 1675), pp. 1, 4–5, 8. The author, generally identified as Wharton, lived in Salem. Wanton was a Scituate merchant and father of the Quaker grandees John and Joseph and the Anglican William, later of Rhode Island. Either Wanton or Wharton was capable of the prank.

34. Fox, *Cain*; George Fox, *Something in Answer to a Letter . . . of John Leverat Governour of Boston to William Coddington Governour of Rode-Island . . . wherein John Leverat justifies Roger Williams's Book of Lyes* (London?, 1678). Groom, *Glass*. Leach, *Flintlock*, p. 195. Fox and Burnyeat, *New England Firebrand*, p. 246.

35. Leach, *Flintlock*, p. 195. Shurtleff, *Massachusetts Records*, 5:134. Besse, *Sufferings*, 2:259–260.

36. *Records*, 2:538–540, 548.

37. Ibid., pp. 549, 567–571.

38. Samuel Deane, *History of Scituate, Massachusetts from Its First Founding to*

1831 (Boston, 1831), p. 51. Pulsifer, *Plymouth Records*, VI,71; Sandw MM, 4/IV/1674, 1/VIII/1675, 4/I/1678, 7/III/, 2/V/1680, 3/IV/1681.

39. O'Callaghan, *Doc. Hist. New York*, 3:605–609.

40. Charles J. Hoadly, ed., *The Public Records of the Colony of Connecticut* (15 vols., Hartford, 1850–90), 3:264.

Chapter 3. *Decline of the Quaker Menace*

1. Watts, *Dissenters*, pp. 200–208, discusses Quaker ability to survive compared to other fringe groups in England.

2. A discussion of testimonies is in Part III.

3. Morton, *New England's Memorial*, pp. 106–110, 151, 157–158. To be fair one should note that one minister, William Hubbard, did not take as harsh a stand on Friends as did Morton. Hubbard was pastor of the church at Ipswich and no doubt had had some difficulties with Quakers. Unlike Morton and the Mathers, he had urged moderation, and in his "General History of New England," not published in his lifetime, he limited his discussion of the Quaker arrival to quoting a letter written by John Endecott and the General Court's 1660 justification of its charges. See above, chapter 2, note 32, for additional information on this point.

4. George Bishop, *New England Judged*, 2:123, 139.

5. Christopher Holder, *Faith and Testimony of the Martyrs* (London?, 1669?), pp. i, 1–4.

6. Coddington, *Demonstration of True Love*, pp. 3–4, 20.

7. George Fox, *Cain Against Abel*, pp. 3–12, 38, 41–48; above, chapter 2, note 34.

8. Fl MM 25/VI/1683.

9. Increase Mather, *Illustrious Providences*, pp. 341–344.

10. George Keith, *The Presbyterian and Independent Churches of New England Brought to a Test* (Philadelphia, 1689), p. 202. Ethyn Williams Kirby, *George Keith (1636–1716)* (New York, 1942), pp. 52–53.

11. Keith, pp. 32–33, 35–38, 125–126, 215–220, 227.

12. Cotton Mather, *Memorable Providences* (Boston, 1689), pp. 1, 3, 7. James Allin, Joshua Moody, Samuel Willard, and Cotton Mather, *The Principles of the Protestant Religion Maintained, And the Churches of New England in the Profession and Exercise thereof Defended* (Boston, 1690), pp. 2–23.

13. Kirby, *Keith*, p. 56. Harold S. Jantz, "Christian Lodowick of Newport and Leipsig," *Rhode Island History*, 3 (1944), 111–112.

14. Jantz, "Christian Lodowick," 3:111. [Christian Lodowick], *A Letter from the Most Ingenious Mr. Lodowick of Rhode Island, Febr. 1. 1691.2* (Boston?, 1692?), pp. 1–3, 5.

15. George Keith, *The Pretended Antidote Proved Poison . . .* (Philadelphia, 1690). George Keith, *A Refutation of Three Opposers of Truth . . .* (Philadelphia, 1690). [George Keith], *The Christian Faith of the People of God, called in Scorn, Quakers in Rhode Island* (Philadelphia, 1692). Kirby, *Keith*, pp. 56–57.

16. Kirby, *Keith*, 57−61. Frederick B. Tolles, *Quakers and the Atlantic Culture* (New York, 1960), pp. 34, 142−143.

17. Thomas Maule, *Truth Held Forth and Maintained* (New York?, 1695); RI MM 22/XI/1688. Lond. eps. rec. I, 21, 301.

18. Maule, *Truth Held Forth*, pp. 20, 26−28, 119.

19. [Thomas Maule], *New England Persecutors Mauled* (New York, 1697), pp. 53−58. NE YM 1699. [Thomas Maule], *An Abstract of a Letter to Cotton Mather in Boston in New-England* (New York?, 1701), p. 6. John Whiting, *Truth and Innocency Defended* . . . (London, 1702), pp. 151−152. Also among these attacks on the Standing Order was Daniel Gould's *A Brief Narration of the Sufferings of the People Called Quakers* . . . (Philadelphia?, 1700), which was in part an attack on Allin, Moody, Willard, and C. Mather, *Principles of the Protestant Religion* (note 10, above).

20. Cotton Mather, *Magnalia Christi Americana; or The Ecclesiastical History of New England* (2 vols., Hartford, Conn., 1852−53), 2:522−525. See also Louis Weeks, III, "Cotton Mather and the Quakers," *Quaker History*, 59 (1970), 24−33.

21. Whiting, *Truth and Innocency*, pp. 12−14, 128−135.

22. [Cotton Mather], *Man of God Furnished* . . . (Boston, 1708), pp. 72−79, 84. John Whiting, *A Just Reprehension of Cotton Mather* (London, 1710), details the delivery of Whiting's *Truth and Innocency*.

23. Patrick Henderson, *Truth and Innocence the Armour and Defense of* . . . *Quakers* . . . (London, 1709). Whiting, *Just Reprehension*.

24. William G. McLoughlin, *New England Dissent 1630−1833: The Baptists and the Separation of Church and State* (2 vols., Cambridge, Mass., 1971), 1:290−292.

25. Ibid., 290.

26. [Cotton Mather], *Three Letters from New-England, Relating to the Controversy of the Present Time* (London, 1721), pp. 12, 16.

27. Daniel Neal, *The History of New-England* . . . (2 vols., London, 1720), 2:291−360. Samuel Sewall MSS, *Massachusetts Historical Society Collections*, 47 (1882), 251−252.

28. [Cotton Mather], *Vital Christianity* . . . (Philadelphia, 1725), pp. 3−4. [Cotton Mather], *Lampidarius* . . . (Boston, 1726), pp. 1−2.

29. [Thomas Chalkley], *A Collection of the Works of* . . . *Thomas Chalkley* . . . (London, 1791), pp. 557−563.

30. George Keith, *A Journal of Travels from New-Hampshire to Caratuck, On the Continent of North-America* (London, 1706), pp. 5−6. [John Richardson], *An Account of* . . . *John Richardson* . . . (2nd ed., London, 1758), pp. 105−123. Alonzo Lewis and James R. Newhall, *History of Lynn* . . . (Boston, 1865), pp. 304−305.

31. Keith, *Journal*, pp. 17−39.

32. Ibid., pp. 44−49.

33. Samuel Bownas, *An Account of the Life of Samuel Bownas* (London, 1759), pp. 74−114. Bownas worked to support himself while imprisoned and was able to have long discussions with visitors. His incarceration was clearly easier

than that of the majority of New York prisoners. For New York jails, see Douglas Greenberg, *Crime and Law Enforcement in the Colony of New York 1691–1776* (Ithaca, 1976), pp. 125–128.

34. Lond mfs 21/III/1708.

35. James Wetmore to the Secretary of the SPG, December 21, 1730, in Robert Boulton, *History of the Protestant Episcopal Church in the County of Westchester* (New York, 1855), p. 255.

36. [James Wetmore], *A Letter from a Minister* (New York, 1730?), p. 9. James Wetmore, *Quakerism: A Judicial Infatuation . . .* (New York, 1731?). Wetmore makes reference to Mott's pamphlet in *Quakerism*.

37. Ibid. pp. 4, 20.

38. N. C. Hunt, *Two Early Political Associations: The Quakers and the Dissenting Deputies in the Age of Sir Robert Walpole* (Oxford, 1961), pp. 55–61. James Wetmore to the Secretary of the SPG, April 3, 1732, in Boulton, *Westchester Episcopal Church,* p. 258.

Part II. Institutions, Growth, and Worship

1. Vann, *English Quakerism,* p. 103. Arnold Lloyd, *Quaker Social History 1669–1738* (New York, 1950). Watts, *Dissent,* pp. 300–302. Vann and Watts point out the key role of Fox in instituting English Quaker business meetings.

2. See the author's article, "The Impact of the Discipline," forthcoming in *Quaker History*.

3. Rufus Jones, *The Later Periods of Quakerism* (2 vols., London, 1921), 1:59–60. Howard H. Brinton, *Friends for Three Hundred Years: The History and Beliefs of the Society of Friends since George Fox Started the Quaker Movement* (New York, 1952), pp. 176–187; Sydney V. James, *A People among Peoples: Quaker Benevolence in Eighteenth-Century America* (Cambridge, Mass., 1963), pp. 141, 247–249, suggests 1760, 1764, 1767, and 1770 as dates for the onset of reform in New England. For New York, James (p. 251) relied on Bliss Forbush, *Elias Hicks: Quaker Liberal* (New York, 1956), pp. 29, 51, 52, which suggests 1776 for that yearly meeting, because of the outbreak of fighting—a conclusion that cannot be supported from New York meeting records.

Chapter 4. Organization and Growth before 1755

1. See above, note 1 of Part II.

2. Tolles, *Quakers,* p. 12. Fox, *Journal,* 2:111.

3. Burnyeat, *Journal,* pp. 196–197.

4. Fox, *Journal,* 2:92–110. Burnyeat, *Journal,* pp. 202–203.

5. Fox, *Journal,* 2:111, refers to the establishment of subordinate meetings "for ordering the affairs of the church, many weighty things were opened and communicated by them, by way of advice, information and instruction in the services relating thereunto; that all might be kept clean, sweet and

savoury amongst them. In these two meetings, several other men's and women's meetings for other parts were agreed and settled." Burnyeat, *Journal,* p. 203, offers similar sentiments.

6. RI MM 26/IV, 24/V, 18/VII/1677. George Fox suggested that Henry Bull should have impounded and not shot the horses, and that he should make restitution. Fox also was critical of the Bulls's marriage so soon after her former husband, Nicholas Easton, had died. George Fox to Christopher Holder, London, 15/IV/1677, A. R. Barclay MSS, transcription, Friends House Library, London.

7. RI MM 30/II/1678, 29/II/1679, 2/I, 27/II, 17/VI/1680, 1/I, 24/II, 21/IV, 31/XI/1681, 25/II, 23/III, 7/IX, 30/XI, 27/XII/1682, 27/I, 11/VII, 19/VIII/1683, 13/VI, 7/VIII, 24/X/1684. Salem Monthly Meeting also had problems in these years, which may have been related Salem MM 6/VI/1680, 10/VIII/1682. There appear to have been similar difficulties in Sandwich, centering on John Jening and Peter Gaunt. Sandw MM 1/V, 2/IV, 1/III, 4/VI, 2/VIII/1681, 1/X, 5/XI, 2/XII/1682, 1/V/1687. The only other schism of significance came over fifty years later when Rhode Island and Salem monthly meetings had to deal with Friends who preached universal redemption. Salem MM 13/VII/1739; RI MM 27/IX/1739, 24/IV/1740.

8. Increase Mather, *Illustrious Providences*, pp. 341–344, 346. Fl MM 26/XII/80.

9. [William Edmundson], *Journal of the Life, Travels, Sufferings . . . of William Edmundson . . .* (London, 1774), p. 105. [Joan Vokins], *God's Mighty Power Magnified . . .* (London, 1691), p. 35. Chalkley, *Works,* p. 22.

10. Thomas E. Drake, *Patterns of Influence in Anglo-American Quakerism* (London, 1958), and Henry J. Cadbury, "Intercolonial Solidarity of American Quakerism," *Pennsylvania Magazine of History and Biography,* 60 (1936), 362–374, set forth similarities of transatlantic Quakerism. For membership rules transmitted by Fox and others, some of which were similar to English rules, some of which applied strictly to the colonial situation, see "Ancient Epistles, Minutes and Advices, or Discipline," New England Yearly Meeting Collection, Rhode Island Historical Society; and Worrall, "Impact of the Discipline."

11. NE YM 1695 agreed to the establishment of the New York body, which first met in 1696: NY YM 1696.

12. RI MM 14/VII/1680, 1/I/1681, 7/VII, 26/IX, 28/X/1708. Fl MM 28/VI/1708. London eps rec II, 27–30.

13. London eps rec II, 302. Richardson, *Account,* p. 83, details advice given on the select meeting in 1702: NE YM 1701. Samuel Bownas reported difficulties with some ministering Friends near Dover in 1703: Bownas, *Journal,* pp. 202–203.

14. Rhode Island Quarterly Meeting was the first quarterly meeting. It was not until 1707 that quarterly meetings as such began to send representatives to the yearly meeting: NE YM 1707.

15. NE YM 1708, 1709. The New Testament basis for dealing with erring members is Matthew 18:15–17.

16. Fl MM 26/XII/1698. NY YM 1746.

17. Burnyeat, *Journal*, p. 197. Pembroke (Scituate) MM 27/VII/1684, 28/-VII/1685.

18. NY YM 1704, 1706.

19. London eps rec, I, 20–21, 302, 343, II, 11, 26. Not all Quakers were free of harassment: Thomas Maule's apple orchard was chopped down, according to John Richardson, *Account*, p. 79. Richardson also noted the large number of converts to Quakerism, p. 108, as had the Rev. Jeremiah Shepherd in 1694, Lewis and Newhall, *Lynn*, p. 296.

20. See, for example, Ezra Stiles's view of the number of Friends on the Narragansett, Franklin Bowditch Dexter, ed., *Extracts from the Itineraries and Other Miscellanies of Ezra Stiles, 1755–1794, with a Selection from His Correspondence* (New Haven, 1916), p. 11, in which Stiles estimated in 1758 seventy-seven families for South Kingston alone, while the monthly meeting that covered most of the Narragansett country had had only thirty-seven marriages between 1743 and 1769, far from the number of marriages needed to support seventy-seven families in the entire area, let alone one town in it. James, *People*, p. 339, suggests that the South Kingston Monthly Meeting had an importance which the foregoing data do not support.

21. Hynchman, *Early Settlers*, pp. 130–137. Other persons identified as Friends apparently were forbidden to hold a meeting by Captain John Gardner in 1680. Gardner also actively opposed the Quaker presence in 1704. He may have allied with the Martha's Vineyard Mayhews to stir up the Indian residents to complain to Governor Joseph Dudley in 1702. Henry Barnard Worth, "Nantucket Lands and Owners," *Nantucket Historical Association,* 2 (1901), 149–150. Florence Mary Bennett Anderson, *A Grandfather for Benjamin Franklin: The Story of a Nantucket Pioneer and His Mates* (Boston, 1940), pp. 24–28, 197–214.

22. Chalkley, *Works,* pp. 19–20. Richardson, *Account,* pp. 86–92. [Thomas Story], *Journal of the Life of Thomas Story . . .* (Newcastle upon Tyne, 1747), pp. 350–359. Samuel Bownas also visited Nantucket in 1702, although not with the same effect as Richardson: Bownas, *Life,* pp. 114–115.

23. Myron Samuel Dudley, ed., "Timothy White Papers 1725–1755," *Nantucket Historical Association,* 1 (1898), 13, mentions opposition on the island to a mandatory salary for clergy. Thomas Story made a strong case against "Hireling Priests, the Merchants of Babylon, their Doctrine and Maintenance . . .": Story, *Journal,* p. 353. For discussion of the struggle against church taxes, see Chapter 7.

24. Lond. eps sent, II, 499, to NE YM, 18/V/1735 counseled "Now we doubt not but that Province Friends are duly Sensible of the priviledges they Enjoy, so they will demean themselves with Gratitute accordingly." Richardson, *Account*, p. 233.

25. Bownas, *Life,* p. 212. George J. Willauer, Jr., "Irish Friends Report on

Their Missions to America," *Quaker History,* 59 (1970), 15–23.

26. Mary Weston's Journal, transcript, Friends House Library, pp. 44–68, 125–133.

27. J. S. Rowntree, *Quakerism Past and Present* (London, 1859), p. 80. William Beck and T. Frederick Ball, *The London Friends' Meetings* . . . (London, 1869), data from table between pp. 90 and 91. Worrall, "Impact of the Discipline," for marriage data for the Irish monthly meetings of Carlow, Cork, Dublin, Edenderry, Lisburn, Mountmellick, Moate, and Wexford, indicates that decline began later in Ireland (ca. 1720) than Ball, Beck, and Rowntree found for England (ca. 1680), a situation confirmed in a very few English meetings by Richard T. Vann, *Social Development,* p. 162. The difference may arise from the fact that Vann and Worrall basically depended on monthly meeting records, if available, rather than marriage registers.

28. Merchant Walter Newberry was the father of Thomas Richardson's first wife and for a time was his business partner.

29. Zuckerman, *Peaceable Kingdoms,* shows the consensual basis of New England town government.

30. Elizabeth Isichei, *Victorian Quakers* (Oxford, 1970), pp. 80–82, discusses how the yearly meeting clerk and a few other weighty Friends dominated the yearly meeting for much of the nineteenth century.

31. Thomas Rodman was first appointed clerk of Flushing Monthly Meeting in 1733 Fl MM 1/IX/1733.

32. See Appendices A and B.

33. NE YM, 1733–1738. Discipline, New England Yearly Meeting, MS, Quaker Collection, Haverford College Library.

34. Appendix C. Where minutes of New York meetings were missing, the author made conservative estimates of the probable number of marriages in these meetings. The percentage increase as a result in total marriages is indicated on the chart.

35. Fl MM 2/III/1734; Wy MM 24/VII/1735; NY YM 1746.

36. Fl MM 6/XII/1723, 7/III/1724.

37. NE YM 1729; Fl MM 2/III/1734, 6/IX/1753.

38. NY YM 1746.

Chapter 5. Reform and Worship

1. NE YM 1754. Peleg Smith of Dartmouth Monthly Meeting was vastly impressed by Fothergill and his companions Joshua Dixon and Thomas Goodwin, who, he thought, "declared to us the Whole Councel of god as they Received of him which I believe Will be of great advantage to some amoung us and Especially in that of Regulations the discipline in the Church." Peleg Smith to Grace [Mo?]sher, Dartmouth, 11/VIII/1755, Peleg Smith MSS, Old Dartmouth Historical Society.

2. James, *People,* pp. 159–162.

3. Ibid. Samuel Fothergill to Israel Pemberton, Flushing, 26/V/1755 in George Crosfield, ed., *Memoirs of the Life and Gospel of Samuel Fothergill* . . .

(Liverpool, 1843), p. 187. Fothergill made a similar reference to those who were "the Head, but are the Tail" in England, Fothergill to John Churchman, 26/X/1756 Robson MSS, Friends House Library. Edward Milligan, Librarian, Friends House Library, London brought this to my attention.

4. Wy MM 29/I/1766, 1761–1767. Fl MM 5/V/1763, 6/XI/1766. NY YM 1773, 1774.

5. NE YM 1756, 1757, 1760.

6. NY YM 1758, 1759, 1763. Fl MM 5/I/1763. Purch QM 3/V/1760.

7. NY YM 1759. Purchase Quarterly Meeting had proposed the establishment of a meeting for sufferings, 6/V/1758.

8. NE YM 1760. NY YM 1763.

9. For a discussion of antislavery actions in these meetings, see Chapter 9.

10. RI MM 28/VI/1711. NE YM 1712.

11. See Vann, *Social Development,* chapter 4.

12. NY YM 1756, 1772, 1773, 1774.

13. SK MM 1/IX/1755: "it is agreed by this meeting that for the futer the visitors of Each meeting Do visit the families of such who were married among friends that have not cut themselves off by Transgression those who are Children of Friends and Read the Queries to them and Such who are willing to be in observation of Such Queries and have a Desire to be under the Care of Friends in order that the monthly meeting may have a Right Sence of the Conduct of Such." James, *People,* pp. 248–249 also considers this question, although since he had not read Sandwich and Nantucket records, he was not able to place New England's membership decision in a sufficiently broad context.

14. Sandw MM 3/I/1755. Nant MM 10/III/1755. Smithfield MM 30/V/1765.

15. NE YM 1774.

16. See above, Chapter 4, note 27.

17. Jack D. Marietta, "Ecclesiastical Discipline in the Society of Friends, 1682–1776" (Ph.D. dissertation, Stanford University, 1968), pp. 148–149 and Appendix B, pp. 172–179, which also emphasizes that there was an increased number of dealings in Pennsylvania after 1730, in sharp contrast to New England.

18. See Appendix D. James, *People,* pp. 248–249 states that the extension of the Pennsylvania revival came first to New England because of tumults there and really got under way because of the visit of John Woolman and the retirement of Thomas Richardson as clerk in 1760. Because of the nature of his study, James did not study disownments in detail and as a result his attention focused on the rhetorical aspects of reform. See also above, Part II, note 3.

19. See Appendix E. Data for older meetings after 1790 were gathered for another study. As this study terminates in approximately 1789, data for Maine and New York meetings do not go beyond 1789. Unlike data for marriages, there are no estimates made for dealings where minutes are missing.

20. See Appendices F and G.
21. See Appendix C.
22. See Appendices E, H, and I. Appendix H indicates that there could be substantial differences between monthly meetings; the effect overall was, however, as indicated in the text. Jones, *Quakers in Colonies,* pp. 133–134, discusses the effect of Sands.
23. Nant MM 29/VII/1762, 28/V/1764, 29/VII/1765. Frost, *Quaker Family,* p. 36. Frost's discussion of Quaker worship in his chapter 2 is the best I have encountered for colonial Friends.
24. Nant MM 25/IV/1711, 30/II/1716 note the first meeting house and its enlargement.
25. As quoted in Forbush, *Elias Hicks,* p. 67.
26. As quoted by Henry J. Cadbury, "Now and Then," *Friends Intelligencer,* October 1, 1919; also quoted in part by Frost, *Quaker Family*, pp. 36–37, who identifies the year as 1750.
27. Irish Half-Yearly National Meeting, 8, 9/IX/1699.

Part III. Testimonies and Politics

1. McLoughlin, *Dissent.* Edwin Scott Gaustad, *Dissent in American Religion* (Chicago, 1973), pp. 133–136, does study pacifism in the Mennonite context, among other matters. Still needed for American religious history is a study on the order of Watts, *Dissenters,* which treats admirably the history of dissent in England from the Reformation through the late eighteenth century.

Chapter 6. Quaker Politics and Oaths

1. *Calendar of State Papers Colonial: 1697–98,* 521, 1071; *1700,* 14, ix; *1704–05,* 1424, xxxvi.
2. Ibid., *1697–98,* 521.
3. Bartlett, *Rhode Island Records,* 4:454, 456, 461.
4. Ibid., pp. 491, 496.
5. SK MM 29/I/1770; 29/XI/1773. NE YM 1778. Some Friends, probably in Rhode Island, had again served in political office in 1778, a situation that led the yearly meeting to issue a stern demand for their withdrawal.
6. Ellis Ames, Abner C. Goodell, John H. Clifford, eds., *The Acts and Resolves Public and Private of the Massachusetts Bay* . . . (5 vols., Boston, 1869–86), 1:14.
7. NE YM 1702. Dtmth MM 25/III/1701. Edward M. Cook, Jr., *The Fathers of the Towns: Leadership and Community Structure in Eighteenth-Century New England* (Baltimore, 1976), pp. 136–138, details Quaker participation in the government of some New England towns.
8. Salem Monthly Meeting in 1717 was concerned about the hazard of members serving as constables, and directed consultation with the monthly meeting before taking office, presumably because of the danger of having to

arrest other Quakers who refused to pay a church tax: Salem MM 9/III/1717. For dissenting towns like Dartmouth and Tiverton, this was not a problem, as those towns resisted the tax.

9. *Journals of the House of Representatives, Massachusetts* (33 vols., 1919–57), 12:65, 20:19. *Mass. Acts,* 3:126–127, 362. *Laws of the Commonwealth of Massachusetts Passed from the Year 1780, to the End of the Year 1800 . . .* (2 vols., Boston, 1801), 2:797–798. Dtmth MM 18/V/1737.

10. *Jrl. Mass. H. of R.,* 17:132, 151. Governor Belcher had made the proposal.

11. Charles B. Kinney, *Church and State: The Struggle for Separation in New Hampshire* (New York, 1955), p. 49. *Acts and Laws Passed by the General Court or Assembly . . . of New Hampshire . . .* (Boston, 1726), pp. 1, 71.

12. *Acts and Laws . . .,* pp. 79–81. *Acts and Laws of . . . New Hampshire . . .* (Portsmouth, 1761), pp. 72–74, 127–129. Kinney, *Separation,* pp. 49, 59.

13. Nathaniel Bouton, *Provincial Papers. Documents and Records Relating to the Province of New Hampshire . . .* (12 vols., Concord, 1867–83), 4:776, 5:135, 225.

14. For detail on this point, see Patricia U. Bonomi, *A Factious People: Politics and Society in Colonial New York* (New York, 1971).

15. *Acts of the Assembly, Passed in the Province of New-York, From 1691, to 1718* (London, 1719), pp. 8, 29–32.

16. Earl of Bellomont to Lords of Trade, April 27, 1699, O'Callahan, *Docs. Rel. N.Y.,* 4:509. Cornbury to Lords of Trade, September 27, 1702, and petition of Quakers in New York Province to Cornbury, October 2, 1702, Public Record Office, C.O. 5, 1047, 68, XV.

17. Rip Van Dam complaint vs. Cosby, attached to Morris to Council of Trade, Morrisania, December 15, 1733, *Cal. St. P. Col.,* 1733, 441, xxvi. Cosby to Council of Trade, June 10, 1735, ibid., 1734–35, 591. See ibid., 443, for the New York Council's reply to Van Dam.

18. Fl MM 29/III/1692, 28/IX/1696, 29/III/1714. For the New Jersey alliances of Lewis Morris see John E. Pomfret, *Colonial New Jersey: A History* (New York, 1973), pp. 79–85. Bonomi, *Factious People,* pp. 69, 170, 255.

19. Fl MM 6/VII/1750.

20. One factor in the differing disownment patterns in New York and New England mentioned in Chapter 5 may have been that New York Friends were not involved in government. That hypothesis must be qualified, however, because English and Irish Friends were not in government either in the eighteenth century but disowned many of their members throughout the century.

21. *Laws of the State of New York . . .* (2 vols., New York, 1789), 1:27, 2:63–64.

Chapter 7. Church Taxes

1. Basic to any study of the struggle to rid New England of a tax-supported church is McLoughlin, *Dissent;* also useful is Susan Martha Reed, *Church*

and State in Massachusetts 1691–1740 (Urbana, Ill., 1914). Zuckerman, *Peaceable Kingdoms,* assesses town autonomy, although not in the case of church taxes.

2. Some relief may have been given even before the arrival of Andros: Lond. eps rec, I, 21, 58–59 (Rhode Island epistles of 1686 and 1687).

3. Ames, *Mass. Acts,* 1:14.

4. Ibid., pp. 62–63.

5. Ibid., pp. 216–217. McLoughlin, *Dissent,* pp. 124–127.

6. NE YM 1696.

7. Lond eps rec, I, 302–303.

8. Lond eps sent, I, 368–369.

9. Conn. MSS Code, no. 179, 195.

10. Hoadly, *Public Records of . . . Connecticut,* 3:264, 4:161, 182, 191, 201, 214–215, 253, 261–262, 281, 332, 343, 362, 396. *Acts and Laws of . . . Connecticut . . .* (Boston, 1702), p. 42. Bownas, *Life,* pp. 96–106. Edmundson, *Journal,* pp. 95–98. John Rogers, *An Epistle to the Churches of Christ Call'd Quakers* (New York, 1705). Ellen Star Brinton, "The Rogerenes," *New England Quarterly,* 16 (1943), 3–19. John R. Bolles and Anna B. Williams, *The Rogerenes: Some Hitherto Unpublished Annals Belonging to the Colonial History of Connecticut* (Boston, 1904).

11. *Cal. St. P. Col.,* 1704–05, nos. 1060, 1100. Lond mfs 12/IX/1703. Sydney V. James, *Colonial Rhode Island: A History* (New York, 1975), chapter 7. Michael Garibaldi Hall, *Edward Randolph and the American Colonies 1676–1703* (New York, 1969), pp. 203–213.

12. Lond mfs 19/IX, 26/IX, 17/X/1703, 2/VII/1704. *Cal. St. P. Col.,* 1706–1708, no. 511.

13. Ashurst's arithmetic was at least as bad as English Quaker knowledge of New England: he should have said forty-two years. Also he was apparently ignorant of the fact that printing the code made its provisions current whether enforced or not. Lond mfs 28/XII/1705. *Cal. St. P. Col., 1704–1705,* nos. 1100, 1153, 1356.

14. *Cal. St. P. Col.* 1704–05, no. 1362, 1706–08, nos. 511, 730.

15. Ibid., no. 790. Lond mfs 3/XI/1706.

16. For town autonomy, see Zuckerman, *Peaceable Kindgdoms.*

17. Ames, *Mass. Acts,* 1:505–506, 597–598.

18. McLoughlin, *Dissent,* 1:16. Governor Dudley mistakenly informed the Board of Trade that 60 pounds was to be added to Dartmouth rates, *Cal. St. P. Col.* 1708–09, no. 391.

19. Ibid., Dtmth MM 20/VII/1708.

20. McLoughlin, *Dissent,* 1:180–181. RI MM 28/X/1708. At least one of those who sent in a petition on October 28, Joseph Wanton, was a resident of Tiverton, and all were Quakers. McLoughlin indicates that the assessors were only from Dartmouth. Rhode Island Monthly Meeting sent 20 shillings for the support of the prisoners and also a leading member, John Borden, to see that the prisoners would be well cared for.

21. *Cal. St. P. Col., 1706–1708,* no. 511, 1708–09, no. 391. P.R.O.C.O.

5/184, nos. 114, 156, 157. *Massachusetts Historical Society Collections*, 7th series, vols. 7–8 (1911–12), *Diary of Cotton Mather 1681–1708*, pp. 537, 557, June 30, 1718, and October 2, 1718. Mather mentioned that Tiverton was to be cared for—"miserable Tiverton" he stated in October when other clergymen had visited the town.

22. *Mass. Acts*, 2:26–27. McLoughlin, *Dissent*, 1:186–187.

23. *Jrl. Mass. H. of R.*, 1:217–218. Lond mfs 5/X, 12/X, 21/X/1718, 16/VII/1720. McLoughlin, *Dissent*, 1:187–190.

24. McLoughlin, pp. 190–192. Hunt, *Political Associations*, pp. 55–56. In addition to Partridge, another active member of the meeting for sufferings was Walter Newberry, father of Richardson's first wife and his onetime business partner who had just retired to London.

25. Lond mfs 11/VIII, 25/VIII, 20/X/1723, 3/V, 23/VIII/1724. McLoughlin, *Dissent*, 1:191–194.

26. McLoughlin, 1:191–194. *Cal. St. P. Col.*, *1724–1725*, no. 198. *Acts of the Privy Council, Colonial Series*, 3:58.

27. For Anglican pressure for relief from taxes to support Congregationalists, see McLoughlin, *Dissent*, 1, chapter 11.

28. *Mass. Acts*, 2:494–495.

29. Ibid., pp. 619–620. *Jrl. Mass. H. of R.*, 10:199, 241, 301. Jonathan Belcher to Richard Partridge, Boston, January 3, 1731/32, April 27, 1732, May 7, 1740, *Mass. Hist. Soc. Colls.*, 56:31, 82, 57:282. Richard Partridge to Josa [Josiah] Foster, London 6/VI/1737, Portfolio 41, no. 34, Friends House Library.

30. *Jrl. Mass. H. of R.*, 16:126, 131; 20:365–366. Smithfield MM 27/IV, 28/IX/1769, 28/V/1772.

31. Obl MM, List of families, III, 1760. Richard L. Bushman, *From Puritan to Yankee: Character and Social Order in Connecticut, 1690–1765* (New York, 1970), pp. 165, 168. McLoughlin, *Dissent*, chapter 15.

32. Bouton, *N.H. Prov. Papers*, 16:575–576. McLoughlin, *Dissent*, 2:835. Kinney, *Separation*, pp. 35–37.

33. McLoughlin, *Dissent*, 2:835. Kinney, pp. 35–37.

34. Kinney, pp. 48–49. Bouton, *N.H. Prov. Papers*, 4:537, 592, 597. Dover MM 23/IV/1733. Hampt MM 18/X/1701.

35. Bouton, *N.H. Prov. Papers*, 12:137.

36. Jeremy Belknap, *The History of New Hampshire* (3 vols., Philadelphia and Boston, 1784–92), 3:350–354. Bouton, *N.H. Prov. Papers*, 5:225, 704. It is possible that some Friends paid for the cost of building meeting houses in newly settled towns, much as some New Hampshire Friends hired replacements to go to war. One surmises that the truth of the matter is that in most instances the community did not require Friends to pay. Evidence, if any, may exist in town records not examined for this study.

37. Kammen, *New York*, pp. 136–137.

38. Ibid., pp. 85–86. *N.Y. Acts 1691–1718*, pp. 19–21.

39. Petition of Quakers in New York Province to Lord Cornbury, New York, October 2, 1702, P.R.O., C.O.5/1047 no. 68, xv. Kammen, *New York*,

pp. 220–222. Though Jamaica Presbyterians won control in 1732, they lost again in 1768. One wonders to what extent the Quaker petition might have been writen as a counter to George Keith. If so, it was of limited effectiveness, as the subsequent imprisonment of Samuel Bownas for a year indicates.

Chapter 8. Peace Testimony

1. Peter Brock, *Pacifism in the United States: From the Colonial Era to the First World War* (Princeton, 1968), is the best study on American pacifism and capably deals with colonial pacifism as an aspect of religious dissent. Less successful is James, *People,* p. 143, whose view of Quaker pacifism does not consider changes which this Quaker testimony underwent.

2. Bartlett, *Rhode Island Records,* 2:567–571.

3. Ibid., 2:273, 276; 3:340–341.

4. RI MM 17/III/1709, 26/IX/1734. NE YM 1735. Bartlett, *Rhode Island Records,* 4:457. For background on the Wantons, see John Russell Bartlett, *History of the Wanton Family of Newport, Rhode-Island* (Providence, 1878), and Deane, *Scituate.* Bartlett used much of pp. 371–377 of Deane's work verbatim without attribution.

5. Bartlett, *Rhode Island Records,* 5:145–148. Smithfield MM 28/XI/1754, 24/IX, 25/III, 28/XI/1773. Smithfield MM Box 28/I/1773. Richardson was treasurer from 1748 until his death in 1761. Stephen Hopkins was governor 1755–1764 and 1767.

6. RI MM 30/VIII/1757, 25/XII/1759, 26/II, 25/III, 27/V/1760.

7. RI MM 13/X/1698. Bartlett, *Rhode Island Records,* 3:433, 4:433, 438.

8. RI MM 15/VI/1704, 21/III/1706. Lieutenant Governor Walter Clarke was one of the petitioners.

9. Richardson, *Account,* pp. 130–131.

10. Deane, *Scituate,* pp. 50–51. *Mass. Acts,* 1:128–129, 133–134.

11. Brock, *Pacifism,* p. 44, alleges that Nantucket Friends had participated in privateering. Brock does not offer any evidence on this matter, nor have I encountered any. John Smith, *A Narrative of Some Sufferings for His Christian Peaceable Testimony by John Smith . . .* (Philadelphia, 1800), pp. 6–9. Dtmth MM 20/IX/1704, 19/I/1750. Story, *Life,* pp. 266–270, 308–312.

12. Bouton, *N.H. Prov. Papers,* 3:311. *N.H. Acts* (1726), pp. 91–97, 145.

13. Story, *Life,* pp. 314–320. Bownas, *Journal,* pp. 183–184. Chalkley, *Works,* pp. 40–45.

14. Fl MM report of sufferings 1675 following 29/X/1677. O'Callahan, *Doc. Hist. N.Y.,* 3:607–609. Lond eps rec, I, 215. As William Morris helped supervise the erection of Manhattan's English church in 1697, he eventually left Quakers and may even have done so by 1686: Thomas F. Archdeacon, *New York City, 1664–1710: Conquest and Change* (Ithaca, 1976), p. 128.

15. Lond eps sent, II, 102. Lond eps rec, II, 292, 379, III, 73. Wy MM 3/IX/1730.

16. *Laws of New York, from . . . 1752, to 1762* (2 vols., New York, 1762),

2:43–45, 55–56. Wy MM 26/III, 30/IV, 3/V/1755. NY YM 1755–1762. O'Callaghan, *Doc. Hist. N.Y.*, 3:1027–30.

17. *Jrl. Mass. H. of R.*, 32:341, 362, 378.

18. Ibid., pp. 378–80, 388, 395. *Mass. Acts*, 3:915–916.

19. *Mass. Acts*, pp. 967–978, 1055.

20. Dtmth MM 1/VI/1757. *Mass. Acts*, 4:49–50, 90–91, 142, 215, 237, 337.

21. *Mass. Acts*, p. 119.

22. Nant MM 27/IX/1756. Dtmth MM 20/II, 15/III/1758. Sandw MM 3/III/1758. RI QM 7/IV/1757. Lond eps sent IV, 107.

23. Bouton, *N.H. Prov. Papers*, 6:670–671, 707.

24. Ibid., 6:761–764, 766–768, 837; 7:121. Some persons in Brentwood, New Hampshire, who called themselves Quakers had served in the army and in 1764 received credit for their service by act of the provincial legislature; and the town had relief from Quaker tax assessed. These were schismatics who had been disowned by Dover Monthly Meeting and so are not counted as Friends, nor does their military service represent a compromise of Quaker principles.

25. See Mack Thompson, *Moses Brown: Reluctant Reformer* (Chapel Hill, 1962), chapter 6, and Brock, *Pacifism*, p. 259.

26. Lond eps sent, V, 26. Arthur J. Mekeel, "The Society of Friends (Quakers) and the American Revolution," (Ph.D. dissertation, Harvard University, 1940), is the best detailed source on Quakers in the period of the War for Independence.

27. NY YM 1777. The yearly meeting stated that persons who took the affirmation to the state government "thereby acted inconsistant with our Christian Testimony & Principles by therein being concerned in setting up & putting down the Powers of the World."

28. Arthur J. Mekeel, "New York Quakers in the American Revolution," *Bulletin of Friends Historical Association*, 29 (1940), 47–55.

29. RI MM 28/I/1777. The address to General Henry Clinton began: "We the Kings peacable & Loyal Subjects being deeply affected with the unhappy Commotions which now prevail around us . . ." went on to note that Quakers had not deviated from their loyalty to the king, noted that Clinton's arrival filled them "with thankfull hearts," and concluded by requesting "the protection of our persons & properties & indulgence in the enjoyment of our Religious Liberties . . ."

30. Mekeel, "Quakers in Revolution," pp. 146–148. NE mfs 12/VII, 11/IX/1775. Alexander Starbuck, *The History of Nantucket: County, Island, and Town Including Genealogies of First Settlers* (Rutland, Vt., 1969), pp. 185, 225–227, chapter 5. *Memorandum Written by William Rotch In the Eightieth Year of his Age* (Boston and New York, 1916).

31. Mekeel, "Quakers in Revolution," pp. 253–254, 257. NE mfs 13/-XI/1780, 1/IV/1781. Thompson, *Moses Brown*, pp. 144–145.

32. Mekeel, "Quakers in Revolution," pp. 151–153. [Timothy Davis], *A Letter*

from a Friend to Some of His Intimate Friends on the Subject of Paying Taxes (Watertown, Mass., 1776), pp. 1–3, 6–8.

33. NE mfs 12/III, 13/V, 12/VI, 12/VIII/1776.

34. Mekeel, "Quakers in Revolution," pp. 151–153. NE YM 1778. Sandw MM 5/VI/1795.

35. Thompson, *Moses Brown*, pp. 144–145. SK MM 25/VI/1781. NE mfs 10/XII/1788. Forrest McDonald, *The Formation of the American Republic*, *1776–1790* (New York, 1965), pp. 119–127, details the speculative background of the 1786 currency as well as its ties to wartime expenditures. See also James, *Rhode Island*, pp. 366–370.

36. Wy MM 30/III, 29/VI/1785. There could be vast differences in sufferings, as in 1783, when Westbury Monthly Meeting reported total sufferings of £49/4/9, Oblong, £2076/9/6, and The Creek and East Hoosuck inclusive, £1302/9/6.

37. NY mfs 31/III/1778. NY YM 1779, 1780. Fl MM 1/IV/1778.

38. NE YM 1761. A. Day Bradley, "New York Friends and the Confiscated Loyalist Estates," *Quaker History*, 61 (1972), 36–39. Mekeel, "Quakers in Revolution," pp. 360–363.

39. One thinks especially of Narragansett land in the case of land taken from Indians by at best dubious means. James, *Rhode Island*, p. 66.

40. *New York Laws, 1789*, 1:13. Mekeel, "Quakers in Revolution," pp. 260–262. NY mfs 10/VIII/1782.

Chapter 9. Philanthropy

1. "Ancient Epistles," pp. 1, 2, 5.

2. The usage of "poverty" here is relative: poverty clearly meant one thing in 1680 and something else in the mid-eighteenth century.

3. Sandw MM 2/VII/1673. RI MM 16/VII/1677, 11/VIII, 6/X/1681, 29/IX/1687, 18/XII/1689. Fl MM 30/X/1776, 14/VIII/1784.

4. RI MM 26/V/1752. Nant MM 21/VI/1773. Salem MM 9/III/1780. Smithfield MM 27/VIII/1772. Fl MM 2/IX/1756. Perhaps the fact that few New York Friends lived in an urban environment before 1756 delayed the establishment of the first committee to care for the poor.

5. NE YM 1697, 1698. One of the many problems with New York records is indicated here: they contain no reference to the assistance given to those New England Friends, although New England records indicate receipt of funds.

6. Dtmth MM 20/X, 21/XII/1708.

7. NE YM 1751. Dtmth MM 14/IV/1760. A similar case occurred when Lydia Norton was cared for by Salem Quarterly Meeting until her son took her into his home. In itself this demonstrates that charity was the primary responsibility of the meeting if family members lived in other areas. Salem QM 9/II, 10/VII/1744, 5/V, 9/VII/1745, 14/II, 14/V/1745, 15/-VII/1746.

8. NE YM 1698. Pembroke MM 6/XII/1691. RI MM 20/VII/1698. Salem MM 9/III/1758. Peleg Slocum, a member of Darmouth Monthly Meeting, while far from pleased with the relief act, informed Friend Samuel Pope of Boston: "I think it the duty of Christians to be Gratfull toward their benifactors which I believe the General Court hath passed Several Acts in order to favour friends . . ." Peleg Smith to Samuel Pope [n.p.], Peleg Smith MSS, Old Dartmouth Historical Society, 3/V/1758.

9. NE mfs 14/VIII, 11/IX/1775, 12/III/1776. Thompson, *Moses Brown,* pp. 115–117, 130–131.

10. Henry J. Cadbury, "Quaker Relief during the Siege of Boston," Publications of the Colonial Society of Massachusetts, *Transactions,* 34(1938), 39– 179.

11. NY mfs 1/VIII/1776, 2/II, 2/VII, 3/XII/1777.

12. James, *People,* chapter 11.

13. Account from Stephen Blizard to Abraham Redwood, Antigua, April 13, 1755, Newport Historical Society, Vault A, Box 36, folder 5. Estate of George Hunt, 1761 Newport HS, Vault A, Box 45, folder 22. RI MM 28/VII/1772, 25/VIII/1772, 29/IX/1772. Thomas E. Drake, *Quakers and Slavery in America* (New Haven, 1950), pp. 9–10. Elizabeth Donnan, ed., *Documents Illustrative of the History of the Slave Trade to America* (4 vols., Washington, 1930–1935), vol. 3, (1932) *New England and the Middle Colonies,* pp. 183, 203, 213, 216, 475, 476, 485. Donnan misidentified Joseph Wanton as a Friend. She confused him with the Joseph Wanton of Tiverton, born in 1705 and unlikely to be commanding a slaver off Africa at age 53 in 1758. The Joseph in question seems to have been a 1730 graduate of Harvard. J. William Frost, "Origins of Quaker Antislavery," paper delivered at the Conference of Quaker Historians, Richmond, Indiana, July 10, 1978, convincingly demonstrated that Quaker beliefs and practices, not outside influences, determined Quaker antislavery.

14. Ancient Epistles, pp. 2, 3, 6.

15. Ibid., p. 51. Drake, *Quakers and Slavery,* pp. 11–14. George Keith apostatized in 1691 and criticized Quakers for holding slaves. Germantown Friends had made similar arguments in 1688.

16. Thomas Richardson to James Took, Boston, 9/VI/1712, Richardson account book. Thomas Richardson to Abraham Borden, Newport 30/XI/1715. Thomas Richardson to Daniel Lawrence, Newport 26/IX/1716, Richardson letterbook 1715–19. Thomas Richardson to Benjamin Borden, Newport 6/V/1739, letterbook 1737–1741. Thomas Richardson to Richard Partridge, Newport 4/IV/1750, letterbook 1751–1761, Richardson MSS, Newport HS.

17. Edward Besam to Abraham Redwood, Antigua, February 15, 1729. Jonas Langford, Jr., to Abraham Redwood, Antigua, May 14, 1730. William Mackinnon and Stephen Blizard to Abraham Redwood, Antigua, April 11, 1765. William Mackinnon to Abraham Redwood, Antigua, May 9, 1766, MSS, Newport HS, Vault A, Box 30, folders 5 and 6. Copy of will of Joseph

Wanton of Tiverton, R.I., 14/VI/1749, S. A. G. Smith MSS, indicates that Wanton, a Quaker minister, presumably like others in his family, held many slaves. RI MM 29/III/1776 indicates that Joseph Jacob, Newport merchant active in meeting affairs, held slaves. Thomas Robinson to William Stead, 3/V/1755, Thomas Robinson letterbook, transcript S. A. G. Smith MSS, indicates Robinson was involved in the slave trade.

18. Donnan, *Documents on Slave Trade,* 3:117, see note 13 above. Thomas Robinson to William Stead, [Newport?], May 3, 1755, Thomas Robinson letterbook, transcript, S. A. G. Smith MSS. That slave trading was far from profitable for Rhode Islanders like the Browns of Providence is indicated in James B. Hedges, *The Browns of Providence Plantations: Colonial Years* (Cambridge, Mass., 1952), esp. chapter 4, p. 80.

19. Donnan, *Documents on Slave Trade,* 3:475, 476, 485.

20. James, *People,* pp. 338–339, in bibliographic comments, indicated that he found urban meeting records more useful than rural in studying Quaker antislavery and philanthropy. Although one cannot find names of country Friends who opposed slavery (to use Jack Marietta's phrase, they were probably people who did not count), as indicated below, antislavery proposals came again and again from rural meetings, not urban meetings like Rhode Island Monthly Meeting.

21. Dtmth MM 30/III/1711, 15/I/1714, NE YM 1717.

22. RI MM 27/XI/1715, 30/VIII, 27/IX/1716; EG MM 3/XI/1716, 17/VII/1717. Nant MM 26/IX/1716. Dtmth MM 19/I, 17/X/1716.

23. Fl QM 23/XII/1716. NY YM 1717.

24. Nant MM 29/II/1717. NE YM 1717. NE YM of ministers and elders 1717.

25. Benjamin Lay, *All Slave-Keepers That Keep the Innocent in Bondage Apostates* . . . (Philadelphia, 1737), pp. 6–11.

26. NY YM 1718, Lond eps sent, 2:296–297.

27. Sandiford was an immigrant English Quaker who published a tract against slavery in 1729. Drake, *Quakers and Slavery,* pp. 39–42.

28. Ibid., pp. 37–38. Nantucket was not, strictly speaking, rural. Its whaling interests had not yet made it an international trading center like Newport and New York.

29. Salem QM 8/IX/1731. Dover MM 4/IX/1731. Dover Monthly Meeting had reached the decision to forbid slavery and the trade for its members who did not yet own slaves before asking the advice of the quarterly meeting.

30. NE YM 1742, 1743, 1744. Smithfield MM 25/IX/1742, 27/XI/1742. RI QM 7/II/1743.

31. James, *People,* pp. 128, 137. For the numbers of slaves crossing to North America, see Philip D. Curtin, *The Atlantic Slave Trade: A Census* (Madison, 1969), p. 140.

32. Curtin, pp. 136, 141. Frost, "Origins," disagrees with the contention that reform had a direct tie to antislavery.

33. NE YM 1760. RI MM 29/III/1763, 27/X/1772.

34. Edwin Cady, *John Woolman* (New York, 1965), pp. 100–101. Drake, *Quakers and Slavery,* pp. 62–63. New England Yearly Meeting Book of Discipline 1760, MS, RIHS.

35. As already indicated, the elderly Thomas Richardson stepped down as clerk of the yearly meeting in 1760. He died the following year. See RI MM 27/XII/1774, 28/II/1775, 28/III/1775 with regard to dealings with elderly members.

36. South Kingston MM 27/IX/1760, 26/VII/1761. As in note 20 above; James, *People,* p. 339, contends that South Kingston Monthly Meeting members were a cut above those of other rural monthly meetings. I have found no evidence either in meeting records or elsewhere to sustain his assertion.

37. Dtmth MM 18/VIII, 28/X/1760. Nant MM 29/XII/1760. RI MM 24/VI, 29/VII/1760, 25/VIII, 29/IX/1772.

38. Alexander McAlister to Abraham Redwood, Antigua, February 19, 1769. William Mackinnon and Stephen Blizard to Abraham Redwood, Antigua, April 11, 1765, MSS Newport HS, Vault A, Box 36, folder 6.

39. RI QM 13/IV/1769, 12/IV/1770. NE YM 1770 contains this revision to the tenth query "and do they give those that are young such an education as becomes Christians, and are the others encouraged in a Religious and virtuous life, And are all set at Liberty that are of an age capacity and ability's suitable for freedom."

40. RI MM 30/VII/1771. RI QM 8/IV/1773. NE YM 1773. The new tenth query, mandating manumission and clarifying the 1770 query, stated: "Are friends clear of Importing, Buying or any way purchasing disposing or holding of mankind as Slaves, And are all those who have been held in a State of Slavery discharged therefrom."

41. The meeting took Hopkins under dealing in September 1772. The meeting decided to disown him in March but did not read his disownment and thus expel him from the meeting until October 1773—hardly a hasty decision. Smithfield MM 24/IX/1772, 25/III, 28/XI/1773.

42. NE YM epistle to London, 1775. Dover MM 18/X, 20/XII/1777. Manumission papers follow the meeting for 21/XI/1778. Of the nine papers, Moses Brown was a witness to four of them.

43. Lond eps rec, IV, 23–24. Fl MM 5/IX, 2/X, 7/XI/1765. Obl MM 16/IV/1767. NY YM 1768, 1771, 1774. Purch MM 10/I, 20/XI/1782. Gary B. Nash, "Slaves and Slaveowners in Colonial Philadelphia," *William and Mary Quarterly,* 3d. ser., 20 (1973), 223–256.

44. *N. Y. Acts to 1718,* p. 237. *N. Y. Acts to 1752,* p. 196. *N. Y. Acts to 1789,* pp. 253, 255–256.

45. NE YM 1775, 1776.

46. Thompson, *Moses Brown,* pp. 181–192. NE mfs 23/II/1784, 9/VI/1787, 9/I, 9/IV, 11/VI/1788. Arthur Zilversmit, *The First Emancipation: The Abolition of Slavery in the North* (Chicago, 1967), pp. 115–124, 156–157.

Part IV. Quakers in the World

Chapter 10. Economic and Social Conditions

1. For an example of widening the gap between the upper and lower segments of society, see James A. Henretta, "Economic Development and Social Structure in Colonial Boston," *William and Mary Quarterly,* 3d. ser., 22 (1965), 75–92.

2. A helpful discussion of Rhode Island social and economic life is in James, *Rhode Island,* chapters 8 and 10. RI MM 27/XII/1704, 22/III/1705.

3. Joseph Wanton had ample means when he died. He left 1900 pounds Rhode Island currency in cash to specified heirs, his unspecified Negroes (no number indicated), a homestead farm, his 1/13 share of the training and burial place, 1/13 of the land laid out for a minister who had never been called, a 120 acre farm, two lots of 120 and 50 acres, 1/30 of Cranberry Neck and buildings. The 50-acre lot was to be sold to provide the cash legacies. Photocopy of Joseph Wanton's will, Tiverton, 14/VI/1749, S. A. G. Smith MSS.

4. RI MM 26/V/1752, 28/V/1782.

5. Lewis Morris [Jr.] to Joshua Delaplaine, Morrisania, March 20, 1752, Joshua Delaplaine MSS, N.Y. Hist. Soc. Isabella had requested that Delaplaine make the coffin of black walnut, lined with calico.

6. Robert V. Wells, *The Population of the British Colonies in America before 1776: A Survey of Census Data* (Princeton, 1975), p. 87. Nant MM 26/VII, 30/IX, 30/XII/1754, 28/VII, 31/XII/1755, 27/VII/1761. NE YM 1768, 1769. Zuckerman, *Peaceable Kingdoms,* pp. 89–90.

7. The Dartmouth assessment in 1771 found Joseph Rotch and Sons to have 14,924 feet of wharf, 3 warehouses, 1 ropewalk, 683 tons of vessels, £4000 in stock, and £1500 at interest. John Hancock had 22,672 feet of wharf, 594 tons of vessels, £7000 in stock, and £11,000 at interest.

8. For Moses Brown, see Thompson, *Moses Brown,* and Hedges, *Browns.* Concerning farms surrounding Providence, see James, *Rhode Island,* p. 257.

9. James, pp. 250–257. Jackson Turner Main, *The Social Structure of Revolutionary America* (Princeton, 1965), pp. 22–23.

10. W. L. Fisher to Thomas Rotch, Philadelphia, 14/II/1823, Rotch MSS, Massillon Public Library. Abigail Robinson to Mary R. Morton, Newport 3/XI/1823, Henry A. Wood II MSS.

11. Rhode Island Monthly Meeting's share of the Rhode Island Quarterly Meeting contribution to the yearly meeting treasury dropped from 50 percent in 1774 to 16 percent in 1785. In Salem Quarterly Meeting, meetings shared virtually equally in expenses immediately after the war in 1783. But even the quarter share supposed to be contributed by Salem to the yearly meeting was difficult. In 1781 Salem was deficient a total of £21/9/2. The quarterly meeting's assessment was reduced to 20 percent by 1790.

12. New England migrants, primarily from Dartmouth and Nantucket, com-

prised 11 of the 17 families and 15 of the 26 individuals who moved into
Nine Partners and Oblong Monthly Meetings between 1770 and 1774—a
ratio essentially the same as in earlier years. In the five years in question,
immigration of Friends to these meetings more than doubled. Between
1775 and 1779 numbers more than tripled; most of them came in 1775 and
1776 from Dartmouth and Nantucket to Nine Partners Monthly Meeting.
Fifty-three of the 66 families and 45 of the 66 individuals (persons who did
not come with families) came from New England. Lockridge, *New England
Town,* chapter 8, and James A. Henretta, *The Evolution of American Society
1700–1815: An Interdisciplinary Analysis* (Lexington, Mass., 1973), pp.
128, 135–136, discuss tensions that were the result of land shortage.

13. Daniel Merritt account book, New York Historical Society. Warren H.
Wilson, *Quaker Hill: A Sociological Study* (New York, 1907), pp. 20–24.
James H. Smith, *History of Dutchess County, New York* (Syracuse, 1882), p.
63.

Chapter 11. Retrospect and Prospect

1. W. R. Ward, *Religion and Society in England 1790–1850* (New York,
1973), pp. 21–26, discusses English opposition to unitarian attempts to
have the Test and Corporation Acts repealed. William Rathbone, a Quaker
who supported Priestley, later found disfavor among orthodox Friends for
supporting the Irish New Lights, whose views were apparently similar to
those of Job Scott discussed below. Rufus M. Jones, *Later Quakerism,* Vol.
1, chapter 9. Doherty, *Hicksite Separation,* pp. 18, 20–23.

2. Doherty, passim.

3. Smithfield MM 26/XI/1773, 31/III, 28/IV/1774.

4. Jerome H. Wood, Jr., "For Truth and Reputation: New England Friends'
Dispute with Isaac Backus," *New England Quarterly,* 50 (1978), 458–463.
Isaac Backus, *A History of New England with Particular Reference to the Denomination of Christians Called Baptists* (2nd ed., Newton, Mass., 1871), pp.
92, 97, 245–287.

5. Job Scott, *The Works of That Eminent Minister of the Gospel, Job Scott, Late of
Providence Rhode Island,* ed. John Comly (2 vols., Philadelphia, 1831),
1:199.

6. Ibid., pp. 275, 486, 491.

7. Ibid., pp. 501, 516–517.

8. William Rotch, Senior, to Samuel Rodman, Dunkirk, France, 15/XII/-
1792, ODHS: "I have long been expecting Job Scott, but if he is detained
for want of a clear vission in the two thou mentions I doubt his reaching this
country soon." Scott, *Works,* 2:179, Job Scott to Daniel Anthony, and
Family, London, 23/II/1793: "I am very apprehensive that my detention
in New England has put me by the first right time for Ireland." Edmond
Prior to Moses Brown, New York, 7/III/1797: "Jobs Sentiments have on
some Subjects been as it were new on the prospect of things before him,

some of these we are warranted in Saying, became cause of Concern to many Friends in England and Ireland, and to Some of the most Sensible and experienced there, were exceptionable, but this we mention wholly in Confidence to thee." Moses Brown MSS, RIHS.

9. Moses Brown to Edmund Prior, Providence, 18/V/1792, Moses Brown MSS, RIHS.

10. NE mfs, 8/V, 20/X/1792, 12/II, 10/IV/1793.

11. Not discussed here is the case of Jemima Wilkinson. Disowned in 1776 before she set up her small sect, her effect on Friends in the northern yearly meetings was minimal, essentially confined to Smithfield Monthly Meeting and not of substantial effect on it. For a detailed discussion, see Herbert Wisby, *Pioneer Prophetess: Jemima Wilkinson, the Public Universal Friend* (Ithaca, 1964), pp. 6–12.

12. Jeanette Carter Gadt, "Women and Protestant Culture: The Quaker Dissent from Puritanism" (Ph.D. dissertation, University of California, Los Angeles, 1974), chapters 2, 3. See above, chapter 4, note 30.

13. NY YM 1749, 1781. Smithfield MM 25/IV/1771. Fl MM 1/VI/1774. Wy MM 20/III/1760.

14. NE YM 1781.

15. NE YM 1708. RI MM 24/XII/1684, 27/II/1703, 25/VI, 30/VII/1771.

16. Dtmth MM 24/VI/1723, 20/VIII/1729, 21/X/1730. Nant MM 30/XII/1754. Joseph Rotch paid for the education of his children by the resident Congregational minister Timothy White in 1742, 1748, and 1749: Myron Samuel Dudley, ed., "Timothy White Papers 1725–1755," *Nantucket Historical Association,* 1, no. 2 (1898), 51, 66, 69.

17. EG MM 19/I/1711, 7/VIII/1760. In rural meetings like South Kingston the small family school continued to be the characteristic mode of education: SK MM 23/III/1796.

18. NE YM 1779.

19. Smithfield MM 25/III/1779. NE YM 1780. East Greenwich Monthly Meeting decided to establish a school in 1780, but apparently it did not last, for the next mention of a monthly meeting school in 1796 indicates that if the school was ever established, it did not last long: "Friends Children have mostly had their Tuition by different Masters in divers places who were not Members of our Society, Some of whom kept nearly all the Time, and others were of Short duration." EG MM 4/IV/1796. Nantucket established a school in 1784 and Lynn Preparative Meeting in 1783. Nant MM 30/VIII/1784, 27/VI/1785. Salem MM 8/V/1783. Lynn Prep M 6/VII/1808.

20. NE YM 1780. NE mfs 13/VI/1782, 11/VI/1783, 4/X, 1/XI/1784, 18/VI/1788.

21. NY YM 1779, 1780.

22. Fl MM 5/VI/1703, 5/III/1709, 6/XII/1780, 4/IV/1787. Wy MM 25/X/1780, 28/III/1781, 30/XI/1782, 31/III/1784, 27/IX/1786, 28/I/1789.

23. Lond eps rec, II, 11. Bownas, *Life,* pp. 171–172. *An Account of the Captivity of Elizabeth Hanson, Late of Kachecky in New-England . . . Taken in Substance from Her Own Mouth, by Samuel Bownas* (London, 1787). SK MM 29/-VIII/1768, 31/VIII/1769. Bartlett, *Rhode Island Docs.*, 6:578–579.

24. 13/VI/1815, Diary of Stephen Gould, The Quaker Collection, Haverford College. Gould misspelled Cuffe's family name.

Glossary

Acknowledgment   The formal apology given by an offender to a business meeting for an infraction of Quaker rules. Also, the formal apology accepted by the business meeting.

Convincement   In general usage, Quaker convincement means conversion. As used in business meeting records, it means recognition as a member. Conversion for Friends meant sanctification, a quest for holiness which would continue after convincement.

Dealing   The process by which a business meeting brought a violator of Quaker rules to account. It was almost always instituted by the monthly meeting.

Declension   The decline of Quakers, as American Quaker reformers after 1750 saw it.

Discipline   Rules established by yearly meetings for members in their jurisdictions.

Disownment   The expulsion from membership of Quakers for violation of rules.

Distraint   The seizure and sale of property for nonpayment of taxes or nonperformance of services.

Engagement (or Affirmation)   Solemn promise to tell the truth in lieu of taking an oath for those who scrupled against swearing.

Inward Light   The light or seed of God that Quakers believed lay within all people, sometimes referred to as the Light Within, or, more recently, as the inner light.

Restoration   The formal restoration to membership of a disowned member on her/his delivery of acceptable acknowledgment.

Sufferings   The financial losses, imprisonments, physical and/or mental abuse endured because of conscientiously observing Quaker practices and beliefs.

Testimonies   Quaker behavioral requirements which in the eighteenth century included such as plain dress and speech, refusal to take an oath, and pacifism.

Yearly Meeting   The annual business meeting for a geographic area that made rules and oversaw their enforcement. Yearly meeting also could refer to yearly revival or general meetings, a custom which fell into disuse after reform came to northeastern Quakers.

Quarterly meeting   The meeting that met quarterly and served as a buffer between the rule-making yearly meeting and the rule-enforcing monthly meetings. It also transmitted information between superior and inferior meetings and discussed issues raised by both.

Monthly meeting   The basic Quaker business meeting which oversaw behavior of it members in terms of Quaker rules, dispensed charity to its members, raised funds to build meetinghouses, and discussed issues of importance.

Meeting for sufferings   The executive committee of the yearly meeting.

Index